80 Years of Yachting

Also by Bill Robinson

ISLANDS

WHERE TO CRUISE

SOUTH TO THE CARIBBEAN

CRUISING: THE BOATS AND THE PLACES

WHERE THE TRADE WINDS BLOW:
A YACHTING GUIDE TO SOUTHERN WATERS

THE CARIBBEAN CRUISING HANDBOOK:
A PLANNING GUIDE FOR CHARTERERS AND PRIVATE OWNERS

80 Years of Yachting

Compiled and Edited by

Bill Robinson

 A Triton Book

DODD, MEAD & COMPANY
NEW YORK

Grateful acknowledgment is made to *Yachting* magazine
for permission to publish all of the articles in this book.

Published by Dodd, Mead & Company, Inc.
71 Fifth Avenue, New York, N.Y. 10003
Distributed in Canada by
McClelland and Stewart Limited, Toronto
Manufactured in the United States of America
First Edition

1   2   3   4   5   6   7   8   9   10

Library of Congress Cataloging-in-Publication Data

80 years of Yachting.
   Includes index
   1. Yachting.   I. Robinson, Bill, 1918–
II. Yachting.   III. Title: Eighty years of Yachting.
GV812.A16   1987   797.1   86-23991
ISBN 0-396-08958-5

Contents

Introduction   ix
  Bill Robinson

PART I
Competitive Events

How *Resolute* Kept the Cup (1920)   3
  Herbert L. Stone

The Kaiser's Ocean Race (1968)   6
  Edmund Randolph

The Fastnet Disaster (1979)   15
  Guy Gurney

Cup Goes Down Under (1983)   23
  Guy Gurney and Jack Somer

PART II
History, Adventure and Hard Chances

Croesus and His Steam Yacht (1907)   33
  Arthur F. Aldridge

The Last of the New Bedford Whalers and The End of
    the *Wanderer* (1924)   41
  William H. Taylor

First Airplane to Bermuda (1930)   45
  Zeh Bouck

The President Goes Cruising (1933)   50
  Paul D. Rust, Jr., and James Roosevelt

The Boat That Came Back (1940)   59
  Joseph Chase Allen

The "Mystery" of the *Mary Celeste* (1940)   62
  Dr. Oliver W. Cobb

End of a Bootlegger (1941)   68
  Vincent Gilpin

The Snatch and the Sunbeam (1943)   74
  Arthur W. Bull

Five Flashes East (1961)   77
  Harold Waters

Captain America Rides Again (1975)   86
  Jeff Hammond

In Their Hour of Triumph (1977)   95
  John Hersey

PART III
The Thinking Cap—Opinions and Expertise

Wanted: Wholesome Boats for the America's Cup (1907)   107
  Sir Thomas Lipton

On Shipyards and Drawbridges (1920)   112
  Catherine Drinker Bowen

Designing an America's Cup Defender (1937)   118
  W. Starling Burgess

Tank Tests in Yacht Designing (1937)   125
  Olin J. Stephens II

From "Golwobblers" to "Mae Wests" (1947)   131
  C. Sherman Hoyt

"Do You Anchor At Night?" (1954)   135
    Ann Davison

Racing Starts & Rounding Buoys (1959)   142
    Bus Mosbacher

Single-Handed Passages (1963)   151
    Francis Chichester

PART IV
Wartime

A Western Ocean Cruise in Wartime (1916)   161
    George H. Dillenback

San Pedro to Key West in Wartime (1942)   184
    Charles Peterson

Squadron "X" (1943)   193
    Hugh B. Cave

In the Path of the Hurricane (1945)   200
    R. F. Hainge

PART V
The Lighter Side

Skippers We Can Live Without (1947)   209
    William H. Taylor

The Crew I Can Do Without (1947)   215
    Alfred F. Loomis

"100 Tons of Bronze, Son" (1964)   221
    Cleveland Amory

PART VI
Cruising

The Cruise of the Yakaboo (1917)   229
    F. W. Fenger

Discovering Islands (1935)   242
    Irving Johnson

Icebound in the Far North (1960)   248
  Donald MacMillan

Into the Solomons (1973)   257
  Harold LaBorde

Deep Sea Passage (1976)   265
  Frank W. Hamilton, Jr.

A Dream Comes True, the Hard Way (1981)   278
  Jack A. Somer

Index   285

Introduction

Browsing through 80 years of back issues of *Yachting* has been a fascinating task, given the accompanying problem of time spent, since the temptation was always there to stop and read almost everything. I happen to have been reading *Yachting* since 1924, and it was an orgy of nostalgia to relive memories and to see the articles and pictures that nurtured the dreams of boyhood, adolescence and the years beyond.

Gradually, out of this vast smorgasbord, a policy was developed to select pieces that seemed most suited for reading and enjoying today, and not just for reasons of historic interest or curiosity. Much of the practical stuff has been completely outdated of course, and while it is historically amusing to see what was said in 1908 about the new gasolene [*sic*] engines, actually reading the article is not very entertaining. The same applies to such later developments as diesel, radio and other electronics, and the availability of new materials. It is surprising, too, to realize that so much of the how-to on seamanship, racing tactics and racing gear has been superseded.

Over the years, there has been, of course, a wealth of cruising material, with some top selections in the following pages, but, especially in the early days of the magazine, accounts were in serial form that eventually ended up as a whole book. The style was leisurely and chatty, making excerpting almost impossible.

It has been instructive to see how often certain themes have recurred. The number one subject, right from an article by Sherman

Hoyt in the first issue in January 1907, has been controversy over rating rules, and a complete book (not very readable today) could be assembled on that whipping boy alone. Similarly, complaints about "freak" boats versus "sound" ones have repeatedly been grist for the mill. Arguments over the merits of certain rigs have been a staple: gaff-vs.-marconi, staysail schooner instead of main and foresail rig, ketch-vs-yawl, cutter or sloop (and just what is a cutter?).

While these have been standbys, there have been changes in emphasis. Canoe racing, rowing, trapshooting, model sailboats, aviation and powerboat racing have all had their day, to be seen no more, and regional news columns, a feature from 1934 to 1978, are gone. Another type of feature that has departed is the pseudonymous column. For years "Cap Stan," "Spun Yarn" and "Boatsteerer" could express all sorts of outrageous opinions and hold forth on pet peeves safe behind the cloak of a pen name, though "Spun Yarn" ended up as the transparent cover for Alf Loomis, one of the magazine's best-known and closely followed writers from the '20s to the '60s.

Yachting has had a history of long runs for many of its personnel. Herb Stone guided its existence from its second year until 1955, Bob Rimington came on the staff in World War II and took over from Herb Stone, running things into the '70s, Bob Bavier's byline first appeared in the '30s when he was in college, and he joined the staff upon graduation in 1940, retiring in 1980. Bill Taylor wrote pieces starting in 1924 and was an editor for over 20 years following World War II, Marcia Wiley started in 1946, and I began writing columns in 1947 and came on the masthead in 1957.

As writers, editors (and sometimes photographers), and always as sailors, these staff members and many more who have worked with them for shorter periods, have shaped the material that appears here. It is a rich heritage, and the hope is that this distillation of a part of it not only will help keep the storied past alive, but will also provide pleasure and entertainment in the present and future.

BILL ROBINSON

PART I
Competitive Events

Through the years, Yachting has "been there" for all the major events and thousands of minor ones. Often, staff members have been competitors, too, as there has never been an editorial staffer who was not an active participant in the sport. Many of these great events, major ones at the time they were held, have faded into the memory of a few contestants or been superseded by more exciting ones later on, and most of the America's Cup campaigns have been memorialized in complete books. Often, accounts of races became rather routine listings of prize winners and their times, not very exciting reading today, but out of this vast store of material "for the record," there have been certain reports that have given the special flavor of one of the major events, or focused on an unusual development, such as the Fastnet tragedy of 1979, and the selections appearing here are typical of them.

1920

How *Resolute* Kept the Cup

Herbert L. Stone

Yachting's editor with the longest tenure tells of the most interesting of Sir Thomas Lipton's five losing challenges.

After the closest and hardest fought series ever sailed for that historic piece of silverware known as the America's Cup, *Resolute*, by slipping over the line ahead of Sir Thomas Lipton's green challenger *Shamrock*, as the sun set and darkness settled over the sea beyond Sandy Hook on July 27th, decided the future of the Cup for the time being, or until another challenge is received for it—from the Irish baronet or someone else.

In spite of the fact that, boat for boat, the contestants were evenly matched and the series had to go to five races for a decision, at one time the challenger having a clear lead of two wins, the races themselves were not particularly interesting, owing to the fickle winds that persisted over the Cup course from July 15th to 27th. On only one day was the wind true throughout and of sufficient strength to give the boats a thorough test on all points of sailing, and on that day a squall near the end of the race spoiled what would have been a very close finish, though the challenger would have been beaten on time. No race was sailed in a strong breeze, and so we are still ignorant of what the *Shamrock* can do in a good breeze to windward. On the only day there was a really strong breeze there was too much of it, and neither skipper cared to send his boat over the course, but quickly assented when the committee asked if they were willing to have the race postponed.

Yet, in spite of the poor winds and the unavoidable flukes of yacht racing, everyone who saw the series off Sandy Hook during those two weeks must be convinced that the fastest boat won. If not, he

Shamrock and *Resolute* (*right*) jockey for a start

must indeed be partisan. On every windward leg of the whole series *Resolute* gained, while in all the other races except the second, *Resolute* either made an actual gain or else more than saved her proportionate time on every leg. The second race, which *Shamrock* won, had no windward leg owing to a shift of wind. On the two reaches in this race, *Shamrock's* gain more than offset her time penalty, though she was favored by shifting breezes, while on the run home in that race *Resolute* saved her time on the green yacht.

Yet *Shamrock* came nearer to winning the Cup than any other yacht that has ever come after it. She put up the best race of any of the four challengers of Sir Thomas Lipton, and there is no denying the fact that she is very fast. At times she showed speed that left the American boat well behind her, yet she did not seem a consistent performer. This may have been due to the flaky winds, which prevented comparison when the two boats were separated by over a quarter of a mile, by reason of their not holding the same wind, and it may have been due to handling. Nicholson, himself, her designer, says that they do not know her thoroughly yet, and have not sailed her enough in all conditions to know what is her best point or what kind of a wind she wants. Owing to the backward season and the difficulty of getting work done in yacht yards, her trials before the

International series were woefully inadequate for the proper collection of data or the drilling of her crew. In the early races of the series her crew were very much slower than *Resolute*'s in handling light sails, and this lost precious seconds. On one occasion it took nine minutes to get a spinnaker set, when it should have been done in two or two and a half minutes. They improved rapidly as the series lengthened, but another month of drilling would have helped them wonderfully.

One thing that was apparent throughout all the races was that barring flukes, the challenger could not give the defender the time allowance with which she was penalized. In this connection Herreshoff naturally had the advantage of Nicholson, as he had built to a known rule, with which he had had lots of experience, and knew how to take every advantage of rating. This he did. Nicholson, on the other hand, building for the first time to the rule, naturally went in for *speed* on a given waterline length, letting his boat take her chances of reasonable penalties. The penalties were too heavy, however—from 6 minutes 40 seconds to 7 minutes 1 second, depending on the club topsail *Shamrock* carried. It is satisfactory to note, however, that the series was decided, except in one race, without the need of handicaps. Of *Resolute*'s three wins, in two she beat the *Shamrock* boat for boat, her chief gains being to windward, while in the other race the boats sailed a dead heat on elapsed time, *Resolute*'s gain to windward, equaling *Shamrock*'s on the run.

Nicholson was also unfamiliar with water conditions off Sandy Hook. Had he known them he would probably not have given his boat the flat ends she had, as these undoubtedly hurt her in the long roll and tumble one finds off the Hook even in light weather. The experience gained of our conditions in these races will undoubtedly enable him to do even better next time. His boat has given us the best battle ever put up for the Cup. Another time we may look for an even more dangerous competitor, if the challenger comes from his board.

The sailing of *Resolute* by Adams and his afterguard was all that could be asked. Their judgment was almost invariably good and the execution was always snappy and without hesitation.

1968

The Kaiser's Ocean Race

Edmund Randolph

Recalling the next famous ocean race, in which the schooner Atlantic *set the transatlantic sailing record that lasted until 1980.*

May 17, 1905, dawned calm and foggy upon New York Harbor, about as unlikely a day for fast sailing as one could imagine. Yet the sailing ships assembled there were drawing widespread attention from both sides of the Atlantic as they inched about, jockeying for the start of a race unique in the annals of yachting.

This was the brainchild of His Imperial Majesty, Wilhelm II, Emperor of Germany. But his interest in it was not entirely sporting, since it was colored by the promotion of an image of himself as a sea lord, in preparation for a great expansion of the German Navy.

In the sporting world of yachting, the Kaiser already had two strikes against him on the technicalities of racing rules, with which he tended to take liberties. One was a tiff in the Queen's Cup race of 1893 around the Isle of Wight when his schooner *Meteor IV* disregarded a course mark. Then there had been bad feeling involved in a 1902 race in the Baltic, wherein the Kaiserlicher had pointedly and permanently disqualified the British yacht *Cicely*, a frequent victor over *Meteor II*, for questionable reasons.

Wilhelm had also behaved badly aboard Sir Thomas Lipton's yacht at Cowes in 1904, been called into the chart room by another guest, Edward, Prince of Wales (his uncle, later King Edward VII) and asked to leave, which he did in a huff.

These incidents and the Kaiser's neurotic behavior at sea—hiding from storms in his cabin—did not endear him to the international yachting fraternity. And so there was some eyebrow raising when he announced, with great fanfare, that he would sponsor an unprecedented open yacht race from Sandy Hook to the Needles, off the Isle of Wight, for a gold cup of his own personal design. This was

6

to be followed by a less arduous race from Dover to Heligoland, and topped off by festivities in Kiel including an imperial reception aboard his 4,000-ton, 382-foot steam yacht, *Hohenzollern.*

Invitations went out to leading international yacht clubs, whose blue water members sat back to ponder. There were some unhappy personal feelings; but then, the Kaiser was offering a mighty interesting proposition. Several sailing yachts had competed in trans-Atlantic crossings, but always singly or in private races between friends. This was to be the first open, free-for-all contest, organized as an event of international interest under world-renowned sponsorship.

The Kaiser's patronage alone, coupled with his delicate position in world affairs, and the hope that, at last, he might be turning toward peaceful pursuits, wreathed the event in an aura of mystery and importance that had never been equalled in the sporting world. There was also a certain nostalgia for the fast-fading era of square sail that added to the appeal of Wilhelm's race.

The German entry, *Hamburg*, was a 140', very fast two-masted schooner owned by a syndicate and commanded by its leader, Adolf Tietjens, though sailed by British Captain James Peters. The Kaiser was not aboard her, but she carried a mysterious passenger who kept

Hohenzollern, the Kaiser's 382-foot yacht

The Empress' bedroom on *Hohenzollern*

strictly to himself and to the company of the afterguard, under two obviously assumed names, and who was generally rumored to be H.R.H. Prince Adalbert, Wilhelm's third son.

Ten other yachts made up the field, all with owners in command, except for New York stockbroker Henry S. Redmond's *Ailsa*, commanded by his representative, Grenville Kane, and sailed by Captain Lem Miller with a crew of 18. Two yachts were British, the other eight American.

Valhalla, the largest entrant, owned by the Earl of Crawford, was the only full-rigged ship in the race, a majestic vessel 245′ o.a., carrying a crew of 66.

Possibly the world's most famous and traveled yacht *Sunbeam* was the other British entry, owned and commanded by the so-called Dean of Deep Sea Yachtsmen, the Right Honourable Lord (later Earl) Brassey. Owner and ship held seniority in the event, he then being in his 70th year, and she having come off the ways in 1874. By 1905 they had cruised together in all the seven seas for 300,000 miles. *Sunbeam*, a three-masted top-sail-yard schooner, measured 170′ o.a.

Newest yacht was Wilson Marshall's two-year-old, 185', three-masted schooner *Atlantic*, sailed by the aggressive, redoubtable and temperamental Scotsman, Captain Charles Barr, most famous professional sailing master of his day. With two mates and a crew of 50, he sailed her to the Needles 22 hours ahead of all competition.

Smallest entry was Dr. Lewis A. Stimson's 108', two-masted schooner *Fleur-de-lis* carrying the only lady among some 300 men in the race, Miss Candace Stimson, the owner's daughter.

Only yawl in the race was *Ailsa*, second smallest yacht, with a water-line exceeding that of *Fleur-de-lis* by only two feet, although her pronounced overhang of 18' forward and 20' aft made her 19' longer overall.

Another large schooner was Chicago packing magnate Allison V. Armour's three-masted, 190' *Utowana*, sailed by Captain J. H. Crawford and a crew of 34.

Robert E. Tod, a Scottish-born New York businessman, sailed his 150', two-masted schooner, *Thistle* with an afterguard of four and a crew of 22.

Commodore George Lauder Jr. of the Indian Harbor YC commanded his trans-Atlantic record-holding, two-masted, 137' schooner *Endymion* with a crew of 26 under Captain James A. Loesch.

The Philadelphia Corinthian YC was represented by Edward R. Coleman's *Hildegarde*, measuring 134' and sailed by Captain S. M. Marsters with two mates and a crew of 24.

Apache was the only barque. The 220', Scottish-built ex-*White Heather* was re-named by her latest owner, Edmund Randolph, a New York stockbroker, who raced her with his captain, J. H. McDonald, two mates, J. K. Gibson and E. S. Estes, seven in the afterguard and a crew of 40.

The three foreign yachts came over well ahead of time. Square sails had a tendency to club together, *Valhalla* and *Sunbeam* anchoring in New York's North River near *Apache* (whose rig was much admired by Lord Brassey), rather than with the other yachts in the Horseshoe, farther down the Bay. *Hamburg* showed a weird offishness and remained aloof from all the others.

The newspapers made much of the good-natured Lord Brassey, who received reporters aboard and also in his Hotel Brevoort suite. His tall, courtly figure was imposing in the full dress uniform of Honorary Commander of the Royal Naval Reserve.

In yachting dress, he ran to a certain distinctive bagginess of trousers, amply cut double-breasted coats and steep-visored caps, rakishly set. His large, dark blue eyes twinkled in a lined, ruddy face trimmed with side whiskers and a fringe beard. He commanded his ship personally in deep water or foul weather, continually checking the rigging for improvements, and making all celestial observations. He knew all his crew personally, participating with them in the morning deck washing, his trouser legs rolled up, barefooted. Yet he always maintained an air of dignity.

Sunbeam was as sturdy and characteristic as her owner. She had been designed and built like an old ship-of-the-line, massive and apparently indestructible. She had a frigate's deck of thick, wide, teak planks, set with squarish, heavy deckhouses. At and above deck level she had windows instead of portholes, and the panes were heavy glass blocks.

Below decks the main cabin, illuminated by big skylights, was like a floating museum. Guests would be shown the cabin where "Lord Tennyson lived for days together," or "dear old Gladstone's room," with some of his books still in it.

Contrasting in cordiality was the German contender. Adolph Tietjens and his afterguard barely exchanged civilities with their fellow yachtsmen. The few pressmen and tradespeople allowed aboard *Hamburg* said of her company that "there was something odd about the way they acted," particularly with regard to a mysterious guest, a 19-year-old boy referred to only as "Mr. Pincinelli, an Italian merchant."

Tietjens gave private, hushed-up entertainments ashore, limited to this young man and other guests, after which "Mr. Pincinelli" booked passage for Germany aboard the steamer *Kaiser Wilhelm II*. Upon boarding the liner, he immediately disappeared into the captain's quarters, where he remained incommunicado until sailing time, under the name of Oberlieutenant R. Glaser, a German Army Officer.

The calm on the morning of May 17 caught some of the yachts offshore, where they had been tuning up, and delayed the start. Meanwhile, a large and restless spectator fleet gathered, proving hazardous and harassing to the sailors when excursion boats popped in and out of the fog, hunting celebrities and thrills for their customers. Everyone wanted to see *Atlantic*, the favorite, under Captain Barr of America's Cup fame; *Endymion*, the current trans-Atlantic champion; *Hamburg*, the mystery ship; *Valhalla*, with all her full square rig set; *Sunbeam*, the most famous. *Fleur-de-lis* drew quite a gallery for carrying the only lady, for being the smallest yacht (ignominiously sideswiped by a scow the night before), and because Dr. Stimson's captain, Tom Bohlin, was known to be the prototype for the famous Gloucester fisherman character, Captain Tom Ohlsen, in the best-selling sea tales of J. B. Connolly.

In the confusion, one of the spectator launches caught fire and her three occupants had to jump overboard, but were fished out safely. Then a postponement of the race was called, and a disillusioned gallery headed for shore.

This postponement and what some considered the ill omens of calm, fog, fire and collision caused nervous tension and discontent. There was trouble aboard *Atlantic*, and the high-strung Captain Barr was just barely persuaded not to quit his job.

Apache's volatile owner developed a touch of gout, and with it an increasingly dim view of the Kaiser and his rule that yachts with auxiliary power remove their propellers. Randolph considered this unsportsmanlike and, in a noble but unfortunate effort to illustrate true sportsmanship, dispensed with *Apache*'s "wireless" also, which was later needed.

After the spectator fleet had disappeared, a light breeze sprang up, dispersing the fog. The postponement was called off, and the starting gun boomed at 1415, with only a handful of spectators and officials present. *Atlantic* was first over the line.

Last across was *Apache*, to the dismay of her owner and seven unhappy guests. They were Royal Phelps Carroll, R. Burnside Potter, W. Gordon Fellowes, J. Borden Harriman, Ralph N. Ellis, Stuyvesant Leroy and the ship's doctor, W. B. Morrie, tending to their gouty host. The big barque maintained this embarrassing position all the way over, slowly but steadily increasing the gap, a fate due partly to the most trying circumstances (which seem to have surrounded her more than any other vessel in the race) and partly to the choice of too northerly a course for that time of year.

As to this course, it is odd that various records, which should be reliable, show discrepancies never explained. *Apache*'s log book has disappeared, but daily fixes from it appear in a German account presented to the New York YC by Commander H. G. Hebbinghaus of the Imperial Navy, then Naval Attaché at the German Embassy in Washington.

According to this account, the yacht seems to have logged 762 statute miles to the noon fix of May 22. However, on that day, she was reported by the steamer *Columbia* at Lat. 40° 29′ N., Lon. 50° 50′ W. and heading for an ice field. The *Columbia*'s fix would have put her about 1,200 miles east of New York, off the Grand Banks, and some 430 miles southeast of Cape Race, an apparently impossible position according to the German records, which show that she did not log this distance until May 26, a discrepancy of some 438 statute miles.

Meanwhile, there was no doubt about *Atlantic*. She was thrashing along on her more southerly course, holding and widening her lead under the determined Captain Barr, who put in by far the most hours as helmsman, especially in heavy weather, and practically lived in hip boots. Although she was a little shy of ballast in the keel, the Scotsman kept her lee railing awash for days at a time (and some of her guests praying below decks) while he drove her for every ounce she was worth.

Somewhere near the middle of the field was tiny *Fluer-de-lis* at about this time, likewise on a somewhat northerly course. She reported battling fogs and furious gales, and dodging icebergs. For three days she was forced to batten down her hatches while her decks were under water and her helmsman was lashed to the wheel.

On Sunday morning, June 4, the New York newspapers concluded that *Apache*, unreported for 13 days, and last seen headed for arctic ice, was sunk. Apparently, they assumed that she had her "wireless" intact and would otherwise have been heard from somehow. Headlines on a front page spread of the "American and Journal" announced, "*APACHE* FEARED LOST IN ICE FIELDS WITH ALL HANDS" over a large picture of the barque and a smaller one purporting to be her owner but which was actually his father. There followed weepy columns about this sporting tragedy and the sad loss of the prominent people, together with a faint hope that some of them might still be picked up in the yacht's lifeboats.

Since all other yachts had finished without sight of, or word from *Apache*, the conclusion was perhaps not unreasonable. But it was happily erroneous.

After the *Columbia*'s sighting and report, the barque was practically becalmed off the Banks on May 24 and 25, so that her run for the latter two days was only 141 miles. During this time, her owner and his friends amused themselves by fishing for cod. Then the wind came up suddenly.

For the next two days, she was buffeted by no less than four heavy gales, culminating in a fierce, icy blow which forced Captain McDonald to heave to for 18 hours on May 27. This reduced her progress on that day to 69 miles, as compared with her previous low point of 68 miles, three days before, from too *little* wind.

By May 28 she was back on course, and from then on, her daily runs kept increasing, to a peak of 271 miles at the noon reckoning of June 2, when she reached her highest latitude, 50° 33′ N. Next day, her run dropped to 190 miles as she neared England.

On Monday morning, June 5, the newspapers published a different story. *Apache* had been sighted and spoken to (wig-wagged) by the steamer *Minnetonka* at a position given as "250 miles west of the Lizard," which should have been her position at noon Sunday, according to the German figures.

Minnetonka had also given the financially bad news of that climactic turn in the Russo-Japanese war: the sinking of the Russian fleet by Admiral Togo in Tsushima Strait on May 27. That did not help Randolph's gouty temper.

Now that there was some definite fix on *Apache*'s whereabouts, after two weeks of anxiety, the Kaiser dispatched a swift destroyer under two senior naval officers, to intercept the beleagured yacht, present congratulations and offer a tow.

Randolph considered the mention of a tow out of order, since he had not abandoned the race, and this offer of help was a little late—coming from one so lacking in sporting sense that he had snatched away *Apache*'s propeller. He wanted no help from the Kaiser, who had not even helped his own first cousin, the Czar, and had probably helped only a crash in Wall Street. He was for dismissing the destroyer forthwith.

Cooler heads on the bridge and in the afterguard suggested that this might be considered a breach of etiquette, since they were all technically guests of the Emperor, and should at least invite his emissaries aboard, even though it meant heaving to again and losing more time, just as they were enjoying their first good sailing.

Etiquette won, but in a specially tailored version. *Apache* came up into the wind and the Germans were welcomed aboard late at night, with the understanding that her owner was unable to receive them personally, being confined to his stateroom on doctor's orders. Captain McDonald played host, offered the hospitality of the ship and had champagne broken out. The party lasted until nearly dawn, somewhat to the annoyance of the owner.

The dawn was that of June 5, on which *Apache* crossed the finish line at 1020, 18 days, 17 hours and 3 min. from Sandy Hook to Lizard Light. Of the expected distance she had hoped to save by sailing the northerly course all but 38 miles had been lost by her being blown off course. Her final track was 2,975 miles, which she covered at an average speed of 6.88 knots.

Atlantic's winning time was 12 days, 4 hours and 1 min., over her southerly track of 3,013 statute miles at an average speed of 10.32 knots.

Following *Atlantic* by 22 hours came *Hamburg*. *Valhalla* placed third, also trailing the winner by nearly two days. Then *Endymion*, *Hildegarde*, *Sunbeam*, little *Fleur-de-lis*, *Ailsa*, *Utowana* and *Thistle*.

The yachts re-grouped at Dover for the race to the little island of Heligoland in the North Sea, slated to start June 17. Bad weather again prevailed, with rain and fog, so that only five of the eleven actually raced. The others, including *Apache*, following along at their leisure. From Heligoland they proceeded through the Kaiser Wilhelm (or Kiel) Canal across Schleswig-Holstein to the port of Kiel, for the Emperor's reception aboard his imposing *Hohenzollern*.

The Ocean Race festivities culminated at the Kaiserlicher YC there, a great dinner being held the night of June 26. Forty battleships, cruisers and other naval vessels were moored hard by, their attention riveted on the clubhouse. When the Kaiser arrived with a bevy of dignitaries, their searchlights were turned on suddenly and focused upon the building for the entire time he was within. When he emerged, all ships broke out into gala lighting, while far out in the harbor a huge edition of the Imperial standard blazed from *Hohenzollern*'s masthead.

Meanwhile, a summer thunderstorm had been in the making, with a background of dark clouds as a perfect setting for the illumination. Just as the Imperial Band strenuously unleashed its patriotic strains, nature joined in homage to Wilhelm with a mighty thunderclap and a bolt of lightning. Then the searchlights followed his launch out to the *Hohenzollern*, serenaded by the strains of "Watch on the Rhine" and Körner's "Battle Song."

All in all, the Ocean Race was a great success for the Kaiser, even though he didn't participate. It was a fine piece of publicity for him and for the German Navy.

Wilson Marshall, winner of the ugly, much-touted golden cup, had every reason to be proud, too. It was the only one of its kind in the world, designed and presented by the Kaiser himself. There was only one thing wrong with this cup, which was not discovered until its donor became our enemy in World War I.

Then, no longer so proud of his trophy, Mr. Marshall decided that it should be melted down, and the gold value invested in war bonds. Only then was it discovered that the cup was indeed, not gold at all, except for a clever job of plating. The rest was pewter.

The Fastnet Disaster

Guy Gurney

*Ocean racing's worst tragedy claims 15 lives and over 20 yachts as a freak
storm scatters the 306-boat fleet*

Three hundred and six yachts started the 1979 Fastnet Race off
Cowes, in Britain's Isle of Wight, on Saturday, August 11. Six days
later, 97 boats had finished. The remaining 209 had either retired,
been abandoned or sunk. Not since the disintegration of the Spanish
Armada in 1588 had a fleet in British waters been so reduced in
numbers by a storm. A total of 15 racing yachtsmen and three other
sailors had died in the course of the storm, which Royal Ocean
Racing Club Secretary Alan Green described as "a freak." No fewer
than 136 individuals were rescued, of whom 75 were lifted from their
yachts or from the water by helicopters. Twenty-four yachts were
lost or abandoned.

After the spray had settled, Ted Turner's 61-foot, S&S-designed
Tenacious emerged as the corrected-time Fastnet winner, followed
by the British Contessa 39 *Eclipse*, skippered by Jeremy Rogers.
Third was the Peterson-designed *Jubile*. In the Admiral's Cup series,
for which the Fastnet was the final and clinching race, the Australian
team of *Ragamuffin*, *Impetuous* and *Police Car* finished first. The
American trio, *Imp*, *Aries* and *Williwaw*, were second, and *Eclipse*
was the first-to-finish of the Admiral's Cuppers.

Before the start, the weather forecast was a moderate one, calling
for southwest winds seven to 16 knots. The actual start was in light
and variable breezes, and by Sunday morning most of the fleet was
tacking slowly along the south coast of England, with insufficient air
to work their way around some of the headlands when the strong
tidal current was against them. At one stage some 40 yachts were
stacked up at Portland Bill waiting for the tide to turn. People had
begun to talk about another slow, boring Fastnet like the previous
three, all held in unusually light airs.

Aboard the Australian Admiral's Cupper *Police Car*, Hood Sail-makers' President Chris Bouzaid remembered, "Since we were at our worst in light and variable winds, due to the boat's fractional rig, we elected to go out in one long board and back to the Lizard on another to miss Portland Bill altogether. Sunday morning we were back at the Lizard and the seas were building, but it was a dead calm. We got all the weather forecast information we could, and it predicted a fresh Force 7 (28–33 knots) with a low coming in."

As the leading boats left Land's End to head northwest across the Irish Sea toward the turning mark at Fastnet Rock, the change of weather became apparent. At 1800 the shipping forecast issued a prediction for the area of Force 6 to 8 (winds to 40 knots) from the south, veering to the west. The wind backed around to the southeast and started to build, the sky turned ominous, and barometers began to drop dramatically, as the racing fleet prepared itself for a good blow.

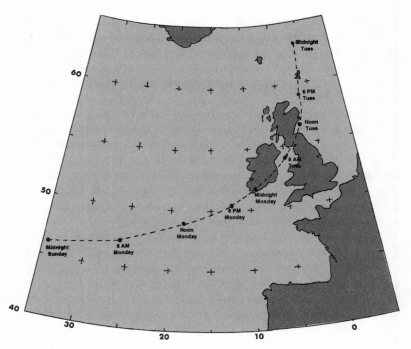

Track of the Fastnet storm

Those listeners able to hear and understand the French marine forecast an hour later were told to expect winds of 41 to 47 knots, a strong gale in Beaufort Scale terms. Aboard many yachts, this was the first indication of a true storm, as opposed to the traditional Fastnet bad weather. Aboard *Police Car*, Chris Bouzaid said that the wind came on quickly: "By Sunday 2100 it had freshened to more than 35 knots and we took our Flanker down after a nosedive told us it was time to get the gear off."

Apparently the result of a collision between a cold front coming down from Iceland and a warm front moving northeastward, the blow caught forecasters totally by surprise, and even the radio-equipped yachts in the fleet had only a couple of hours' warning before the winds were at full strength. (Because of the cost—four times what it is in this country—radio equipment is not required in RORC-sponsored events, except aboard the Admiral's Cup squadron.) As predicted, the wind did shift around to the west, making it vital to round Fastnet Rock early, although some of the fastest boats arrived too early. The two maxi-yachts in the lead, *Condor* and *Kialoa*, were on the wind for about six hours after rounding, until the wind shift. On the eventual corrected-time race winner, Ted Turner's 61-foot *Tenacious*, the navigator was Peter Bowker—one of ocean racing's most experienced contenders: "Well, I nearly got washed overboard as I went up to take a bearing. We were sort of reaching: we got around the rock before the wind came in, and we thought that screwed us because after rounding we were hard on the wind. Then it freed us up, but we were down to just the storm jib and had the main down for five or six hours.

"I had to come on deck to take a radio bearing—I never had to do this in a race before, because I usually use Omni, but Omni, like Loran, is banned in RORC races. I was sitting down to leeward in the cockpit with the Brookes & Gatehouse unit when a wave came up and washed me out of there. I hit the wheel and bent it to hell. I had no harness on—navigators aren't supposed to need harnesses—and I thought I was going over the side for sure. I found myself underwater, tangled with the lifeline, and I was OK, and I had the bearing. When I came up, I still had the headphones on and the compass in my hands, but the B&G box was gone."

Aboard the Two Tonner *Police Car*, conditions appeared even more violent: "We got to the rock with a triple-reefed main and a number four and came back with a beam wind in the most dangerous conditions possible. This was the point at which the smaller boats had real problems, as they were still beating out to the rock in 30-

to 40-foot seas. The tops of the waves were breaking off and sliding down, making it like a beach surf. For the small boats, climbing these seas was nearly impossible without full power. The boats trying to sail with mainsails alone couldn't handle it. We rolled the spar down three times and were racing along waves at 17 knots at times—the waves were breaking all the time, so it was like riding a surfboard, with a maximum wind of 70 knots lasting for about four hours."

The larger boats, including most of the Admiral's Cup contenders, had rounded by the early hours of Tuesday morning, when the worst part of the storm had passed over the general area, accompanied by a violent, 90-degree wind shift to the west. Some vessels near Fastnet Rock, which is only a few miles off the jagged Irish shore, reported very confused seas with large, periodic peaks coming out of a completely different direction from that of the wind-driven wave system. Skippers speculated that these rogue breakers, which were difficult or impossible for a boat to avoid, were rebounding from the Irish coast.

As the head end of the fleet rounded off for a broad reach toward the Scilly Isles under storm jibs alone, the smaller and slower boats found themselves tacking into winds of 70 knots and seas averaging 20 to 30 feet. Many yachts were unable to sail into the steep, plunging seas, and there were numerous reports of boats being repeatedly flattened, with crews and gear tossed about down below. Lying ahull, recommended for extreme weather conditions, was often impossible because with way off, the boats were hurled about to such an extent that stoves and even inboard engines were being broken loose and crewmembers risked serious injury lying in their bunks.

The extreme motion was not confined to the smaller boats, as the 47-foot Admiral's Cupper *Jan Pott* did a 360-degree roll and lost her spar. Other craft reported somersaulting and cartwheeling in the seas. Many radio and masthead electronic units were blown off or broken in knockdowns and, with water inundating the accommodations, many of the transceiver-equipped yachts lost radio communication.

As the smaller boats were hammering their way toward the rock and making very little progress, *Condor* was slipping ahead of *Kialoa*. Neither of the maxi-yachts ever saw the other, and *Condor* elected to go inside the Scilly Isles (a short-cut that wrecked the ill-fated tanker *Torrey Canyon* in 1967), while *Kialoa* took the safer route outside. Her owner-skipper, Jim Kilroy, sustained three broken ribs when two crewmen were pitched on top of him after he had been tossed onto a cockpit winch.

Condor set a 2.2-ounce spinnaker and was going very fast when she took a terrific broach that brought her head-to-wind, with the chute backed and driving her astern at three knots. The helmsman spun her around, the spinnaker filled again, and they were off after what a crewman termed "a perfect three-point turn."

Owner Bob Bell said that if there were another broach like the first, he would take off the spinnaker. About 30 minutes later a second broach put green water over the coffee grinders, and the sail was doused. But *Condor* still chalked up a first-to-finish in record time.

Tuesday ended with the first, larger yachts finishing as the other vessels were still virtually stalled, struggling with winds and seas. The battle was simply too much for some of the boats and their crews; Gear—especially rudders—began to give way under repeated stresses, and crews began to think about leaving their yachts. New Zealander Ron Holland is an outstanding yacht designer and an experienced offshore skipper. Aboard his *Golden Apple of the Sun*, he had a crack crew that included Olympic champion Rodney Patisson and level-rating winner Harry Cudmore. All of them abandoned the rudderless Admiral's Cupper, as Holland explains:

"The main reason was that we had a really bad weather forecast of 48–55 knots again. We had already broken our spinnaker pole trying to steer the boat after losing the rudder in the worst of the storm, and we had no way to steer. We were 40 miles to windward of the Scilly Isles, cold, wet and tired, and there was this helicopter dangling a rope at us. So we said 'screw it' and grabbed it.

"If the wind had been moderating, we might have stayed, but with that forecast we weren't very keen to spend Tuesday night out there. We set the boat up well for the night, with fenders all around it, shut the hatches, put the nav lights on and raised the radar reflector to the masthead. We had an accurate position fix from a cargo ship with sat nav which was standing by. We thought if the weather was fine the boat would be all right on its own and we could pick it up the next day, and if the weather was going to be really bad again, we wouldn't want to be out there anyway." (Subsequently, Holland and his crew did recover *Golden Apple*.)

Other yachts were abandoned in a less calculated fashion, and sometimes in the face of near-suicidal conditions. Chris Bouzaid said of the worst of the storm: "There is no way any kind of life raft would stand up in those conditions, and smart people would stay with the boats. But you really needed total control with the power of a headsail and main." Fatalities occurred as people were thrown out of rafts that flipped over in the heavy seas and high winds. There were reports of canopies blown off the rafts, and the cold water and constant exposure caused hypothermia in many individuals.

English sailor Peter Bruce grew up sailing with his father, renowned racer-author Errol Bruce. Peter was aboard the top-placing British Admiral's Cup yacht, *Eclipse*. "I'm worried by the lack of experience in the fleet generally. Some people don't actually do any offshore racing all year around and just come out for the Fastnet because everyone else does, and it's a sort of end-of-season jamboree. It is increasingly a case of people taking along their 19-year-old daughter, to make it a family outing. People have been predicting for several years that there would be a really heavy Fastnet and that these new attitudes would create problems. We hadn't a good blow for many years now, and in any case people think of safety in numbers, with someone always around to look after you.

"There *have* been gales before—1957, 1961 and 1969—but there was more respect for the sea. Those older boats had less sail, stronger masts, narrower hulls. They were more heavily built and the people had a different attitude toward it. *Eclipse* was one of the light ones, but we had a strong crew: Our weakest members were probably stronger than the skippers of some other boats."

According to Bruce, avoiding panic in extreme conditions is a matter of experience and preparation: "If water starts coming in, you pump it out quickly. You keep on top of the situation. If you have been through it, you're always ready for the next problem. But when the going gets really tough, some can't cope.

"If you have been through this sort of thing before, you know that it always clears up and the sun always comes out, and that keeps you driving through it. Sailing back from the Lizard to the finish was one of the most delightful sails of the season, running with a spinnaker."

Ten of the competing yachts suffered broken rudders, including five Admiral's Cup contenders. Most of the broken rudders were made of light-weight carbon fiber, but at least one was of titanium. This one was aboard the Admiral's Cup boat *Tina*, in which Doug Peterson was a crew member. The titanium blade was attached to the rudder shaft with clamps, rather than by welding, and the blade began to slip on the shaft. The crew tried to steer using a spinnaker pole and made it to Cork in southern Ireland after the wind had moderated to 25 knots. At the height of the storm, they reported, it was nearly impossible to work on deck. The wind was too strong to allow one to stand and the boat was leaping about so wildly that the crew had to crawl hand over hand across the deck.

Derelict *Ariadne* in wake of Fastnet disaster. The yacht was later reported sunk, with two of it's crew members dead, two rescued by another vessel, and one rescued by helicopter.

As Wednesday dawned, the winds fell to Force 6 in most areas, and the remaining competitors raced to the finish as the race and rescue authorities ashore began sorting out the disaster. The rescue effort was one of the largest ever in peacetime, and included units of the Royal Navy, Royal Air Force, Royal National Life-boat Institution (a publicly supported, volunteer search-and-rescue service), fishing boats, coasters and a Netherlands Navy destroyer. This vessel, the *Overijssel*, picked off one crew who were able to step from their yacht as the large ship rolled through 60 degrees to lay her rail down to water level.

Of the 15 dead in the racing fleet, two were Americans—Frank Ferris, skipper of the Carter 35 *Ariadne*, and Robert Robie, one of his crew. The three non-racing fatalities were the entire crew of a small trimaran that set out to track the race unofficially, in the face of warnings that the multihull was unready for the open sea. The sunk and abandoned boats were about equally divided among classes 3, 4 and 5—the smallest in the fleet, with yachts ranging from approximately 30 to 37 feet overall.

Alan Green, RORC Secretary and spokesman, was particularly disturbed at inaccuracies in early news reports, especially those from the United States. He also explained the RORC's point of view regarding its races: "The principle of ocean racing is that yachts must leave port entirely self-sufficient and able to meet any weather. And it is a tradition that RORC races are started at the time advertised, and it is up to the skippers to decide to start and whether to continue the race. . . . There is always the compromise between speed and seaworthiness. The object of our club is to encourage the best combination of speed and seaworthiness. Since the first Fastnet Race in 1925, there has never been a storm like this," Green concluded.

British yachting generally is far less regulated than it is in many other countries, including the United States. While many organizations issue lists of recommended safety equipment, there is no governmentally imposed list of safety gear for yachts, nor is there a single organization comparable to the U.S. Coast Guard, with both law-enforcement and search-and-rescue functions. The policy of leaving most equipment and operational decisions in the hands of individual skippers applies also in offshore racing, where Offshore Racing Council–required equipment lists may or may not apply. The question of how much help additional supervision would have given will obviously be a controversial one. Chris Bouzaid, who did most of his youthful sailing in his native Australia, feels quite strongly: "The lessons on safety procedures are there to learn. All boats should have radios, as we do in Australia. There should also be a strict rule on spade rudders to insure their strength, again like we do in Australia."

Initial investigation has suggested that there may be some problem with the quality of carbon fiber supplied for many of the rudders that failed under storm conditions, rather than with the rudder design itself. Other racers criticized what they felt was an excessively casual attitude toward ensuring that yachts had complied with equipment requirements.

Lost or abandoned:
Class 3
Allamanda—OOD 34, *Griffin*—OOD 34, *Charioteer*—OOD 34, *Festina Tertia*—Contessa 35, *Carmargue*—Buchanan North Sea 34, *Tide Race*—Holland One Ton, *Trophy*—Holman and Pye 37.

Class 4
Adriadne—Carter 35, *Flashlight*—Olson 35, *Hestrul*—Holman and Pye 35, *Polar Bear*—Holman and Pye 33, *Gringo*—Frers 33, *Alvena*—Peterson 33.

Class 5
Billy Bones—Mauric 28, *Bonaventure, Gan-Harlé, Skidbladner*—Ballad, *Maligawa*—Linge 33, *Grimalkin*—C&N 30, *Gunslinger*—Jones 30.

Cup Goes Down Under

Guy Gurney and Jack Somer

The 25th Defense: the Challenge that succeeded where all others failed.

It had to happen sooner or later. The America's Cup has finally departed these shores, after an unbroken run of 132 years of successful defenses. Alan Bond, on his fourth try, has succeeded in capturing the Cup for Australia, and the New York Yacht Club has handed it over to the Royal Perth Yacht Club.

After a summer filled with incident and controversy, the final Cup series was the most exciting ever seen. After breakdowns in the first two races *Australia II* soon found herself 3–1 down in the best-of-seven series, but rallied to draw level and finally win the Cup. Dennis Conner and the crew of *Liberty* sailed magnificently, but found themselves up against a yacht that was significantly faster in most conditions. Yet, ironically, it was not a speed difference in the end that cost them the Cup, but a windshift on the run of the final race, when *Liberty* led by nearly a minute, with one last leg remaining before clinching another successful defense. The Australians snatched the lead and survived a long tacking duel on the final leg to score a stunning victory.

Pandemonium broke out. Surrounded by a fleet of cheering supporters, the triumphant crew was towed slowly back to Newport, where Conner and the crew of *Liberty* were already waiting to give the traditional three cheers to the victors. The scene that followed at the Australian dock was unforgettable, even to a town as accustomed to post-race celebrations as is Newport. One famous international sports photographer, standing beside me, said that he had never seen a celebration like it, even when Italy had won the soccer World Cup.

Under a battery of television lights and flashing strobes, surrounded by a vast crowd of supporters, singing, cheering and endlessly spraying champagne over the crew and each other, Bond stood beaming on the bow of *Australia II*'s tender. Then, in a moment of pure theater, he slowly raised his arms to indicate that the yacht should be hoisted out of the water, to reveal the secret keel to the public gaze for the first time. The crowd went wild, and Australian supporters paddled small boats or swam to the keel to stroke it and kiss it.

Its shape is close to the profile and plan drawings printed in the September 1983 issue of *Yachting*, except that there is no bulb, and the trailing edges of the fins are not swept back. Designer Ben Lexcen describes it as an upside-down keel: in other words, imagine a conventional (but slightly smaller than usual) 12-Meter keel cut off where it meets the hull, and reattached the other way up. Thus it is broader at the base than at the top, both in profile and in end elevation. The wings, which start halfway back along the base of the keel, are each about 3' wide by 6' long, angled down about 20 degrees. They are made of lead, contributing toward the righting moment as well as providing an endplate effect on the keel and increasing the effective draft when heeled.

There is no doubt that Lexcen's radical hull design played a major part in winning the Cup for Australia. Knowing that your yacht is superior in terms of maneuverability, pointing, stiffness and acceleration provides a very large psychological advantage. Throughout the summer the *Australia II* team had worked with quiet confidence, making few mistakes while learning how best to use their powerful weapon. In elimination trials against the six other potential foreign challengers they had won 43 out of 48 races, beating *Victory '83* in the finals 4–1 to become challenger.

If Lexcen is the genius that provided the seeds of success, the experience of three previous challenges enabled Bond to put together an impressive team with no weak links. Skipper John Bertrand, tactician Hugh Treharne and the rest of the crew were as competent as the management team of Bond, Warren Jones and John Longley, all veterans of Bond's original 1974 challenge. Their thoroughness extended to enlisting the services of three helmsmen of eliminated challengers, Terry McLaughlin, Harry Cudmore and Bruno Troublé, to take the wheel of *Challenge 12* on lay days during the Cup series to provide Bertrand with starting practice. The sails, designed by Tom Schnackenberg of North, were certainly as good as those used by *Liberty*, eliminating another weakness of previous challenges.

In comparison, the American yacht showed signs of strain, coming to the starting line with scars on her hull and paint peeling off her mast. For most of the summer honors had been evenly shared by the three potential defenders, and it was only at the end of August that *Liberty* began to win with any consistency. She was probably chosen mainly for the system of multiple rating certificates that designer Johan Valentijn had worked out, which gave her a unique advantage. Her performance could be matched to daily conditions by removing or adding internal ballast and sail area the day before, while retaining an identical 12-Meter rating. It was a controversial but perfectly legal system under the present rule.

Liberty and *Australia II* turned out to be surprisingly evenly matched to windward. *Liberty* tended to drive off for speed while *Australia II* pointed higher, but it was usually when they tacked that the American yacht was at a real disadvantage. On the reaches she tended to gain slightly, but running she lost distance almost every time to the Australians, who were able to point much lower without losing speed. This came as a real surprise, because in the challengers' trials running had been her weak point. Perhaps the foreign yachts were all fast downwind. Throughout the series Conner avoided tacking duels, after early experience showed up *Australia II*'s superiority at them in both light and heavy conditions. It was only in the last beat of the last race that he found that he could match the other yacht tack for tack in medium air.

Many still believe that the winged keel is illegal. During the summer the America's Cup Committee of the NYYC took various steps to prove its illegality, giving the unfortunate impression that they would try anything to hold onto the Cup. Their rather tactless handling of the affair brought them universal public condemnation, and dismayed many of their own members. The committee obviously acted in good faith, but they reached a stage where whatever they did was bound to be wrong in the public view.

They claimed that the keel had been designed by Dutchmen at the Netherlands Ship Model Basin where Lexcen worked on the design, but this was quickly denied. They claimed that the keel was a "peculiarity" under 12-Meter Rule 27, and as such deserved a rating penalty, but the measurement committee which they had appointed (whose decision could not be appealed) disagreed. The NYYC pointed out the advantages of the increased draft produced by *Australia II*'s wings when she heeled—surely this was a "peculiarity"? No more so than *Intrepid*'s two rudders in 1967, said the Australians, and even Olin Stephens agreed with them. The final embarrassing moment for the NYYC came when the Australians revealed that Ed du Moulin, manager of Conner's campaign, had telexed to Holland a request to buy a winged keel design, offering to keep the deal confidential. This revelation somewhat diluted the NYYC case, and they gave up the struggle. No doubt the November meetings of the IYRU will discuss the issue at length. But nothing can detract from a fine effort by the Australians, who by any standards sailed well and deserved to win the Cup.—*G.G.*

Race 1: After a first-day abandonment, the race was held in a fresh 18-knot northeasterly, under a bright New England autumn sky. The Twelves started on starboard tack, with *Australia II* three seconds ahead and to leeward. *Liberty* soon tacked to the favored right side and *Australia II* covered, and for the first time in this agonizingly long campaign the world was able to view them side by side.

These were supposed to be *Liberty*'s conditions and *Australia II*'s nemesis—moderately strong winds and sloppy seas. Yet both John Bertrand, at *Australia II*'s helm, and Dennis Conner, on *Liberty,* seemed to have great difficulty reining in their boats, Conner apparently the worst of it. *Liberty*'s mainsail fluttered; she heeled five degrees more than her rival. Both yachts tracked oddly in the chop and locally shifty winds.

Still, after *Australia II* tacked away onto starboard and then both tacked to cross for the first time, *Liberty* had a slight lead. At the northern end of the course *Australia II* gained the lead on sheer boat speed, crossed *Liberty* and tacked on her weather bow. Bertrand, in command, held Conner away from the mark, carrying him almost into a collision with an anchored Coast Guard cutter, before tacking for the mark to round eight seconds ahead.

Australia II gained two seconds on the first reach, but on the second Conner sailed high for speed and Bertrand hesitated to cover. Within a few hundred yards of the mark Conner gained "mast abeam" and drove over Bertrand to run for the mark and round 16 seconds ahead.

On the second windward leg Conner settled *Liberty* down and picked up 12 seconds. Then at the mark he called for a jibe set to protect the left side of the course, but his crew took about 30 seconds to get *Liberty*'s spinnaker squared and drawing while *Australia II* rounded smoothly with superior speed. Minutes later Conner jibed back to cover (after changing to a lighter chute) and had lost all but inches of the lead. As the two ran for the mark on port, Conner faked a jibe, called his bowman back, then jibed swiftly to starboard. Bertrand, caught unprepared, was forced to head up sharply to clear *Liberty*'s stern. *Australia II* broached; her spinnaker pole flew wildly upward, killing her speed and her steering jammed when a cable pulley bracket bent under the load. *Liberty* rounded 35 seconds ahead. On the final beat Bertrand was forced to steer by trim tab for ten minutes until a jury rig was set. *Liberty* gained 35 seconds to win by 1:10.

Race 2: *Liberty* took the start by five seconds and headed for the right side. But *Australia II*'s mainsail flogged excessively. Prior to the start, the headboard locking device failed, the sail slipped one foot and the sail tore. Despite that, Bertrand was able to lead at the mark by 45 seconds.

On the reaches—while *Australia II* sent a man up the mast to attempt a repair—*Liberty* recouped 24 seconds. The mainsail was by then, according to Alan Bond, held to the headboard by "a one-inch piece of Kevlar."

On the second beat, Conner forced Bertrand into a pair of tacking duels to press his advantage when he saw *Australia*'s boom dragging. Splitting with *Australia II*, *Liberty* rode to a lift, tacked to starboard and crossed one length ahead. Conner immediately tacked on Bertrand's wind and Bertrand was forced to tack sharply under *Liberty*'s stern to clear his air. *Australia II* raised a protest flag on the basis that Conner had not given them room to keep clear. Conner led at the mark by 48 seconds.

On the run, Conner covered but lost 17 seconds as the breeze fell to 10 knots. On the final beat, with a course change to accommodate the veering breeze, Conner kept a loose cover and won by 1:33. The next day the Jury threw out *Australia*'s protest.

Race 3: (The first attempt at a third race was abandoned at 1725 on September 17. *Australia II* was ahead by 5:57 at the fifth mark when time ran out.) In the third race start, Conner forced Bertrand to tack to starboard, but had to luff sharply to avoid hitting the committee boat's anchor rode, thus diminishing his eight-second lead. Ten minutes later *Australia II*, pointing higher and footing faster, crossed *Liberty*, never to be threatened. She showed extraordinary light-air speed and led at the first mark by 1:14. Conner cut that lead to 42 seconds on the reaches, but Bertrand applied a loose cover on the second beat and led by 1:15. *Australia II*, supposedly slow on the run, widened the lead to 2:47 at the fifth mark and eventually finished 3:14 ahead of the burgundy-red American boat, in shifting wind. With predictions of light air, Conner asked for a lay day.

Race 4: Conner took advantage of Bertrand's late tack onto starboard to cross him on port tack with good speed and ahead by six seconds at the gun. *Australia II* tacked on *Liberty*'s hip and both sailed right. But Conner played the shifts better and *Liberty* extended her lead on each successive crossing. Conner, applying a loose cover, rounded 36 seconds ahead.

On the first reach, both set staysails—*Australia II* for the first time—and *Liberty* rounded the wing and leeward marks ahead 48 seconds.

Conner, avoiding extensive tacking duels, applied a loose cover to the second windward mark, losing only two seconds. On the run *Australia II* regained 11 seconds, but could not break through, and Conner rounded in a commanding position. With good boat speed in the freshening afternoon breeze, Conner held Bertrand off and took the gun by 43 seconds.

Race 5: One hour before the start, *Liberty*'s port hydraulic jumper strut extender collapsed as she hit a large wave. A new part was sent from ashore, and Tom Rich and Scott Vogel went up the mast to install it and retune the mast. By the time they returned to the deck, exhausted and bruised, two minutes remained to the first gun. In their haste to bend on the genoa they tore its luff tape and had to hoist Conner's second choice.

Still, at the start Conner held Bertrand at the buoy end of the line, then tacked away on port with good speed. Bertrand mistimed, luffed to slow down but *Australia II* was over early. Bertrand restarted, behind by 37 seconds.

But less than four minutes into the race *Liberty*'s new extender failed (it was too long). She was partially crippled on port tack—with the top of her mast bowed to leeward she lost pointing ability. Conner chose to split tacks rather than cover closely and risk a tacking duel. Halfway up the leg *Australia II*, playing the shifts better, tacked to starboard and a safe leeward on *Liberty*. Conner tacked away and when they crossed again *Australia II* was ahead to stay, opening her lead to 23 seconds. From then on Bertrand made no errors, leading at the wing mark by 23 seconds and the third mark by 18 seconds. On the second beat, with the mark moved to allow for a shift, *Australia II* led by 1:11; at the fifth mark by 52 seconds, and she finished 1:47 ahead of *Liberty*.

Race 6: A cold front moved through New England in the night, then skies brightened as a fresh northwesterly brought unlimited visibility.

Conner avoided a tight circling fight at the start then forced Bertrand on to port tack. Starting eight seconds ahead, *Liberty* soon crossed then covered and both Twelves took a long starboard tack toward Point Judith.

Australia II came back onto port and Conner forced her back onto starboard. On their second crossing Conner refused to cover and remained on port tack for eight minutes. Bertrand sailed into a freshening header, tacking onto port into a lift that never reached *Liberty*. Conner came back on starboard and when the two crossed *Australia II* was well ahead. Bertrand tacked on *Liberty*'s wind and forced Conner back onto port. For the rest of the leg *Australia II*, still in the lift and with a fresher breeze, climbed over *Liberty* and led at the mark by 2:29. Always on the favored end of the still-shifting breeze, *Australia II* opened her lead to 3:46 on the reaching legs. On the second beat *Liberty* gained 24 seconds, but fell behind by 4:08 at the leeward mark. Conner regained 43 seconds on the last leg, as the wind stabilized and the shifts became less important. *Australia II*'s 3:25 victory proved her strength in medium air. Despite their momentum, the Aussies called a lay day to thoroughly check their boat.

Race 7: On Saturday, September 24, the wind was light and shifty and after two false starts, the race was abandoned. Immediately, the *Liberty* syndicate asked for a lay day: Expecting 10- to 12-knot winds they put *Liberty* into her "light mode" for the final race.

That race started in ideal conditions. An eight- to 10-knot southerly filled Rhode Island Sound. Shifty at first, it caused a postponement. But, at 1305 the most crucial sailing race of all time had its start. *Liberty* crossed the line ahead by eight seconds. Conner chose to sail to the right, Bertrand to the left, each in search of the favorable shifts. On their first crossing *Australia* tacked on *Liberty*'s wind, forcing Conner to tack. But Conner returned to starboard, on the inside of a lift, and worked out ahead to round 29 seconds in the lead. His early rounding gave him a 45-second advantage at the wing mark, but Bertrand changed to a lighter spinnaker and gained 22 seconds. Conner found the right breeze on the second beat and widened his lead to 57 seconds.

But history was made on the next leg: the run. Minutes after rounding, *Liberty* jibed to port leaving *Australia II* alone on the right. Bertrand found two freshening shifts and by the time Conner jibed back Bertrand had closed the gap. Passing across *Liberty*'s bow, *Australia II* rounded 21 seconds ahead. Bertrand applied a perfect cover during 47 tacks up to the finish. In desperation, Conner tried to take Bertrand beyond the starboard tack layline into the spectator fleet, but Bertrand wouldn't have it. He tacked first and headed for home and history. *Australia* finished 41 seconds ahead of *Liberty*, and the world's longest winning streak ended at 132 years and 41 seconds.—*J.S.*

PART II
History, Adventure and Hard Chances

Reports on all forms of seafaring have appeared in Yachting, starting with reminiscences, in the early years, of the great days of sail. Herb Stone, editor for so many years, had gone to sea under sail as a young man, had a vast personal knowledge of the subject and a continuing interest in it, and articles he printed in the magazine served as a valuable history of a dying era. Other colorful sea sagas, of wrecks, storms, rum-running and odd bits of history and folklore have enlivened the pages while providing valuable background information and the stuff of dreams and fantasies.

Croesus and His Steam Yacht

Arthur F. Aldridge

What life was like, and what it cost, on the floating palaces of the golden era of luxury yachts in the first decade of the twentieth century

There seems to be no limit to the luxury and comfort that may be found in a steam yacht these days, and as a result a great deal of the romance of yachting has departed. When one sees the luxurious pleasure boat of today and then thinks that in the early days of this country adventurous men crossed the ocean in small sailing craft, almost small enough to be carried on the davits of some of these steamers, one wonders how they did it. Then they had to subsist on food that would not perish by keeping and on water that became tainted. Their bunks were hard and uncomfortable, there was no heat on the boats, and the lights were only the dim flickerings of tiny candles. Navigating instruments were crude, and as those early mariners had to suffer hundreds of untold hardships, it is a wonder that they reached their destination.

A steam yacht now is a palace afloat. Every conceivable comfort can be found on board. The fittings are the most artistic that can be procured. There will be one suite of rooms finished in the style of Louis XIV; the dining saloon will be decorated in the Renaissance style, or in Roccoco or Colonial. The music room will be Italian, the smoking room in Flemish or early English, and the saloon in Byzantine or Venetian.

The furniture will be made specially for the yacht and will match the apartment for which it is intended, and the draperies and hangings, too, will be the most costly that money can buy. This year the centennial of steam navigation is to be celebrated, and no better idea of the progress that has been made in the hundred years can be had than by studying the old *Clermont* and comparing her with one of the modern steam yachts that are to be seen in any harbor during the summer months.

There are eleven yachts in the steam fleet of the New York Yacht Club, each having a gross tonnage of more than 1000 tons. Of these, eight measure more than 300 feet on deck. These eleven yachts have cost their owners from $500,000 to $1,000,000 each. It takes a crew of about sixty men on each yacht to run her, so that the fleet of eleven boats gives employment to about 660 men.

The largest yacht, according to tonnage, is Mr. James Gordon Bennett's *Lysistrata*. Her gross is 1942.75, but so much space is taken up by her powerful engines that her net tonnage is only 626.39 tons. The next largest is *Valiant*, owned by Mr. W. K. Vanderbilt. Her gross is 1823, and net 886. *Lysistrata* is 314 feet 6 inches over all, 285 feet on the waterline, 39 feet 11 inches beam, while *Valiant* is 332 feet over all, 291 feet 3 inches on the waterline, 39 feet 2 inches beam, and she draws 18 feet 4 inches. Each of these yachts is fitted with twin-screw engines, but *Lysistrata* is a much faster boat than *Valiant*, while the latter has much more accommodation.

Three steam vessels are now being built abroad for American yachtsmen which will have the best of everything that can be put into a yacht. Two of these—one for Mr. Eugene Higgins and the other for Mr. C. K. G. Billings—are to be fitted with turbine engines, and will be in the largest vessels of their class.

A steam yacht has everything on board that can be had in a house on shore and often more. First, the vessels are staunchly built, and, in model, are beautiful creations. They will withstand any storms that may cross their tracks and withstand any seas that may run, and are so well adapted to such conditions that those on board feel little more discomfort than they would on one of the big liners. With the improvement in the turbine, which is the engine best adapted for yacht use, there is but little vibration and little noise even when running at full speed.

One of the well-appointed yachts is the *Aztec*, owned by Mr. A. C. Burrage. This vessel was built in this country after designs by William Gardner. She is 260 feet long on deck and 214 feet 7 inches on the waterline, with a beam of 30 feet. Her engines can drive her at the rate of 18.3 nautical miles an hour. There is a double bottom to the hull as a protection against damage by striking a rock or derelict. The space between the bottoms is used for water storage. *Aztec* has twelve staterooms, five bathrooms, a dining saloon, drawing room, library and nursery for the owner and his guests, and there

Aztec's music room

are roomy quarters for the officers, crew and servants. One great advantage is that the owner's quarters are separate from those of his guests, which are reached by a stairway from the after library. This library is finished in Circassian walnut, and the bookcases have leaded glass doors. Forward of the library is the drawing room, finished in white mahogany inlaid with satin wood. From the reception room there is a passageway to the main entrance hall, which is just back of the dining saloon, and from this hall stairs lead to the deck. The hall has an opening into the main gangway, so that guests for dinner can leave their wraps there before entering the dining-room. This room, which is the handsomest one aboard, is finished in waxed, dull-polished teak, inlaid and handsomely carved, and all the furniture and fittings harmonize with the joiner work in the room. There is a sideboard and silver closet at the after end and a fireplace, over which is the owner's coat of arms, at the forward end. In each corner there are cabinets for glass.

On the starboard side of the yacht are the owner's quarters. There is a private study furnished with a safe, a desk and an open fireplace;

the bedroom and the bath. There are three double staterooms for the children, one of which is 15 feet long, and is used as a study or nursery. There is also a room for a valet in this part of the yacht. On the hurricane deck there is an observation room finished in English oak.

Mr. F. M. Smith owns the *Hauoli*, the name being Hawaiian for delight. She can make about twenty nautical miles an hour, and in a race against Mr. Rogers's *Kanawha* for the Lysistrata Cup she was beaten only after a hard contest. This yacht is 211 feet 3 inches long on deck. Henry J. Gielow was her designer. There is a dining-room under the bridge which will accommodate twenty persons. This is finished in paneled mahogany, with handsomely carved moldings. The windows are double, and between the panes are fitted sea shells and weed, so arranged that they give one the impression of being under water.

In the after end of the deck house is the social hall, 22 feet by 14 feet, which may be extended by opening sliding doors leading to a stateroom 10 feet long.

The *Niagara*, owned by Mr. Howard Gould, is another yacht that is American throughout, and she is a fine example of what can be built in this country. Mr. Gould designed the yacht himself; that is, he made the interior plans and then had his naval architect work out the details. She is a large yacht, bark rigged, and has commodious quarters for a big ship's company. The deck saloon is a finely finished room, and is fitted with an orchestrion. The dining saloon is the full width of the yacht, and appears more like a room in a fine country house than on a yacht. This impression is added to by the open fireplace and carved mantle that fill one end of the apartment. There is another and smaller dining-room on the upper deck.

Mr. Gould keeps this vessel in commission nearly the whole year round, as he is fond of making long voyages and is a great fisherman. He has crossed the Atlantic in the yacht several times. One feature of the vessel is a dark room, equipped with everything that a photographer needs, and there is always a camera man aboard to take pictures at the many ports at which the *Niagara* touches.

Mr. J. Pierpont Morgan's *Corsair*, Mr. H. H. Rogers's *Kanawha*, Mr. P. A. B. Widener's *Josephine*, Mr. D. G. Reid's *Rheclair*, Mr. W. B. Leed's *Noma*, Mr. A. S. Bigelow's *Pantooset*, and Col. Oliver H. Payne's *Aphrodite* are all American built. Of the foreign built boats in this country, there are the *Atalanta*, owned by Mr. George J. Gould; Mr. James Gordon Bennett's *Lysistrata*, Mr. A. J. Drexel's

Mr. Howard Gould's *Niagara*

Margarita, Mrs. Robert Goelet's *Nahma*, Commodore Cornelius Vanderbilt's *North Star*, Mr. W. K. Vanderbilt's *Valiant* and Mr. F. W. Vanderbilt's *Warrior*. These vessels are all large enough to cruise about the world.

The *Erin*, Sir Thomas Lipton's well-known steamer, while not quite so large as some others well known on this side of the Atlantic, is one of the most luxuriously appointed craft afloat. She is 264 feet on deck, and is well modeled and well proportioned. She has a sun deck above the houses. On the main deck forward is the office of Sir Thomas, and aft is a music room. Below is the drawing room, a dining saloon and several large staterooms and the suite of apartments used by Sir Thomas. The walls are beautifully paneled with silks of delicate coloring. An open fireplace is at the forward end.

The dining saloon, which is finished in mahogany, has 11 feet of headroom. This room connects with the butler's pantry and thence with the galley. Sir Thomas has entertained more than 100 guests at a time.

Ex-Commodore Morton F. Plant, of the Larchmont Yacht Club, who took the schooner *Ingomar* across the ocean on a cup-hunting expedition, purchased, while abroad, the steam yacht *Venetia*, which is one of the best sea boats in the American pleasure fleet. She is 227 feet on deck, and has a steel deck house covered with teak, which

Mr. J. P. Morgan's *Corsair*

extends fully two-thirds of the length of the yacht. This contains at the forward end the social hall or music room; next aft is the dining-room, large enough for twenty-five persons, then a smoking room, and way aft is the drawing room. Below deck are ten staterooms, all finished in light woods, such as bird's-eye maple, butternut or sycamore, and each has access to a bath room with fresh and salt water supply.

Ex-Commodore Morton F. Plant's *Venetia*

There is a library and an armory on deck, but the show apartment of the yacht is the drawing room, which extends the full width of the yacht, 27 feet. It is a marvel of the joiner's and upholsterer's art, and is most beautifully finished.

There is no limit to what a man can spend who owns a big steam yacht. Those that have been mentioned carry crews numbering from forty to seventy-five men, and the figures given in the following table, which are based on the cost of maintaining a crew of sixty, will give some idea of the cost:

Captain, $3,600 a year.
Chief engineer, $3,000 a year.
First mate, $150 a month.
Second mate, $100 a month.
Third mate, $100 a month.
Assistant engineer, $150 a month.
Second assistant engineer, $100 a month.
Four oilers, $40 a month, $160.
Twelve firemen, $35 a month, $240.
Six quartermasters, $50 a month, $300.
Two boatswains, $35 a month, $70.
Twelve seamen, $35 a month, $420.
Two launchmen, $40 a month, $80.
One steward, $2,500 a year.
Two second stewards, $100 a month, $200.
Bedroom steward, $75 a month.
Chef, $1,800 a year.
Three cooks, $75 a month, $225.
Two scullions, $40 a month, $80.
Four waiters, $40 a month, $160.

If the yacht is in commission for eight months out of the twelve, the pay-roll amounts to $29,780.

These men have to be fed, and sixty cents a day per man is allowed for this, so for the eight months the food bill of the employees will amount to $11,712. The bill for uniforms will use up another $3,000.

The coal bill is a big item. If the yacht runs ten hours a day, it will burn from twenty to twenty-five tons, which will cost about $75 a day, or $18,000 for the time the yacht is in commission. Oil, paint, varnish and other sundries will cost $20 a day, or, say, $5,000 for the season, and docking to clean, painting, repairs and other little things too numerous to mention that an owner has to look out for will add another $5,000 to his annual expenses.

A summary is as follows:

Salary of crew	$29,780
Feeding crew	11,712
Clothing crew	2,775
Coal	18,000
Oil and sundries	5,000
Repairs and docking	5,000
Total	$72,267

It must be remembered that this figure does not include the owner's personal expenses, which may be as much more if he is a lavish entertainer when afloat.

The Last of the New Bedford Whalers and The End of the *Wanderer*

William H. Taylor

As a young newspaperman in New Bedford, before he came to Yachting's *staff, Bill Taylor chronicled the end of an era*

1. The Last of the New Bedford Whalers

For the first time in 150 years New Bedford faces the prospect of being without a representative of its once great whaling fleet at sea. The bark *Wanderer*, last of the old square-rigged whalers, is to be laid up and sold—unless the price of whale oil stages a miraculous come-back. Captain Antone Edwards brought her in last Summer and found no market for his oil. If there had been a chance of profit he planned to take her out again this Spring, but now he has decided against it, and when the *Margaret*, the only New Bedford schooner now at sea, returns this Summer she, too, will be laid up. The *Margaret* is now whaling in southern waters, under the command of Captain Joseph Edwards, a brother of the *Wanderer*'s master.

For several years profits from whaling voyages out of New Bedford have been precarious, for it has been found possible to ship oil east from the Pacific Coast whale fisheries and sell it in the New Bedford market cheaper than local vessels could land it on the dock.

Then, too, there was the question of crews. Time was when boys from the inland sections of New England ran away to New Bedford to compete with local boys for berths aboard the whale ships; but of recent years it has been well nigh impossible to get any crews except Brava Portuguese. Whalers have made a practice of crossing to the Cape Verde Islands with just enough hands to work ship, and there enlisting, by hook or crook, enough men to pull their boats. But lately even the lowly Brava has discovered that there is neither pleasure nor profit in eating whale-oil soaked grub, sleeping in whale-oil soaked bunks, and drinking water out of oil casks for a year, only to find on reaching port that he will have to spend the winter chopping wood over on Sconticut Neck in order to work out his debt to the vessel.

Another difficulty experienced by owners of whaling vessels recently has been the inquisitiveness of customs officials, who have a way of snooping around the incoming whalers and discovering jugs of good St. Croix rum in the flour barrels, and that sort of thing, which means confiscation and sale of the ship. Of course, the owner can get her back at the sale for a low price, but this adds to the expense of whaling, too.

With the end of profit in whaling and the passing of the hardy old breed of Yankee whalemen who once carried the New Bedford house flags into every port and to every unknown island of the seven seas, the whale ships have dropped out of the trade, one by one, until only the *Wanderer* and the *Margaret* remained, and now it is announced that they will not go a-whaling again, unless whale oil rises. The newer vessels, converted Gloucester schooners for the most part, have been sold into the Cape Verde packet trade. Some of the older ones have gone coastwise. Of the old barks that a few years ago still survived, the *Bertha*, the *Alice Knowles* and the *Andrew Hicks* have been lost on the grounds within a few years. The *Charles W. Morgan*, built in the '40's, is retired in her old age to a berth at the end of a Fairhaven wharf. The *Wanderer* may make one more voyage—but it depends on the price of sperm oil.

So, it seems, the whaling fleet of New Bedford is about to go the way of those of Nantucket, Edgartown, and the Connecticut shore ports, leaving nothing in its wake but the Whalemen's Club, where a few old-timers sit and smoke and remember the wild days of their youth. Even the smell of whale oil that used to hang over Pier 3 and Merrill's Wharf half a dozen years ago has been driven out by odors emanating from more modern commerce.

2. The End of the *Wanderer*

The wreck of the bark *Wanderer* on the west shore of Cuttyhunk August 26 was a tragic ending of New Bedford whaling.

Though profits for several years have been slim, Captain Antone

T. Edwards decided to try it once more, and the *Wanderer* was fitted out for a year's cruise on the Platte grounds. Monday morning, August 25, a tug nosed alongside and the old bark was pulled out of her slip and headed down the harbor. It had been heralded as her last trip, and it seemed as though a feeling of apprehension weighed on the crowd of 200 persons, many of them friends and relatives of her Brava crew, who were gathered on the pier to see her off. No enthusiasm, no shouting, only a rather forced demonstration of hat waving at the request of a movie cameraman aboard the tug. A fisherman aboard the schooner *Gleaner* blew his foghorn—the only farewell sound. Tom, the ship's cat, which had made his home aboard her for several weeks and was slated for a sea voyage, deserted the ship at the last minute and was to be seen gazing mournfully after her as she slipped from sight behind the state pier.

Off Butler's Flat, the *Wanderer* passed the whaling schooner *Margaret*, commanded by Captain Edwards' brother, Joseph, leaking badly and just in from a whaling voyage with three hundred barrels of oil in her hold. The light southerly wind prevented the *Wanderer*'s getting to sea that day, and the tug left her lying to an anchor a mile to the westward of Mishaum Ledge bell buoy, at the mouth of Buzzard's Bay. Captain Edwards came back to New Bedford in the tug, intending to return next day and get to sea. First Mate Joseph A. Gomes, a whaleman of many years' experience, remained in command. With him were only 11 men, for the intention was to go first to Brava and there recruit the *Wanderer*'s normal crew of 32 men.

That night the blow predicted for several days struck in, and at daylight next morning a heavy rain, driven by a northeast wind, obscured the *Wanderer* from the sight of those ashore. The wind increased and anxiety began to be felt for her. The New Bedford Towboat Company wanted to send a tug down to her, but their boats were moored above the bridge and by that time the wind was so heavy that the draw tender refused to open the draw, holding that he would be unable to close it again because of the gale.

The bay was white from shore to shore with driven spray, ripped from the tops of the seas and driven horizontally by a gale of hurricane strength. To complicate matters, an old sea was still rolling in from the southward. In the height of the gale the *Wanderer*'s chain cable parted, and about the same time the wind, which in the morning might have carried her clear of shoal water, hauled to the westward.

A second anchor, hastily dropped, met the same fate as the first.

The *Wanderer's* steering gear was put out of commission by the breaking of the quadrant, and nothing remained but to let her drift with the wind straight for the west shore of Cuttyhunk.

Fearing death in the breakers, the dozen men aboard her took to the whaleboats. The first mate's boat made shore in Wash Pond Bend, on Cuttyhunk, with her crew nearly exhausted, but for a time nothing was seen of the other boat, in command of second mate Benjamin Freitas.

The *Wanderer* herself swept straight onto the beach at Cuttyhunk, a few hundred yards south of the lighthouse. Three or four rocks went through her bottom, and the seas pounded and ground her against them. At the time she struck the Cuttyhunk coast, guards reported that she could not last through the night.

In the morning the power lifeboat from Cuttyhunk went out to Sow and Pigs lightship on the chance that the second mate's boat might have reached there, and sure enough the whaleboat was moored astern of the lightship, with all hands safe aboard the ship.

That was two weeks ago, and for the next two days, while the sea was still running, it was continually said she could not last another tide. She is still there, a biscuit toss from dry land, leaning heavily to starboard against two big rocks. She has been stripped of everything valuable that could be moved except her spars. Her rudder is on the beach near her. Her foremast has gone through her bottom, but is still standing, held at a slight angle by her port shrouds. Her martingale stays are gone. Her deck house is racked and splintered and her wooden canopies sagged by the weight of the seas that broke over her. Her new pine sheathing is ripped off the exposed port side. Her back is broken somewhere forward of the mainmast and a part of her stern is gone. But the stout old hull, built 46 years ago at Mattapoisett, still hangs together waiting for another storm to end her existence.

1930

First Airplane to Bermuda

Zeh Bouck

A bit out of Yachting*'s usual line, but a remarkable, little-known episode*

With the Bermuda races in the immediate offing, when a large fleet will set sail for the "Onion Patch," the story is aptly told of the three April fools in a tub—W. H. (Bill) Alexander, Captain Lewis A. Yancey, and the writer. On the morning of April first, at 9:37 to be exact, the airplane *Pilot Radio* took off from Flushing Bay, Long Island Sound, for the Bermuda Islands—not always the easiest place to find by boat and, as our navigator will tell you, a tricky dot in the ocean to find by air. The take-off itself partook of the inauspiciousness of the day, and it was not until the fifth attempt that we were able to lift her—after draining approximately fifteen gallons of gasoline, throwing overboard a kit of spare pontoon parts and jettisoning our anchor. The Sound was glassy calm and stuck to the floats like glue. It was the rolling wake of a Clason Point ferry and the churning froth behind a friendly and cooperative seaplane that finally got us up on the step and to flying speed.

The airplane was a Stinson SM-1F six-passenger monoplane modified especially for the Bermuda flight and motored with the Wright J-6 300 h.p. Whirlwind. The *Pilot Radio* was equipped with Edo floats, and double wing gas tanks, giving a total gas capacity of 200 gallons, or, conservatively estimated, fuel for twelve hours' cruising at 100 miles per hour. Provision was made for replenishing oil from within the cabin. We carried five days' rations. The radio room was located just abaft the main cabin, and was comfortably equipped with short and long wave transmitting and receiving apparatus, covering one frequency in all definitely demarcated bands between 20 and 1100 meters. The plane is ordinarily used as a flying laboratory by the Pilot Radio and Tube Corporation of Brooklyn, and the radio equipment was designed and built in their laboratories.

The pyralin top over the cabin was arranged so that it could slide back, opening the top of the plane for the taking of sights. (It is needless to point out to the experienced navigator that the refraction occasioned by even a thin sheet of practically any transparent material would be sufficient to render the best sights hopelessly inaccurate.)

The labors of the crew were definitely assigned and agreed upon. Alexander was to fly the plane and nothing else. Yancey's job was navigation, and mine was to maintain radio communication with radio station WHD, and assist the navigator occasionally by taking drift sights, the mountings for the Pioneer drift and speed indicator being located outside of the radio shack window. An interesting point is that, in an emergency, any one of us three could have pinch-hit for another.

As Bill cleared the East River bridges, the rest of the crew went into action. Lon (his name in its entirety being Lewis Alonzo Yancey) directed Bill to swing around over a string of buoys in Lower New York Bay which, by luck, line up exactly 138 degrees true—the course to Bermuda. I crawled back into the radio cabin, settled myself comfortably for a day's work, reeled out the antenna, and established communication with the New York station. A few minutes later we took our departure from Scotland Lightship. At noon we were over the Gulf Stream with a noticeable rise in temperature, and increased bumpiness which added considerably to the difficulties of taking sights.

Yancey navigated by the Marc St. Hilaire method, following the usual shipboard procedure. The sights were taken with a bubble sextant, and lines of position established. Successive lines were brought up in accordance with the intervening dead reckoning. Of course, sights were taken much more frequently than on shipboard, as our position was changing at a rate of about 85 nautical miles per hour with a correspondingly rapid variation in the sun's azimuth. Twenty-four sights were taken between the time of our departure from Scotland Lightship and sundown. Three Longines chronographs were used as chronometers. In passing, it may be remarked that taking sights from an airplane with a bubble sextant is a ticklish and exasperating proposition, quite comparable to similar efforts on board a 36-footer.

And so passed the day, with Bill fighting a cross wind that gave us at times a 20-degree drift and slowed us down considerably below our normal cruising speed.

By five o'clock it became apparent that we could not make the Islands before dark, and we decided to set her down on the ocean rather than risk a landing in Hamilton Harbor at night. The sea looked calm from 1500 feet, and Dr. Kimball, our Palladium of the weather bureau, assured us of continued good weather for another 24 hours.

And set her down we did—Bill doing one of the finest flying jobs it has ever been my pleasure to witness and my discomfort to experience. A fair ground swell was running, heaving in no particular sequence, and water is a hard thing to hit at 60 miles per hour. That the pontoons stood the gaff still remains amazing to me.

The moment *Pilot Radio* came to rest, Yancey climbed down on the floats and threw out two ten-quart pails for a sea anchor. With absolutely no wind these were useless for the first six hours, and half the time we were broached to the swell, rolling one minute, pitching the next—a motion that was disconcerting, to say the least.

We alighted on the ocean at 6:00 P.M. New York time—7:00 o'clock Bermuda time, and just dark. By rigging up an emergency antenna we could have maintained communication with New York throughout the night, but it seemed useless; so, before coming down, we told WHD to sign off until five A.M. the following morning.

We maintained three watches throughout the night. Mine was the first. At nine o'clock, just as the stingy sector of the moon dipped below the water, I first sighted the lights of the *Lady Somers*, bound from Bermuda to Halifax. We saw them again two hours later, and at 1:00 A.M. decided to signal her on the possibility that she might be a boat out from Bermuda looking for us.

Lon opened the top of the plane and fired three Very cartridges at 15-minute intervals. At the end of half an hour she was noticeably nearer, and we could tell by her mast lights that she was heading for us. When these lights worked their way out of line, we would give her another shot, and a second or two later, would see her lights swing around dead for us again. We signaled her first with blinker, and shortly after, when she hove-to at 3:00 A.M., we hailed her.

An unmistakeably British voice from the deck wanted to know if we wished aid, and seemed rather amazed when informed that we did not. We requested that they report us "okay," and proceeding to Bermuda at sunrise, and then asked for the bearing and distance to Bermuda. There was a five-minute pause while they ran up their dead reckoning, and then the voice from the deck informed us that we were 60 miles north of Bermuda, true. This checked very closely with our own calculations. Then we heard the bells in the engine room, and the *Lady Somers* crept away into the dark.

At daybreak I cleaned up the cabin, the contents of which had been rather indiscriminately tossed about during the night, while Bill climbed down on the floats and tightened up a cross wire. At 5:40 we took off. A slight wind had come up during the latter part of the night, and the swells were still running high. Bill again displayed his mastership of a difficult situation, and the plane took a strenuous licking. But we got off—and for the first time in the history of flying a plane had lived out the night on the open sea and taken off again.

As soon as we had made altitude, I went back to the radio cabin, let down the antenna, and was immediately in communication with *The New York Times*. At 6:17 I sent in my last message: "Bermuda sighted dead ahead, 6:15." A terse but eloquent tribute to the ability of our navigator.

I reeled in the antenna and crawled up forward to watch the Islands grow from a smudge on the horizon to the familiar line of green just about seven miles ahead of us. At this moment, I asked Bill how much gas we had.

"About one hour," he replied after a quick glance at one of the wing gauges.

"Fine!" I said. "I'll tell you what we'll do. Jazz over Harrington Sound on your left there, and we'll straff Tom Moore's house. Then we'll fly down over Elbow Beach, across to the hotel, down Front Street in Hamilton, and put her down just off the Inverurie."

"Okay," says Bill.

"Put . . . put . . . put," says the motor, and conked, with the Islands still five miles away. There was no doubt what had happened. Once having heard that sound, it is as easily forgotten as the shake of a rattlesnake's tail. We were definitely out of gas. A dirty gas gauge had deceived Bill a moment before. We do not know to this day where it all went. He set her down again, just inside the reefs, about five miles from the Islands, our flying time being exactly nine hours and twenty minutes.

Yancey ran out the pails and caught them on the reefs just a few feet below the pontoons. These held us for a quarter of an hour—until the rope sawed through on the jagged coral. Then we started drifting, at about five miles an hour, toward New York City. The Islands were definitely retreating. We ran out an emergency antenna, and were about to call for help, when Bill's genius rose to the situation. He figured that rocking around out there, as we had been doing for the past half hour, we might have sloshed a quart of gasoline down into the equalizing tank. Lon cranked the engine. She took instantly, and Bill gave her the gun with Lon climbing through the door, and ten fathoms of rope and radio antenna streaming out behind. We had two minutes of gas—enough to set down definitely in the steamer channel just off Shelley's Bay.

Here Percy Tucker came up to us with his speed boat, and ran back to St. Georges for gas. A few minutes later Roddy Williams' *Golden Wedding* barged up alongside with Reggie Darrell at the helm and J. P. Hand on board—not to mention "Bing" Morris of the Hamilton Hotel, newspaper men and photographers. After a bit of general hand-shaking, J. P. Hand put us under arrest for flying over Bermuda without a permit, and general lack of clearance papers and similar diplomatic necessities. With "J. P.," and Percy Tucker's seven and a half gallons of gas, we flew the length of the Islands, and then set the *Pilot Radio* down, ultimately and safely, in Hamilton Harbor. A boatload of cocktails and ale put out from the Inverurie, all of which livened up our brief period of incarceration. And when the medical and custom authorities finally passed us, we were met at the dock by a host of Bermudian friends, somewhat hazily remembered through the mist of Martini drys.

We were unable to make the return flight due to a strut fitting on the forward port longeron which had practically pulled out, making it hazardous, if not impossible, to take off with a full load. No facilities for repairs are available in Bermuda.

With the probable erection of a radio beacon in Bermuda, within the next two years, I am assured that Bermuda will be well equipped in the way of maintenance and hangar facilities for aerial visitors. Aside from being of considerable assistance to fliers, such a beacon will be equally useful to small and large boat pilots, leading them unerringly to the Islands from at least 200 miles at sea. Radio receiving equipment, requiring no experience to operate, will be available for boats and planes at a cost well under one hundred dollars. Navigating either an airplane or yacht to Bermuda will then be simple and sure, and the already popular islands will have a constantly growing transient population.

1933

The President Goes Cruising

Paul D. Rust, Jr., and James Roosevelt

The whole nation was watching when Franklin D. Roosevelt took a vacation cruise along the New England coast in the schooner Amberjack II

The President of the United States wants to take a cruise Down East. The message rang throughout the country; the Navy Department speculated, sportsmen rejoiced, and everyone admired the simplicity of such a vacation. All interest focused upon the boat which the nation's leader would sail.

The *Amberjack II*, a 45-foot schooner, was chosen. This boat, owned by Paul D. Rust, Jr., was built in 1931 by George Lawley & Sons. The seaworthiness of this little vessel had been most satisfactorily proved in the Transatlantic Race to England and subsequent races both in British and American waters.

The *Amberjack*, having a Marconi main, gaff fore, and double headsails, is powered with a 40-horse Scripps motor. As to the interior, a crew of seven, including one paid hand, can be very comfortably accommodated. Two of the afterguard sleep in a moderate-sized quarter stateroom, four in the spacious main cabin, and the "crew" forward. Under the bunks in the main cabin are two 100-gallon water tanks. The galley, located just forward of amidships on the port side, is equipped with a Shipmate coal stove. In general, *Amberjack's* layout is the usual one of an auxiliary cruiser of this size.

Early in May the *Amberjack* went into commission. The following month was spent in preparation for the President's cruise. Supplies, consisting mainly of canned foods, such as corned beef hash, peas, stewed corn, tomatoes, and various fruits, were systematically stowed in the lockers and under the bunks, for nothing can be more

President Franklin Roosevelt at *Amberjack*'s helm (*Courtesy of the New York Yacht Club*)

disconcerting to a cook at sea than to search every locker, and sometimes the bilges, before being able to find a can of beans. As a result, an entry was made in the back of the log book which told where everything had been hidden away. Then followed a few days spent in bending on a new suit of canvas and in taking shakedown trips in Massachusetts Bay.

At last, on the evening of June 14th, the *Cuyahoga*, a 125-foot navy radio communications ship, which was to be *Amberjack's* escort, dropped anchor at the mouth of Marblehead harbor. Last minute provisions were put aboard. The crew, James Roosevelt, Amyas Ames, George Briggs, Paul Rust, and a Navy bosun's mate, were ready to set sail for Marion, Mass., where the President was to join the ship and become the skipper. But, as every old hand knows, no cruise is perfect without delays. At almost the moment of weighing anchor, James Roosevelt's house in New Hampshire burned down, and all plans were thrown into confusion. "Jimmie" immediately rushed home while the rest of the crew stood by awaiting orders. Finally, after many messages and telephone calls, word came through to proceed to Marion without him.

Shortly before midnight we signaled our convoy to get underway and follow us to Cape Cod. Because of extremely light airs we told the chief in charge of the *Cuyahoga* that it would probably take us somewhere between eight and ten hours to make the run from Marblehead to the eastern entrance of the Cape Cod Canal. But during the mid-watch, a beautiful quartering breeze sprang up which lasted throughout the run, and instead of taking ten hours, we made the trip in just over six. At daybreak we began to search the horizon for our Diesel escort, but she was nowhere to be seen. Upon reaching the canal, where we thought she might be awaiting our arrival, they told us she had not been seen. The tide being to our advantage, we ran through in short order, shot out into Buzzard's Bay, rounded up, put on full sail, and laid a course for Marion. From the east end of the bay, looking toward Marion, we could faintly distinguish the outlines of two large vessels. Just at this moment someone below turned on the radio. The early morning news flash informed us that two destroyers, the *Ellis* and the *Bernadou*, were lying off Marion harbor awaiting the President's arrival, that the *Amberjack* had left Marblehead the evening before, and that Congress was still in a turmoil.

This pre-breakfast news concerning Congress certainly did not add to our appetites, for we had all been anxiously praying that that august body would tire of arguing and let our skipper-to-be start his vacation. Within the hour we slid quietly under the bow of the *Ellis*, up the narrow channel and dropped the hook in Marion harbor. The anchor was scarcely on bottom when the yacht club launch came alongside to put us aboard the *Ellis*. At the head of the gangway we were greeted by Captain Vernon, the President's naval aide, who wanted to know what we had done with our convoy. Before we could give him an answer, a communications officer delivered a message from the *Cuyahoga* which read—"Searching Massachusetts Bay for *Amberjack*. Request orders." Puffed out a little with pardonable pride at having run away from a naval escort, we began to laugh, but soon realized from the expressions on the faces of the officers that in the Navy this was no joke. A wireless was dispatched to the *Cuyahoga* and she duly joined the little fleet.

During the afternoon, a most congenial little man came aboard, said his name was John Cutter, and wanted to know where to put his things. We had read in the papers a few days before that there was a friend of Mr. Roosevelt's who would join the ship, but where he would meet us and what he would be like afforded quite a topic of conversation. Little did we think when Mr. Cutter joined the ship that he was the person whom we would all learn to respect so highly for his excellent cooking and to like for his continuous good humor.

Saturday afternoon, June 17th, the once quiet little whaling village of Marion was in an uproar. The houses and shops were decorated and draped with flags, the streets and waterfront were jammed with people. Just after three o'clock *Amberjack* was brought alongside Dr. McDonald's dock, the same dock from which many an old whaler had cast off in years gone by. Navy gigs and launches buzzed all over the tiny harbor.

At four, word came through from Groton that Mr. Roosevelt and James were on their way by automobile and should arrive within an hour and a half. At six, a strong rain squall, which lasted but a few minutes, whipped the shallow waters of the harbor into a foaming mass of spray. On the heels of the flurry, the President and his son, sitting in the back seat of an open car, drove quietly into the yard. The car stopped for a few minutes while the President greeted some of his old friends, and then proceeded down to the dock where the *Amberjack* was lying.

The engine was running. Each member of the crew had some particular job; two were on the bow and stern lines, one on the main signal halliards, ready to hoist the President's flag as soon as he stepped on board, and Rust was at the wheel prepared to get underway as soon as the gangplank had been removed.

All went smoothly and we shoved off amidst a burst of applause and cheering, took a short spin around the harbor and then picked up our mooring. As the little *Amberjack* settled back on her chain in the quiet water, and the sun went down behind the old sail lofts on shore, it seemed as though the world had been left behind. The President gave a sigh of contentment and said nothing for a few moments while he sat taking in that peaceful scene.

With characteristic spontaneity, Mr. Roosevelt, the President of a few moments ago, now "The Skipper," came out of his reverie to greet his old friend, Dr. McDonald, who was just coming aboard. The host for the evening provided a most delicious dinner, which his housekeeper had prepared. For over an hour a small motor launch was busily engaged in bringing first one hot course and then another from the house to the boat. At last, the finishing touch, the housekeeper herself came out with a tremendous shortcake which she presented to Mr. Roosevelt, much to his enjoyment.

By midnight, we had all turned in for a good night's sleep, but in the morning even the skipper complained that one of the lobsters eaten the night before had sneaked up and bitten him viciously about 4:00 A.M.

At six o'clock the first hand to awake could be heard endeavoring to crawl from his bunk. By 6:15 three or four of the outfit were in swimming and the most tremendous racket could be heard on deck, but the skipper continued to sleep on. By seven o'clock an entirely "New Deal," a vacation, had started for the President. Those of us who are unaccustomed to tremendous publicity could hardly call the reception that the skipper got when he came on deck a vacation. At eight o'clock, after a good breakfast of eggs, bacon and coffee, the skipper put his head out of the main companionway, to be greeted by a swarm of photographers, each one more anxious than the other to get the closest "shot." For almost an hour these men continued to scrap for a front row seat.

Just before nine, our scheduled hour of departure, when the skipper's anxiety to get underway could be held in check no longer, he asked the photographers to leave and gave the order to hoist sail. With a beautiful nor'west breeze and all our kites flying, we ran out of Marion, across Buzzard's Bay for Naushon Island. How many who see this, whether casual readers, old-time racing men or deep sea cruisers, can picture a President of the United States sitting at the wheel of a small boat, quietly giving orders in a manner that stamped him as a real sailor. From the moment we weighed anchor, every one of us knew that he was, in reality, the skipper.

Arriving off Naushon, we ducked into Woods Hole Passage and left our destroyer escorts looking like a couple of suspicious bulldogs, while their pup, the *Cuyahoga*, followed us through and anchored nearby. Here we were met by Mr. W. Cameron Forbes, who escorted us into his beautiful little landlocked basin, Hadley's harbor. After the skipper had had a visit with Mr. Forbes and the crew a horseback ride ashore, we set sail for Nantucket. Upon leaving Hadley's and entering Woods Hole Passage, a series of squalls overtook us, so that we were forced to douse the main and run wing and wing under the fore and forestaysail. After we had slipped past Woods Hole and scudded part way down Nantucket Sound, the weather ahead looked so dirty that the skipper thought it wise to put into Edgartown for the night.

Just before turning into that snug little harbor, the skipper decided to notify the escorts of our change in plans. Where were they? Oh, yes, there they were, just astern, although up to that time no one had so much as given them a thought. We counted; one, two—one bulldog, two bulldogs. But where was the little white puppy? Great hilarity took place on deck. Perhaps the *Amberjack* had once again run away from the *Cuyahoga*. Not so, however, for, just dropping anchor, who should loom up astern but our long lost pet.

It might be interesting to know that from Woods Hole Passage to Squash River Bell, off Edgartown, we averaged 5½ knots under our meager spread of canvas. But our speed could by no means be entirely attributed to the force of the wind. Those of you who know sailing realize what a large part helmsmanship and trim of sails play in keeping a boat footing. In both of these respects Mr. Roosevelt is most adept.

Six A.M. found us underway again. The skipper remained in his bunk, enjoying the luxury of a much deserved rest. Edgartown had been wonderfully quiet and peaceful. A long day's run around the Cape to Provincetown lay ahead, thus an early start. What a run! Scarcely had we poked our nose into Nantucket Sound than a strong east wind and head sea started to make up. By the time we had reached Handkerchief Shoal Lightvessel it was blowing hard. The little press boats, which thus far in the story have been neglected, were making bad weather of it astern. So, once again, excellent judgment on the part of the skipper came into play, and we put the helm up and ran into Nantucket.

There, for the first time since leaving Marion, we realized that the President was on board. To us, at that time, he was only a fine sailor, and a pleasant, congenial companion. Upon entering Nantucket harbor we were suddenly aroused from our quiet contemplation of the weather by the blowing of whistles, ringing of bells and the enthusiastic cheering of throngs. The President of the United States was visiting one of the quaintest and oldest ports in the country. Hundreds of small boats, overcrowded with people, buzzed around our little craft. Some were just sightseers, some only curious; but the great majority were there whole-heartedly to welcome their "friend." So great was the confusion that even before we had come to anchor, the destroyers were forced to send in some small motor launches in order to keep the crowds at a safe distance.

In the early afternoon it was decided that those who were so inclined should go ashore to replenish the cook's greatly depleted store of food. Needless to say, every one of us was extremely anxious to see the island, so we left the President in the company of a couple of old friends with the intention of wandering around the town by ourselves.

One of the navy launches set us ashore on the yacht club float, and there, much to our amazement, we were greeted by the mayor, the commodore of the club and a group of distinguished citizens. After a most enjoyable drive with our pleasant hosts, we returned to the boat, having forgotten nearly everything we were originally dispatched to purchase.

As our longest and most strenuous day lay ahead, everyone turned in early that evening. Shortly after four bells next morning, our government anchor watch, consisting of one secret service man and two naval guards, were sent back to their respective ships while we prepared to get underway. It was a beautiful morning. The clouds and rain squalls of the evening before had completely disappeared, and the skipper's prayer for a following wind had been answered.

The breeze, although well astern, became extremely light shortly before noon. With little or nothing to do and the sun blazing down upon us, we stripped to the waist and enjoyed a real baking. While drifting along in this lazy fashion we gradually became conscious of the distant hum of an aeroplane. Before we realized it, the plane was upon us and was recognized as the President's private ship. Within half an hour of our first realization that a plane was nearby, Assistant Secretary of State Raymond Moley was aboard the *Amberjack*. It was a unique place for such an important conference.

After two solid hours of weighty discussions with the President, Mr. Moley returned to the plane which carried him back to Washington. The rest of the day was divided between shifting light sails and sleeping.

Originally, the plan had been to put in at Provincetown for at least one night, but, as the sun sank below the precipitous dunes of Cape Cod, a beautiful quartering breeze overtook us and it was decided to push on to Gloucester. With the skipper at the wheel, and after a wonderful evening sail, we rounded up just under the lee of Gloucester breakwater, lowered our canvas, dropped anchor and turned in.

The morning of June 21st found Mr. Roosevelt returning the call of those hardy men of the "Banks," the Gloucester fishermen who had visited him in Washington scarcely two months before. That was a pleasant and memorable day for everyone. Early that morning, small boats, crowded with people, appeared from every nook in the harbor and by nine o'clock nearly every craft in Gloucester swarmed about the *Amberjack*. The climax of the visit occurred when the veteran sea captains of Gloucester came aboard and presented Mr. Roosevelt with an oil painting of the *Gertrude L. Thebaud*, the shooner in which they had made their voyage to Washington.

Just after noon, with a number of the President's friends aboard, we ran from Gloucester through the Annisquam River into Ipswich Bay. There his guests left us, we picked up the destroyers which were unable to negotiate the river and had gone around Cape Ann, and laid course for Little Harbor, N. H. At colors that evening we were anchored in that delightful spot.

From that, our first anchorage outside of Massachusetts waters, we moved along to Chandler's Cove, on Great Chebeag Island, just to the eastward of Portland, Maine. That little spot was picked out for its apparent solitude, but, upon approaching our anchorage, what should greet us but one of Portland's fire boats which laid down an exquisite barrage of sea water.

Early the next morning, the number of our crew was increased by three when Franklin, Jr., John Roosevelt, and one of their schoolmates, Drexel Paul, joined the ship. Probably the hardest and most exciting day's sail followed. It was blowing a fresh breeze out of the northwest and, with full sail, plus the fisherman staysail, we logged nearly eight knots all the way to Pulpit Harbor, a tiny landlocked indentation on the northwestern side of North Haven.

The trip around North Haven, through Deer Island Thoroughfare to Southwest Harbor was magnificent. The Skipper appeared to have enjoyed that day more than any of the others on the cruise, for East Penobscot, Blue Hill and Frenchman's bays all lie in the most beautiful part of the Maine coast. It was well after dark before we came to anchor at Southwest Harbor.

The cruise thus far had been too perfect. We felt that something must be in store for us and our suspicions were confirmed within the next few hours. A heavy, damp, penetrating blanket of fog dropped over us and for the next few days held the *Amberjack* in Roque Island which we had barely made before it shut in thick. The skipper, always a true sailor, not only enjoyed the fog and the absolute rest which it afforded him, but went so far as to say that it had been made to order. He despatched the *Bernadou* to take "Jimmy" to Boston for a meeting which he had to attend and bring Ambassador Norman Davis to Roque Island. When James Roosevelt returned with Mr. Davis the fog was so thick that the *Bernadou* was unable, because of outlying islands, to get within four or five miles of our anchorage. One of the small boats from the *Ellis* was sent off to bring these two to the anchorage, and for a few hours that morning the United States had an Ambassador at Large in more ways than one.

Pleasant times always come to an end too quickly. The date set for the termination of the cruise was Thursday, June 29th, and fog or no fog, the skipper had to be at Campobello. By eight bells that morning we were underway. Our small detachment of the navy was most apprehensive as to the advisability of the President setting out in such miserably thick weather. However, under his skillful handling and clever piloting we got away from the anchorage and worked through the maze of little channels formed by the surrounding islands, along the coast, and out of the fog into Lubec Narrows.

Just twelve years had slipped away since Mr. Roosevelt's last visit to Campobello. The setting for the return to his boyhood home was perfect. The tide and wind were fair and the sun was shining brightly overhead as we sailed up the Narrows, past the quaint little town of Lubec. Upon rounding Quoddy Light a most impressive spectacle came into view. There, just ahead, in the middle of the bay which was filled with boats of every size and type, were the new 10,000-ton cruiser *Indianapolis* and our two destroyers. As we sailed quietly along thousands of people rushed to the waterfront, whistles blew, and on the deck of the *Indianapolis*, the "Star Spangled Banner" was struck up, while the entire crew manned the rail. Then there was the roar of the twenty-one gun salute. When going by the docks and piers at Eastport, a whole fishing fleet of some fifty boats, dressed for the occasion, paraded past. Seldom, if ever, has any man looked so happy, proud and pleased, as did the President, sitting at the wheel, greeting his friends.

Promptly at four o'clock, as he had promised, our skipper took the *Amberjack* alongside the dock at Welch Pool, on Campobello Island and disembarked.

One of the most interesting and pleasing cruises of all time had ended, and we, the crew, were mighty sad at seeing the skipper go over the side.

1940

The Boat That Came Back

Joseph Chase Allen

A tale with a touch of the supernatural

For genuine good companionship with the last reef shaken out, nothing can beat a group of yachtsmen and fishermen in a gam. Naturally, the group has to be one which approaches a hand-picked grade because the members of neither faction will really loosen up and unburden their souls unless they possess a wholesome and sincere respect for the other. But this condition is found frequently in certain soundings. And speaking of souls, here is the gist of a discussion by one such group and the yarn that wound up the session in the cabin of a little cruiser swinging to her anchor behind the breakwater at Vineyard Haven.

Of course, poets and an occasional superstitious sailor will talk about the soul of a ship or boat. Very well-ballasted master mariners will solemnly assure anyone that there is more to a vessel than mere wood and iron. No one laughs at this because any boat owner or sailor who possesses a trace of the tincture of Stockholm tar in his veins will, sooner or later, develop an affection for his boat, however large or small, which reveals to him all the oddities of her character, her likes and dislikes—God knows every vessel has them—and various other things that no landsman could understand or appreciate.

But souls in ships? The idea is fantastic in the extreme. A man-made fabric of wood and metal, having any sense of feeling, capabilities of showing emotion or developing a will of its own? Heavens, no! That's exactly what any one of these most salt-loving seamen will say when actually pinned down to brass grommets and the load line. Why, even Frankenstein's monster, modeled as nearly as possible after man, seemed to have precious little soul, so how the devil could a vessel have one? And so went the discussion, while pipe after pipe burned out, was reloaded and burned again. And then this yarn was spun, not as an argument but merely one of those things. Explain it if you can. But you can't; there are too many similar occurrences after you pass the four-fathom sounding, and few men attempt to account for anything unusual beyond that depth of water.

Old man Charlie Anderson was one of those longshore characters that may be found in any port, however small or large. A man of considerable age, whiskery, wearing patched pants and paddling around in a skiff or sailing a little round-bottomed boat. Sometimes he went fishing, more often he collected junk. And, although he was credited with considerable wealth, he was always out of tobacco for the corncob pipe that never left his lips except to be filled.

All hands knew old Anderson, liked him and favored him whenever they could, by giving him anything that was due to be junked or by passing him a line when he wanted a tow. In this way he came into possession of many a small boat, skiffs, dories and the like and, being a clever workman, he would spend his winters "bringing them back to life" as he termed it—which was pretty nearly correct at that. Given a castoff tholepin hole, old Anderson could build a boat around it—and a pretty good boat she'd be, too.

Most of these boats were sold after they had been rebuilt but, when one day someone gave him a battered trawl dory with the bottom and lower strake rotted off, old Anderson expressed unusual gratification and declared that he had wanted something like that for a long time. He coopered and tinkered for months on the thing and finally brought her forth, narrowed, shortened, lowered on the side, with a new bottom, new thwarts and the whole boat bright and shining with fresh paint.

"Tight as a cup, solid as a log and safe as a church," he chuckled, and he was right at that. He kept this boat, using her season after season, and his apparent fondness for the thing attracted the attention of various of the gang who thought at times that the old man was getting careless in his old age. Observing that he had her barely touched upon the beach while he cleaned a mess of fish, someone said to him: "Charlie, you'll lose that boat, leaving her like that. The wake of a passing launch will float her off, the tide will take her and then she'll be gone."

Old Anderson chuckled. "She won't leave me! I saved her from the wood pile and she knows it. I don't have to worry about losing that boat!" And, to demonstrate his point, he shoved the dory out into a four-knot tide that was sweeping through the anchorage basin. The dory shot out into the current, seemed to hesitate for just an instant, then dipped her bow a trifle and sagged gently inshore until her nose hit the beach only a few feet away from where old Anderson was standing.

This yarn was told and retold and, as often as anyone approached the old man with a query as to its truth, he would give them a similar demonstration. Three times the boys stole the dory at night, taking her from Anderson's little dock and mooring her half a mile away. Each time she parted her warps and drifted back to the dock again.

Then Anderson died. They sold the dory to a fisherman, who used her and bragged about her good points. But he just couldn't keep her made fast. Knots loosened, warps parted and finally he moored her with a chain, only to discover her gone the next morning with the staple pulled out of the oak pile. And each time he went looking for her, he found her stranded on the beach in front of Anderson's old shack.

Pulling out the staple was the last straw, however, and he hauled that dory on to the beach, filled her full of driftwood and burned her to ashes. Just the head of the stem was left, a six-inch piece of oak and a daub of green paint. It was the end of Anderson's dory when the next full tide made and washed everything clear.

But, a few days later, someone, cruising the beach in the vicinity of Anderson's dock, picked up the piece of stem, stranded, right there where the dory had always laid. He dropped it as if it were hot although it would have made a fine stick of stovewood.

1940

The "Mystery" of the *Mary Celeste*

Dr. Oliver W. Cobb

A relative of her captain gives the family's official version of the highly publicized mystery, and incidentally uses the correct spelling, "Mary," not the often misused "Marie"

Because of my personal knowledge of and relation to Captain Benjamin S. Briggs and his wife Sarah Everson (Cobb), who were cousins of mine, and my long acquaintance with their families, I feel compelled to write the story of the loss of the brig *Mary Celeste* and shed some much needed light on the so-called mystery surrounding the disappearance of the captain and crew of that vessel. I desire to get before the reading public the truth so far as we know it regarding the fate of those who were on board the *Mary Celeste*, November 24th, 1872.

The story is founded on my personal knowledge, the record of the Admiralty Court at Gibraltar, the letters of Mr. Sprague (the American Consul at Gibraltar), the family records at Marion, Massachusetts, and the inscriptions on the monument on the Briggs burial lot in the Evergreen Cemetery at Marion.

In 1863, Captain Benjamin S. Briggs married Sarah Everson Cobb. He was then in command of the three-masted schooner *Forest King* and for their honeymoon he took his wife with him on a voyage to Mediterranean ports. Later, Captain Briggs commanded the bark *Arthur* and Sarah continued to sail with him until 1865, when she came home to Marion and a son, Arthur, was born to them at Rose Cottage, the home of the Briggs family. After this event, Mrs. Briggs continued to sail with her husband in the *Arthur* and later in the brig *Sea Foam*. On one of these voyages they were at Fiume, Austria, where Captain Briggs picked up a sword with the cross of

Navarre on the hilt. This sword later appears on board the *Mary Celeste*.

In the summer of 1872, on my return from a voyage to the Mediterranean in the brig *Julia A. Hallock*, I was again at Rose Cottage, Marion. Captain Ben and Sarah, now with two children, lived next door. At this time, Captain Briggs was looking for a business on shore as he wished to be with his family. As he found nothing but the sea to satisfy him, he bought the brig *Mary Celeste* and, as his wife was ready to go with him, he had some changes made in the arrangement of the cabin in order to make things more convenient for her. Sarah took along her sewing machine and her melodeon. The brig was chartered for the Mediterranean with a full cargo consisting of 1700 barrels of alcohol, valued at about $38,000. They expected to be very comfortable. I well remember the plans for this voyage. Captain Ben told Sarah that Mr. Richardson was going with him as mate; he had been with Captain Briggs before this. They were taking their younger child, Sophia Matilda, now two years old, with them and leaving Arthur, now seven, to live with his grandmother so that he might go to school. The *Mary Celeste* cleared from the Custom House at New York, November 7th, 1872, with the following on board: Captain Benjamin S. Briggs, Mate Albert G. Richardson, Second Mate Andrew Gilling, Cook E. W. Head, Seamen Volkert Lorenzeau, Arien Harens, Bos Larensen, Gottlieb Goodschoad, and the captain's wife and two-year-old daughter.

A little less than a month later, on December 4th, 1872, Captain Morehouse of the British brig *Dei Gratia*, on her way to Gibraltar, saw the *Mary Celeste* headed westerly with a northerly wind with but three sails set. As it was evident to him that something was wrong with the vessel, he sent his mate, Mr. Deveau, to investigate.

Mr. Deveau found no one on board. The yawl boat was gone. The boat had been carried across the main hatch and, as the section of the rail abreast the hatch had been taken out and lay on deck, it was evident that the boat had been launched from the port side.

The fore hatch lay upside down on deck. The upper topsail and the foresail had blown away. The lower topsail, jib and foretopmast staysail were set. All other sails were furled except that the main staysail was loose on top of the forward house. Water was in the forward house, sloshing about up to the sill. Some water was found between decks, and three-and-one-half feet of water in the lower hold. There had evidently been some water in the cabin as some things there were wet. The beds were made and there was what appeared to be the impress of a child's head on the pillow of the captain's bed.

The log book lay open on the mate's desk and the last entry reads: "Weather, fine; wind, light; St. Mary's Island distant about six miles. Latitude 37° N, longitude 25° 02″ W." And the date: November 24th, 1872. St. Mary's Island mentioned was evidently Santa Maria, the southeasterly island of the Azores group. On the book lay a sheet of paper on which Mr. Richardson had begun a letter to his wife. He had written only four words, "Fannie My Dear Wife. . . ." Evidently he wanted to have a letter ready to mail on arrival at Gibraltar. If he had only written a few more words, his letter might possibly have shed some light on the story of the *Mary Celeste*.

We are quite dependent upon the evidence of the salvors as we try to construct the story. We must be mindful of the fact that Mr. Deveau and the two sailors who with him brought the *Mary Celeste* to Gibraltar, where they went into the Admiralty Court suing for salvage compensation, were coached by an attorney, and it was or seemed to be to their advantage to make the situation or condition as bad for the vessel as possible. I suspect that there was some "window dressing." There must have been some reason why Captain Morehouse of the *Dei Gratia* stipulated that he was not to be called into court.

It is interesting to read the evidence given by these men. They all say that the lower topsail was "hanging by the four corners." It always did depend on those four corners except that it would have rope yarn rovings securing the head of the sail to the jackstay on the yard. One man says that all the cabin windows were covered with canvas and boards nailed on outside. Another said the windows on one side only were like this and he was very sure there was only glass in the other windows. One was sure that the standing rigging was in good shape while another said that it needed much work to put it in order. All said that the binnacle which had been between two cleats on top of the house was displaced and the compass broken. One said that the cleats were broken, but the man who replaced the binnacle said that the cleats were all right and that the binnacle slipped in between the cleats and that it was only perhaps ten minutes' work to replace it. A spare compass was found in the cabin. Much was said about the water in the hold, between decks, and in the forward house. Some things were wet in the cabin. Now, three-and-one-half feet of water in an empty hold would be quite a bit of water but in a hold filled with barrels closely packed and chocked with wood it means comparatively little water. Very little water would remain between decks. As to the water in the forward house, the door of which was open, if even a moderate sea came on deck it could easily slop over the sill into the galley and stay there. The fore hatch being off, any quantity of water that was shipped would go into the hold. As the doors of the forward companionway to the cabin were open, some water would be likely to get into the cabin.

Contrary to many reports, there was no cooked food found on board the vessel but enough provisions to last her crew for six months.

One man said that there was no sign of a boat being carried across the main hatch, and another said that certain rough timbers lashed across the hatch showed beyond a doubt that the boat had been carried there. One man said that "the peak halliards were gone"; another that, "they were broken and gone." And yet no one seems to have thought that when the boat left the vessel the peak halliards might have been taken as a tow rope.

As the entry in the log book made at noon, November 24th, indicates light southerly wind, the *Mary Celeste* was then probably under full sail. This enables us to reconstruct what probably happened. At some time after noon of November 24th, Captain Briggs determined to take in sail. He may have interrupted Mr. Richardson's letter writing. The royal and topgallant sail, the flying jib, main topmast staysail, middle staysail, gaff topsail and the mainsail were furled.

The vessel was still on the starboard tack as is shown by the jibs being set on the port side. That the yards were braced around so as to back the squaresails is evident from the position of the yards when the salvors went on board. The movable section of the rail abreast the main hatch had been taken out and laid on deck where Mr. Deveau said that he left it until he went on board the second time. All the above movements indicate good seamanship and preparation to leave the vessel. We do not know why, but I think that the cargo of alcohol, having been loaded in cold weather at New York early in November and the vessel having crossed the Gulf Stream and being now in comparatively warm weather, there may have been some leakage and gas may have accumulated in the hold. The captain, having care for his wife and daughter, was probably unjustifiably alarmed and, fearing a fire or an explosion, determined to take his people in the boat away from the vessel until the immediate danger should pass.

Knowing what the duty of each man would be, it is comparatively easy to reconstruct the scene with the evidence which we have. The boat was launched on the port side. The captain got his wife and daughter into the boat and left them in charge of Mr. Richardson with one sailor in the boat while the captain went for his chronometer, sextant, *Nautical Almanac* and the ship's papers.

Mr. Gilling with one sailor would be getting the peak halliard ready to use as a tow rope. Another sailor would tend the painter of the boat and a fourth sailor would be at the wheel. The cook gathered up what cooked food he had on hand and some canned goods.

There is some evidence of haste in the act of leaving the vessel. The sailors left their pipes. The main staysail was not furled. The wheel was left loose. The binnacle was displaced and the compass broken, probably in a clumsy attempt to get the compass quickly.

It may well have been that just at that time came an explosion which might have accounted for the fore hatch being upside down on deck, as found. It was currently reported at the time that the captain left his watch and money in his desk and that money was found in the sailors' chests by the salvors—probably small sums of money if any, and the captain's watch probably became a keepsake for somebody. These articles do not appear in the court record and are not mentioned in the memorandum of personal effects which Mr. Sprague, the American Consul, submitted.

Whatever happened, it is evident that the boat with ten people in her left the vessel and that the peak halliard was taken as a tow line and as a means of bringing the boat back to the *Mary Celeste* in case no explosion or fire had destroyed the vessel. Probably a fresh northerly wind sprang up, filled the squaresails and the vessel gathered way quickly. The peak halliard, made fast at the usual place on the gaff, would be brought at an acute angle across the bulwarks at the gangway. With the heavy boat standing still at the end, I do not wonder that the halliard parted. This would tally exactly with the evidence given in court that "the peak halliard was broken and gone." This fact was impressed upon the sailors as they had to get up a coil or rope from the lazarette and reeve off a new peak halliard before they could set the mainsail.

When the tow rope parted, these people were left in an open boat on the ocean as the brig sailed away from them. The wind that took the vessel away may have caused sea enough to wreck them. They perished—let us hope quickly. Nothing has appeared in all these sixty-seven years to tell us of their end. What we know and can surmise from the facts has been told here.

The sword with the cross of Navarre on the hilt, which "Frederick Solly Flood, Esquire, Advocate, and Proctor for the Queen in Her Office of Admiralty" at Gibraltar sought to prove had been used for some nefarious purpose, was not listed by the American Consul among the effects of Captain Briggs. It remained on board the *Mary Celeste* until after a subsequent voyage when George Orr took it home with him to Rerton, N. B. I am told that the sword is still in the family of Captain Orr, at Rerton.

The *Mary Celeste* was built at Spencer Island and registered at Parrsboro, N. S., as the *Amazon*, a single-deck vessel with cabin and forward house on deck, a half-brig rig with a large single topsail. The first captain died three days after he took command. A year later, in 1862, she was at Marseilles, France, and a painting of the vessel was made. This picture is now owned by Mr. R. Lester Dewis, of West Advocate, N. S.

In 1867 the *Amazon* was wrecked in Glace Bay, Newfoundland. As Glace Bay was prohibited by the insurance people and the cost of refloating seemed to be excessive, the owners abandoned her to the salvors. The brig was finally floated, sold to American owners, taken to an American port, an upper deck was added, the forward house raised to stand on the upper deck, a lower topsail yard was added, dividing the topsail. The name was changed to *Mary Celeste* and she was given American registry. The above changes had increased her tonnage measurement from 198.42 to 268 tons.

Captain Briggs bought this vessel in the fall of 1872, and you have read the story of his disaster.

In the following two or three years, the *Mary Celeste* made various voyages and finally was loaded with a cargo of doubtful value on which excessive insurance had been placed. The vessel was wrecked on the coast of Haiti under suspicious circumstances. The insurers refused to pay and charged the captain with *barratry*. For various reasons, the trial was postponed. Two years passed and the captain died, not having been brought to trial.

1941

End of a Bootlegger

Vincent Gilpin

When sail was used in an earlier era of smuggling operations

This yarn concerns one of the most picturesque phases of bootleg-ging—the actual smuggling of liquor into the country—and the natural difficulty of getting such first-hand narratives makes it valuable as a bit of light on the prohibition epoch.

The vessel in the case was *Kona*, a shoal draft, ketch-rigged sailing yacht with gasoline auxiliary, built in 1909 for F. G. Griswold of New York. Mr. Griswold was a well-known sportsman, a friend of Pierre Lorillard and his circle, a great horseman and yachtsman, devoted to sea fishing, especially for tarpon. There is excellent tarpon fishing on the south coast of Cuba, where most of the inlets are shallow and the usual seagoing yacht of deep draft inconvenient, so he went to R. M. Munroe, a leading designer of able centerboard craft, for a boat in which he could cruise to Nova Scotia in summer and to Cuba in winter. *Kona* was the result. She was one of the "Presto boats" originated by Commodore Munroe, essentially round-bilged sharpies; 72 feet long, with beam of 17 feet, she drew 4 feet.

There has been much argument over the virtues of shoal draft at sea and it is said that Griswold's skipper, Dahlberg, an old blue water sailor who had never been in a centerboard boat, almost refused to take charge of her. But, after a few voyages, he became a confirmed and enthusiastic advocate of her and her type for any and all conditions—a judgment amply confirmed by her history, for Dahlberg sailed her 40,000 miles for Mr. Griswold. This is the story of her end.

At the opening of the first world war, she was laid up and was finally sold to a firm in Savannah for the ostensible purpose of charter to yachtsmen. Their chief business, however, was rum-run-ning, and *Kona* was of convenient size for the work. Her shoal draft enabled her to cross the Bahama Banks, take shelter in their many

68

small and shallow harbors and to use the smaller and less frequented inlets on our Atlantic Coast; her strength and ability at sea had been amply demonstrated.

So *Kona* became one of that furtive fleet in which secrecy was the price of life, whose history is a blank, whose numbers are unknown, whose fate is not on record save as one of them might fall into the hands of the law. They loved the dark and times of storm and stress were chosen for their voyages, since these offered the best chance for slipping unnoticed into some obscure inlet. Such a vessel as *Kona*, under sail, could live and carry a good freight in weather conditions quite impossible for the Coast Guard chasers, in which both strength and safety were of necessity somewhat sacrificed for speed.

She made many voyages between the Bahamas and St. Catherine's Sound, where two rivers, the Medway and the Newport, offered plenty of discreet places for unloading, fairly near Savannah; between them lies Liberty County, Georgia, and perhaps its name was considered auspicious. But, at last, after a terrific gale which made the heaviest surf ever seen (November 2nd, 1921) the Coast Guard discovered bits of wreckage at the St. John's River entrance which were identified as the sole remains of *Kona*. With the fragments were many cases of whiskey, sufficient evidence of her errand. Her crew was nowhere to be found and it was assumed that they had drowned.

That, it seemed, was all that ever would be known of the good old boat. Mr. Griswold had published a book on his experiences in her—one of a series on his many outdoor interests—and now added a footnote regretfully recording her disreputable end. But a chain of circumstances was to open a rift in the cloud of oblivion that blotted *Kona* out and reveal to one interested person a vivid picture of her end. The following letter explains itself.

Portland, May 25, 1922

My dear Frank:

Last winter, as you know, we went to Nassau. J. Smith met us and we put a native boat in commission and cruised a month in her, mostly in the waters of Andros.

I made inquiries about *Kona* as soon as I arrived and found a rich sportsman and wholesale liquor dealer who knew her well, but they were all close mouthed about her end—if, indeed, they knew the details. A few days later we were hunting up a native pilot and interviewed a man called "Te"; he had a cough and J. was afraid he might have T.B. I said to him: "You don't seem very strong," and he said "I'll be all right soon—I was shipwrecked last November and I've been sick." I said: "Were you one of the crew of the *Kona*?" and he said "Yes." So we engaged him and he turned out rather better than the average pilot. Well, the story came out after we got to sea; he spun the yarn for me three times and it always checked up. The last day before the cruise ended, I went over it again with him, telling him I wanted to put it down for the man who built and sailed the *Kona* 40,000 miles. Well, here it goes, to close your log.

October 29, 1921 (Saturday). At Stirrup Cay. Ship's company included the captain (a white man from Florida who had been for some time employed by a firm in Savannah as master of one or another of their rum vessels; he had been skipper of *Kona* since they put her into the business—at first, they used her as a yacht and let her on charter); mate, colored, afterward drowned; engineer, white; Te; another seaman, and the cook, afterward drowned. Finished loading 1150 cases of liquor sent down from Nassau about 8:30 P.M. All day the glass had been jumping and dropping a tenth—one of the most definite signs of a hurricane. Set in to rain about 7:30 P.M. Got under way before 9:00, bound for Savannah, course NW½W for Eight Mile Rock, Grand Bahama. Came up on the Rock between midnight and 1:00 A.M. and anchored off Rody Rocks on account of rain and threatening weather; lay there till morning.

October 30th. Got under way about 7:00 A.M. and laid a course to Sandy Cay, on north shore of Grand Bahama. Got there about 9:00 A.M. and anchored again. Weather conditions pointed to a hurricane, but one that was slow in gathering. About 1:00 P.M., the captain decided to chance it, saying: "Let's make hay while the sun shines," which Te thought was a poor joke. The skipper added: "The American people need that booze." Got under way with all sail and motor, laying course NNW for St. Catherine's. The weather was a succession of squalls from the eastward and ENE. During the afternoon, the weather made up so bad that they put back and ran under Settlement Point at the west end of Grand Bahama. Anchored at 6:00 P.M. and lay there all night.

October 31st. Got under way about 6:00 A.M. and laid course NNW for St. Catherine's and American coast. Sailed all day, with weather growing steadily heavier, and kept on all night with things very bad.

November 1st (Tuesday). This morning the captain made out by dead reckoning that he had gone 265 miles of the 366 from St. Catherine's to Memory Rock. Wind increasing in violence and sea rising. About 11:00 A.M., with the skipper at the wheel, a sea struck *Kona* under the quarter; he swung his wheel over to pay her off before the sea and gave her too much, so that she ran off before the wind and jibed the mainsail, parting the peak halliards. The peak dropped and, owing to the lack of ratlines, no one could go aloft to reeve new ones. Te and the mate climbed the hoops and rode the sail down to the deck. The sail was stowed and they went on, under forestaysail and mizzen. Up to this time, *Kona* had been carrying her full mainsail, and the captain had refused to reef, although urged to do so by the crew. The ship, with her cargo, was very stiff and carried her sail well.

Just before nightfall, the ship was still holding her course, and the skipper asked Te what he thought of the weather. Te said he thought the heaviest part of the hurricane would catch them about 11:00 P.M., and advised the skipper to run off and try for Rumsey or Fernandina; he decided, however, to hold on. About 8:00 P.M., the mizzen was taken in and the ship put before the wind under the forestaysail, on a course NW by W. About 8:30 P.M., the boats were swept away from their davits; they had been swung in and lashed to the trunk with canvas bands. Toward 9:00 P.M., the crew jettisoned 300 cases stowed near the engine room. The ship, lightened by the stern, made better weather. Toward 11:20 P.M., the skipper ordered the forestaysail jibed, of which only a small patch was set. He crawled forward over the deckhouse and cut his legs and stomach on the glass of some broken demijohns that had been lashed on the forward deck. At 11:30, Te picked up a light under the lee bow. He tells the story as follows:

"Old Te, what light you t'ink dot is?" asked the captain. I said: "Dot's St. John's bar light, Jacksonville." Captain said no more and kept runnin' wid de light under lee. So den I went below and said to engineer: "If I was you, I'd get some dry canvas and cover de whole engine." De engineer say: "You don't know a dam ting." I went on deck, and de captain say: "Now we're approachin' de danger. Have you ever been over St. John's bar?" I look, and see de Jacksonville light under de lee beam, and de red light at de north end of de bar under our lee bow. "Captain," I say, "you can't run over de bar, we'll all be lost. We've got to try to weather off de jetty—we must get under power."

De captain order de engineer to get under power but de engine only went "*cluck—cluck*." De engineer tried it three times but it wouldn't go. Den we set de mizzen but she wouldn't answer, and we kept bearin' to leeward. Just about tree-quarters of de way from de sout' end of de jetty we struck. "*Bam!*" we struck again, and again de suction carried us off. "*Bam!*" we struck de third time, and I sprang off for de rocks. It was just midnight.

When I got on de rocks, I see de captain, de engineer and Sam, de other hand, all near me in de hollow of de rocks. We could talk but de seas washed over us. I didn't see de cook. At de time we got to de danger, three times I went to de galley and told him to come out but he said he was all right. He was drownded. At de third smash on de rocks, de vessel went to pieces; de mainmast broke in four pieces, and next day her centerboard was on de jetty. Pretty soon I saw de mate to de nort'east on de jetty and I hail him; I ask him how it was where he was. He made no answer—never made no answer. I said to de captain: "I gwine where de mate is, seems like de sea ain't so heavy." "Old Te," he say, "I'd hold what I got." I say "Captain, I gwine where de mate is" and I start crawlin'. I heard a sea comin' and it washed me off on de inside of de jetty. I hear de captain say: "Old Te is gone." "Yes," I say to myself, "I'm gone." But de suction brought me back and I got my clothes off and went swimmin' and divin' to de westward. Finally, after an hour or more, I come on de sand and lay down beside a log till mornin'.

When it come light, I was lookin' to de sout'east and I heard a voice say: "Hello, old Te," and I saw Sam. He ask me how I get ashore and I say: "Why you ask me how I got ashore? You know how I got washed off." He tell me he get washed off ten minutes later and swim along and get on de same piece of sand. After a while we see de captain and de engineer walkin' de jetty toward shore, toward a fisherman's hut, but de mate wasn't with them. Sam went to look for him and come back after a while wid a bottle of whiskey he pick up. While I was takin' a drink, I see somet'ing I took for a log in de water. Sam went to see what it was and found it was de mate, but he was afraid to touch him. Den I went and pulled him out de water and up on de sand. Den we saw de pilot boat comin' for de wreck and I said: "Dis is no place for us; let's make our escape or dey'll make us prisoners." So we went down de jetty to de fisherman's hut and dere we found de captain and de engineer.

That concludes Te's narrative of the wreck. That night, it seems, the fisherman took the captain ashore and paid his fare to Savannah; the following Friday, the owner sent a boat that brought a suit of clothes for each of the three survivors still with the fisherman and took them to Jacksonville. Te was there in hiding till Sunday night, when he went to Savannah. A couple of weeks later, he got a berth in a booze ship and worked his way back to Nassau. His legs were badly scarred from the broken glass that cut him during the gale when I saw him and got the above narrative from him. He is positive there was no drinking during the voyage. He speaks highly of the captain. He says *Kona* behaved wonderfully during the gale and, but for the lost peak halliards, would have had no trouble in weathering the jetty. This long account may bore you, but I took it down, as it was a first hand story of the loss of your old ship, and I believe substantially correct.

Faithfully yours,

DAVID GRAY.

P.S. According to Te, the fisherman was the only one to profit from the wreck. He picked up 1700 quarts of whiskey and announced that he was going to drink it all. From what old Te told me of his four days naked in the hut, the fisherman made a good start.

1943

The Snatch and the Sunbeam

Arthur W. Bull

A yarn concerning some clever nautical detective work

We had made a fast passage across Georgian Bay and now were secure in Western Islands Harbor for the night, lying between two small islands with a line around a tree on each.

We had had a good dinner, dishes were done and highballs were coming up. Everyone had that peaceful, contented feeling except Hank, who had one end of the table covered with papers and books, trying to find what was wrong with his afternoon sight. Of course, we knew just where we were but Hank had studied navigation during the winter and was giving his new sextant a workout on this trip. His last sight had shown us 85 miles from the dead reckoning position and, since that put us outside the Bay, the oldtimers were riding him a bit. At least they were until the skipper said: "Don't let 'em kid you, Hank. Most everything you learn comes in handy some day, even navigation, the way it saved Bill Prince's $50,000." Then he told us the rest of the story.

"Probably most of you never heard of the Prince kidnaping. They're one of those quiet families who don't often get in the newspapers. About ten years ago, when kidnaping was quite a racket in Chicago, a gang put the snatch on Bill. He was driving home from the yacht club one night when a car forced his to the curb. He forgot about arguing when a couple of guns were pointed at him and he was slugged from behind. When he came to, quite a while later, he found he was bound, gagged, blindfolded and going places in the trunk compartment of a car. That kept up for three or four hours. Then two men dragged him out of the trunk, carried him a few feet and lowered him into a small boat. After a short row, the boat

grounded and Bill was hoisted out, carried into a building, up a
ladder and dumped on a cot. When they took off the ropes and gag
and blindfold he asked for water and an explanation. 'Listen, fella;
you're going to be here a few days so just take it easy. We'll take
good care of you and, if your old man comes through with the cash,
you'll be home okay in a week. But don't try any funny business.'

"After they had gone down the ladder and pulled the hatch cover
over the hole a light came on. Bill was in an attic which had a rough
floor laid over the joists. The roof sloped down to the eaves so there
was full headroom only in the center of the space, and there were
no windows. There were a couple of blankets on the cot so he
decided a little sleep would help.

"He was awakened by the hatch cover being pushed back. A plate
of food and a cup of coffee were slid onto the floor and then the
cover was replaced. He felt better after the meal.

"Things went on that way for a couple of days. Food and water
were passed to him without a chance to see his captors' faces. In the
room below, a radio played continually with someone changing it to
cover the newscasts. Bill figured they must have made contact with
his family by now. He hadn't any doubt that his father would meet
the demands if it were at all possible. He dozed, read and listened
to the radio. When the time signal came through, he checked his
watch. It was forty seconds slow.

"Little dots of sunlight came through nail holes or chinks in the
shingles and moved slowly across the floor. Bill started thinking
about sundials. He was wondering if he could check his watch that
way too, when a better idea came along. He had correct time from
the radio and, if he could get the angle between a horizontal line
and one of the sunbeams which came through those tiny holes in the
roof, he would have data from which his position could be calculated
once he got back to his *Nautical Almanac* and navigation tables. The
more he thought about it, the better it looked.

"He unraveled some long threads from the blanket. He found a
heavy nail and used it as a weight or plumb bob to get a vertical
line, which he fastened into the roof alongside one of the holes. Then
he stretched another thread along the floor and carefully adjusted its
height on two sticks until it was touching the plumb line and exactly
perpendicular to it. This was necessary because he was pretty sure
the floor would not be level. When the spot of sunlight crossed the
horizontal string in the late afternoon he marked the spot on the
string and recorded the correct time. With a long sliver divided as a
rule he got the relative lengths of the vertical and horizontal strings

which, with the sunbeam, made up his triangle. The ratio of these lengths would be the tangent of the observed angle. In the next two days, with this substitute for a sextant and with two more horizontal strings, he got eight morning, noon or evening 'sights'. He wrote his data on scraps of magazine pages which he slipped inside his coat lining.

"Meanwhile, the captors had told him to copy a note they had written so they could take it to his father. Next day they got the money. The gang figured that if they returned Bill in good condition they could repeat the performance on other likely prospects. That night they turned off his light, came up the ladder, gagged and blindfolded him again. After another short boat trip they set off in the car. Bill was now sure he had been on an island. Just before daylight, they tied him up and dumped him along the road near Elkhart, Indiana. A milkman pulled Bill out of the ditch. He got to a phone, called his family and they picked him up.

"Two days later, Bill and a pilot were flying over northern Michigan. He had drawn a circle around the intersections of his lines of position, including enough additional area to allow for his probable error. There were three lakes in this circle but only one had an island. That evening Bill and four state police slipped over to the island and, sure enough, it was the place. They nabbed the gang and recovered the ransom. So, as I said before, Hank, navigation may be helpful some time."

1961

Five Flashes East

Harold Waters

Exciting action from rum-running days in Florida

Such was the signal made at night by the "rummys," as we of the Coast Guard called our wily opponents of the rum-running fraternity during the early rip-roaring days of National Aridity, to indicate that the area was clear of Coast Guardsmen and that it was perfectly safe to come in and unload contraband. The latter usually consisted of Scotch, bourbon and Bacardi rum, all destined for thirsty vacationers along Florida's booming Gold Coast. Made with a powerful flashlight, the signal was beamed eastwards in the direction of the Bahamas.

Then the smuggler, generally a squat, light gray flyer with rakish lines, and with all navigational lights extinguished, would come ghosting into the beach, hatches open for the business at hand. A human chain would emerge from the shadows, splashing out to the rummy, her high speed motors turning over slowly in readiness for a quick getaway should anything go awry.

There was little danger of that, however; not with hard-eyed syndicate gunmen keeping a wary eye peeled for hijackers. There was little to be feared from the Coast Guard, so thinly spread were our anti-smuggling forces in those early days of the Dry era. In a few minutes, the contraband would be aboard waiting trucks. The rummy, mission completed, would then turn on her lights and race eastwards at over 30 knots, back to the Bahamian supply base.

The southeast coast of Florida is made to order for smuggling. A long chain of sandy beaches, indented here and there with inlets, rivers and artificial harbors, stretches from Palm Beach to Miami Beach. Only the very lightest of surf laps at the beaches, thanks again to the Bahamas, whose big off-lying islands serve as a breakwater. Close at hand, only 55 miles east of Miami Beach is Bimini, a British possession. A mere 90 miles from Key West is Havana, Cuba. In those days it served as a center for just about every kind of smuggling operation in the book.

Bimini, 55 miles east of Miami Beach, was the main supply depot for Florida-based rummys. It was a permanently anchored Rum Row, whose coral strand swarmed with the very elite of Queer Street: whisky barons, gambling kings and queens, con men, bunco artists, promoters of every shade and hue. Unlike the big Rum Rows of the New England seaboard—concentrations of rum-laden ships of foreign registry which hovered offshore doing a highly lucrative business with shore-based contact boats and were vulnerable to blockade and dispersion—Bimini simply could not be "dispersed."

There was no ducking our duty in the matter, even had we so wished. We certainly had our hands full carrying out our normal Coast Guard chores such as International Ice Patrol, Bering Sea Patrol, the destruction of derelicts and other drifting hazards to navigation. Yet, as the politically powerful Dry lobbies were quick to point out to the Commandant of the Coast Guard, the suppression of smuggling was the very reason for the Coast Guard's founding back in 1790, when the first Secretary of the Treasury, Alexander Hamilton, established a small fleet of Revenue Cutters for the express purpose of stamping out a lively smuggling traffic that was defrauding the infant nation of its rightful revenues.

Our Commandant's reply was brief and to the point. "Give us the tools, and we'll get on with the job."

The Dry lobbies lived up to their word. A reluctant Congress was blackjacked into appropriating huge sums for building and fitting out a Dry Armada. From a normal strength of 4,000 officers and men, the Coast Guard mushroomed up to 14,000. New ships, ranging in size from fast 38′ picket boats to 165′ steel-hulled patrol boats began to slide down the launching ways. Twenty-five destroyers mounting the same guns they had used against German U-boats were borrowed from the Navy. Workhorse of this new fleet was a sturdy wooden-hulled patrol boat, 75′ overall and called by us a "six-bitter." The six-bitter, manned by a crew of eight and mounting a one-pounder rapid fire gun and two Lewis machine guns, was a jack-of-all-trades craft.

The effect of this tremendous expansion was immediate. First to feel the blow were the big Rum Rows of the North, which found themselves under close blockade for the first time. No longer could shore-based contact boats speed out at will to pick up cargos of hooch.

Bases were set up in Florida, at Fernadina, St. Petersburg, and Fort Lauderdale. This was not exactly greeted with cheers by the locals, who made it pointedly plain that we were about as welcome as lepers at a fiesta.

The rummys were invested with a certain glamour by an openly sympathetic press. They were compared with the gay and daredevilish blockade runners of the War Between the States, who had also used the Bahamas as a base. Gush-type journalists played rummys up as romantic types, debonair fellows who were in the trade just for the sport of it, all of which was sheer unadulterated malarkey. Truth is, rummy flotillas were owned and rigidly controlled by mobster syndicates who brooked no nonsense on the part of hirelings. Any skipper who refused to take orders, who talked too much, or was suspected of executing a double-cross, was harshly dealt with—like being encased in a "concrete overcoat" and dropped into the indigo depths of the Gulf Stream. One of the most ruthless of rummy entrepreneurs was a woman, Spanish Marie. She was known to be somewhat rough on lovers, regarding them as perfectly expendable. At least five fetched up in concrete overcoats.

No sooner had we established the bases than the U.S. Government, unwittingly it must be assumed, decided to set up a free navigational aid service for our opponents. This was a chain of powerful aerial beacons flashing skywards all through the night along the entire length of the Florida peninsula. These beacons were plainly visible from both Bimini and Gun Cay. A rummy skipper didn't need a compass; all he had to do was steer toward the flashing light nearest his destination.

At first, the only rummys we caught were daylight-runners. These were generally slow craft or lame ducks whose motors had failed. The flyers raced right on, showing their heels to our slower six-bitters. Even the captured rummys lived to run another day. This was because of the law making it mandatory for seized craft to be sold at public auction. The original owners were always on hand at these auctions, bidding back their craft at ridiculously low figures. Woe betide any dewey-eyed outsider who had ideas about bidding on a seized rummy. A cold-eyed syndicate man would give him the word on that, making it very plain that any such rashness could only lead to mayhem.

This was a pretty sore point with us. It was not unusual for our side to catch the same rummy twice, or even three or four times, and often with its original crew, who were out on bail. Yet we continued to make progress, achingly slow as it was, and meanwhile the rummys were being made increasingly aware of the fact that we meant business.

The development of an Intelligence Section marked the turning of the tide in our favor. Known rummys were placed on what was called a suspected list; their ownership was inquired into, their movements closely watched, and shipyards frequented by them came under close surveillance. The main rummy lairs of Bimini, Gun Cay and Havana were infiltrated by Coast Guard agents.

In the case of captured rummys, some of our people were at first not inclined to regard them as common criminals. Seldom was it that rummy prisoners were placed in irons following capture. This practice, unwise to begin with, was to have serious consequences for one six-bitter crew, resulting in a massacre that is remembered to this day.

The incident occurred on Aug. 7, 1927, when the Six-Bitter No. 249, under the command of Boatswain Sydney Sanderlin, an easygoing warrant officer from North Carolina, was bound from Base Six, Fort Lauderdale, to Bimini, with a lone passenger aboard. The latter was Robert K. Webster, an agent of the U.S. Secret Service.

The Government of the Bahamas, which for some years now had been cashing in on the bonanza resulting from Prohibition, suddenly awoke to the fact that all that glitters is not exactly gold, and that one illicit operation usually brings on another. Bimini, it appeared, was in fiscal trouble of a sort. Not because of any slackening off in business, but because of a sudden flood of "funny money" from across the Gulf Stream. Stateside counterfeiters had taken a hand in the game along Bimini's many-faceted strand. Ironically, Bahamian authorities appealed for help from the very same government whose laws they had been so cheerfully helping to flout. The Secret Service has the job of guarding the nation's money against counterfeiters.

Halfway across the Gulf Stream, No. 249 sighted a small motorboat heading in the direction of Florida. There was only one thing for Skipper Sanderlin to do, and he did it; go on an intercepting course.

Despite a series of unmistakable heave-to signals, the motorboat continued holding to her course and speed.

"Fire a blank charge!" ordered Sanderlin.

The gun boomed out its warning message, but it brought no response.

"Use the Lewis gun! Short bursts just ahead of the bows! We don't want to fire into her unless we have to." Skipper Sanderlin was like that, chary of hurting anybody unless forced to do so.

The machine gun bursts did it. The small motorboat changed course and headed over to us. There were no other ships in sight, just the six-bitter and the motorboat, whose number was V13997. Her homeport was Miami and aboard were two men, James Horace Alderman and Robert K. Weech. Alderman was the elder, a sinister-looking type in his late 30's; Weech was in his early 20's. A search disclosed a small amount of contraband, 20 sacks of whisky.

"Looks like I'll have to take you in," Sanderlin told the two rummys.

"But it's such a small amount," protested Alderman. "Why can't you just take the booze and let us go."

By way of reply, Sanderlin gestured for them to come aboard. Entering the pilot house, Sanderlin went over to the radio telephone and started to raise the Base, but before he got through, a bullet intervened, killing him. Alderman had picked up one of four unguarded .45 caliber pistols lying on a chart desk in the pilothouse and fired it into Sanderlin's back.

What followed was a wild, bloody flashback to the days of the old Spanish Main. Alderman raced out of the pilothouse and fired another shot at Victor Lamby, a young machinist's mate, who fell back into the engineroom, mortally stricken.

Waving his gun at the others, Alderman herded them up forward and announced his murderous intentions. The six-bitter was to be set afire and all hands were to perish in the blaze and explosion. This was to be accomplished by Weech going down into the engineroom and rupturing a gasoline line so that the bilges would flood. Then Weech was to board the motorboat and start the motor in preparation for a quick getaway. Following this, Weech was to re-board No. 249 and, at a given signal from Alderman, throw a piece of lighted cotton waste below, thus igniting the gasoline, causing an explosion.

By this time, according to Alderman's reasoning, he and Weech would have had time to board their own craft and make a safe getaway. The plan might very well have worked but for the timorous Weech, who was plainly not up to it.

"There's a wounded man down in the engineroom," he demurred. "You know, that guy you plugged."

"Kill the bastard off!" raged Alderman. "He's gonna die anyhow, just like these other sons of bitches," he went on, waving his pistols at his prisoners up in the bows, "are gonna die. Don't be so goddam chicken-hearted about it!"

But it was too much for the nervous Weech who left the dying

Lamby strictly alone. Leaping back aboard the motorboat, Weech put on another bad show in his efforts to start the motor. His awkwardness drew a salvo of curses from his partner.

At this point Agent Webster, seeking to reason with the killer, pointed out that what he proposed to do was senseless; that he should at least give them a fighting chance for their lives by letting them lower the six-bitter's dinghy.

"You're gonna fry here along with the rest of these goddamn Coast Guard snoopers!" snarled Alderman. "An' it won't be very long before you do!" Whereupon he again addressed himself to the nervous Weech, urging him in the most abusive manner to get on with the job of starting the motor.

Realizing that Alderman meant what he said, and that there was only one thing to do if a wholesale massacre were to be averted, the gallant Webster, with a cry of "Let's get him, boys!" led a sudden charge. Alderman fired at the Secret Serviceman, hitting him in the heart and killing him instantly, then fired at Jody Hollingsworth, the six-bitter's cook, hitting him twice and knocking him overboard. By this time, the others were upon the killer, who was subdued and put in irons. Weech gave up meekly.

While this was going on, Hollingsworth had drifted off, blood spurting from his wounds. Miraculously, he remained afloat and was recovered just in time as ominous dorsal fins heralded the arrival of sharks. Lamby died a few hours later, but Hollingsworth survived his wounds. Alderman was subsequently hanged. Weech, who turned state's evidence, got off with the very light sentence of one year and a day. Rummys were henceforth treated as common felons.

As our offensive got into high gear, we received reports of shark-mutilated bodies drifting inshore along the Florida Keys. Our first reaction was that the bodies were either those of aliens who had been jettisoned by runners or the consequence of intramural clashes among rummys. It turned out that we were wrong on both counts. An investigation conducted by Coast Guard Intelligence determined that a new and certainly more sinister element had entered the picture—the hijacker. At first we were accused of being responsible for these grisly killings as a way of evening the score for the Alderman affair, and an ugly situation developed at Key West one night when an inflamed mob threatened to lynch the entire crew of our six-bitter after a fire-gutted rummy craft had drifted in with three charred bodies, all bound and gagged. The victims were Conchs, as Key Westers were called.

Holding the mob at bay with his one-pounder and machine guns, our skipper hurriedly got his six-bitter underway, well clear of the land. Months went by before Intelligence was able to convince the citizens of Key West that the cold-blooded massacre was the work of hijackers.

One night off Palm Beach one of our six-bitters chanced upon what appeared to be a hijack operation. Tommy gun tracers were lighting up the darkened sea. The situation was not at all clear to our skipper as to who was who, so he kept his craft well out of the line of fire, intending to close in afterwards, only it didn't work out like that. After the battle had raged on for 30 minutes, both boats caught fire, and our skipper made a Solomon-like decision. Realizing that he would have nothing to show for it if both boats sank, he decided to help put out the fires. Turning on his own navigational lights, he moved in only to receive the surprise of his Coast Guard life. Both boats were rummys, and the battle had been one great tragic mistake for them. Each had mistaken the other in the dark for a hijacker. Luckily for both parties, there were no serious casualties, and our skipper had a word of advice for the disgruntled rummys. "What you guys ought to do, is to get together on a set of recognition signals."

Then there were the unhappy hijackers who were stalking their "prey" one night, only to be blown out of the water. The prey in this instance was one of our six-bitters.

More woes for rummys followed our setting up of a "Dirty Tricks" department. By now they were using radio for eluding our flotillas, and counteracting the infiltration of their own ranks by Coast Guard Intelligence agents posing as bonafide rummys. Under the new system, rummys were not given their destinations until they had cleared Bahamian waters. The orders were dispatched by secret radio codes from clandestine stations along the Florida shoreline. The locations of these stations soon became known to our radio experts, and our cryptographic wizards did the rest, cracking all the secret rummy codes aboard a six-bitter fitted out as a floating "Black Chamber."

Strange things began to happen to rummys as they came ghosting in of nights, only to be greeted by sandpounders with drawn guns, and flotillas of six-bitters and picket boats backing them against the beach. Much to the consternation of the big syndicates, these ambushes were happening with such alarming frequency that they suspected a sell-out on the part of their own people, an illusion which we did nothing to dispel.

Scuttlebutt had three perfectly innocent rummy radio operators hauled before syndicate courts on charges of selling secret codes to the Coast Guard and being given the concrete overcoat treatment.

By a stroke of incredibly good fortune, plus an assist from our Dirty Tricks Department, the Queen of the rummys, the notorious "Spanish Marie" herself, fell into our hands. She happened to be aboard one of her own boats, *Kid Boots*, when it was lured into an ambush at Coconut Grove, just south of Miami. In expressive language, Spanish Marie let us know what she thought of the new Coast Guard tactics.

The loss of so many boats in so short a time began to hurt the rummys, for even in those freewheeling days a 50-foot flyer powered with twin Liberties or triple Fiats ran as high as $50,000. Once seized, both the craft and her cargo became Government prizes under a new law that scuttled the practice of allowing rummys to buy their boats back. The Coast Guard was now allowed to keep captured boats, and in many cases they were pressed into service as anti-smuggling craft. But what really finished the rummys was a Special Patrol Force for Floridian waters. This armada began to arrive early in 1928. It included 12 destroyers, nine 125′ patrol boats, 25 six-bitters, two big ocean-going cutters, and a flight of amphibian planes. In addition, whole platoons of sandpounders were shipped south to reinforce lifesaving stations.

A destroyer blockade strangled Bimini and Gun Cay right away, and the big offshore patrol boats mounted guard over the approaches to Key West. The few rummys who managed to elude the destroyers were usually bagged by a picket line of six-bitters waiting for them half way across the Gulf Stream, and the handful who managed to get all the way across invariably ran into ambuscades set up by picket boats and sandpounders.

First to feel the full effect of our massed onslaught were the fast rummys of the daylight runs, especially now that we had planes aloft. Nor was there much relief for night-running rummys. The few who tried it were invariably caught in the glare of powerful searchlights or illuminated by bursting star shells. Even the old dodge of "belling the cat" no longer worked. This was a dodge designed to lure a blockading ship off station with a fast boat racing out of Bahamian waters oblivious to warning signals. When the blockading vessel took up the pursuit and started to fire lethal stuff, the boat would heave to and an examination would disclose that the craft was empty of contraband. In the meantime perhaps as many as six loaded rummys would race merrily out of Bimini and/or Gun Cay, but there were now simply too many Coast Guard "cats to bell." Besides, it had become too risky with the dread possibility of being blasted out of the water by a four-inch shell from a destroyer, and the price of whisky and rum tripled and quadrupled along the Gold Coast.

Some smuggling did persist right up to the bitter end of Prohibition, in 1933, but only a mere trickle compared with before. Rum-running never recovered from the advent of our Special Patrol Force.

1975

Captain America Rides Again

Jeff Hammond

An intimate account of what it's like to sail in an ocean race with Ted Turner

It is the first morning of the Miami–Montego Bay Race, and Ted Turner's red-hulled *Tenacious* is screaming around the north side of the Bahamian island of Eleuthera, a mark of the course. With her leader at the helm, the boat slips closer and closer to land as he attempts to clear the island's reefs by as slim a margin as possible.

All of a sudden, with the boat roaring along at eight knots, a loud BANG issues from below. Its meaning is unmistakable. The boat shudders, then obediently plunges on.

Turner: "Damn the coral heads! Full speed ahead!"

Peter Bowker, veteran ocean racer acting as cook, drops his chores below, sticks his head through the hatch to look around casually and then observes, with a twinkle in his eye, "If you haven't hit a bit of coral, then you haven't come close enough."

Turner: "Does this mean we have to re-round Eleuthera?"

Bowker: "Just don't hit Cuba."

And *Tenacious* charges on, Turner in his element again.

If you will recall, last summer, after years of craving a shot at defending the America's Cup, R. E. "Ted" Turner got his chance. Then he got his comeuppance. The man who had been heralded for years by the yachting press for his winning ways (and quotable quotes) met near total disaster. He even lost the dubious honor of going down with his flaming red ship, *Mariner*, that chore having been masterfully handled by Dennis Conner. Turner's reputation had been badly tarnished; he was without a boat, and—for a short while—he was even speechless.

Ted Turner

But Turner is talking once again. He now says, and I quote, "After last summer the only thing I had left was tan-ass-sit-ee." That's more or less the way he says tenacity, giving it emphasis by dragging the word out from the bottom of his throat in his Georgia accent for just as long as its few syllables will allow. He tells his story often, of course, and his listeners usually warm to the mental image of Turner rising like a phoenix from the ashes of defeat to once again valiantly challenge men in sailing ships. "TENACIOUS" was painted on the transom of Turner's new boat lest anyone forget the story.

Under that name, "Earth" had originally been written as the hailing port, suggested by Turner before the disaster at Newport. But, having had his comeuppance, a measure of humility had followed. He ordered "Earth" scrubbed off and "USA" painted in its place.

Then, in the 1975 SORC, *Tenacious* won class in every race plus two overalls, was second in another, and was later picked for the U.S. Admiral's Cup team. Ah, sweet victory. Humility bites the dust and Captain America, that legendary superhuman hero of the comic books, rides again.

Now Turner is racing to Jamaica. I'm aboard because, as my host has so succinctly put it, he "could use some good press." Since I could use a good story, I go along. Most of what follows is more or less true. Apologies to those who might hanker for a "how-to" article, because this is not one and much fascinating "go-fast" material has been, regretfully, left out. But hear now, some tales of Captain America in action.

Listen: It is 1030 the morning of the Miami–Montego Bay Race start, an event Turner has won twice and sailed in five times. The start is at noon. At 1031, with most of the crew aboard, Turner starts the engine, throws it in gear and simultaneously screams, "We're leavin'—we're leavin'!" in his peculiarly piercing voice over the protests of two crewmen on the pier frantically trying to untie the dock lines.

Turner's cries have alerted everyone at the Miami Marina and they trundle down for the amusement of watching Captain America leave the dock. Since the boat is in gear, the dock lines are jammed, tautly resisting the best efforts of the men trying to free them. Turner begins to limber up his tongue for a long ocean race by using it to lash his tardy crew into action. As the crowd merrily watches the scrambling aboard *Tenacious*, Turner shouts, "I told you we were leaving on time, and now we're late!" The lines are finally freed on board and cast ashore, never to be seen again, and the boat squirts out of her slip.

With 30 minutes to go before the start, *Tenacious* has already run the line four times and changed headsails thrice. Now Turner begins his pre-race ritual of sailing back and forth across the line until his crewmen are draped over their winch handles like Salvador Dali clocks. Even though these men have been grinding their hearts out, the captain is not satisfied with their slothful behavior and heaps up generous servings of verbal abuse for their consumption. Later, it is said that he does this to get their adrenalin running and to get their attention, much as a farmer might use a two-by-four on his mule. In the process he uses lots of four-letter words, three-letter words and hyphenated words. Occasionally, he even uses longer words; after all, he is a high school graduate. And he is probably also a good Scrabble player. You will, however, be spared the specifics of most of Turner's rhetoric.

Also on board is the designer of the boat, German Frers. German is pronounced "hair-mon." Designers of racing boats rarely make long ocean passages after they become successful. It is, after all, a miserable way to travel. The crew is somewhat awed to have German aboard, not only because he is an outstanding designer, but also because he is a fine helmsman. However, over the next few days awe will melt into familiarity and he will be called first "Herman"; then "Herman-the-German." The crew will delight in telling him what they would change about the boat as every detail of *Tenacious* is hashed out. German will probably not change a thing on his next boat. Except the sliding door to the head which German himself will go crashing through, from the inside out, two nights later while perched on the facilities when the boat tacks.

Like an army, an ocean-racing crew travels on its belly. Turner knows this and has enlisted Bowker as cook. Like Turner, Bowker has become a legend in his own time. Incidentally, Bowker has just stowed $250 worth of food which he purchased in large part with his own money. (One assumes that he was repaid.) He will make these supplies last 12 men six days, which works out to $3.33 per man per day, but don't let that get around.

By late afternoon Captain America has repaired below for a glass of iced tea. Feeling a different motion to the boat he asks from his bunk: "Are we being faired?"

Bowker in the galley relays the message up the hatch: "Are we being faired?"

A crewman sitting near the hatch says to the helmsman: "Are we being faired?"

The helmsman says: "What does 'faired' mean?"

Listen: At night crewmen on deck are issued flashlights. They are expected to use them. Constantly. To insure that this is done, Turner does not sleep a wink the first night on his off-watch and pokes his head up through the hatch every five minutes and looks around, rather like a groundhog vainly searching for his shadow. He then plays the light over the main and moans that nobody is watching the sail. In fact, it has just been trimmed seconds before. Then he looks at the genoa. More cries of anguish that no one is paying any attention. He has a deckload of laggards who are only out for an evening cruise.

Actually, most of these men have sailed with him for years all over the world and two spent all summer with him in *Mariner*. They have heard it all before, and no one thinks much of it as he snorts and drops below, only to pop up three minutes later like toast from a toaster. Occasionally, one of the crew eases the genoa sheet slightly as the glow from Turner's $2 cigar emerges from the hatch, thus allowing him the pleasure of re-trimming the sail to his own taste.

Listen: It is the second night out, and Captain America takes command, outfitted in full battle dress—his blue and white striped railroad engineer's cap with the NYYC burgee pinned in front, a red windbreaker and blue shorts specially made of yacht duck with padding in the seat. He has decided to go behind Cat I. instead of beating around it to the east. He reckons this course will save nine miles. It will also, in fact, take *Tenacious* over a patch marked "Shoaling Reported" on the chart.

Unbeknownst to the men on *Tenacious*, there is a 1½-knot current between Cat I. and Eleuthera and the boat is being set toward a spot on the chart marked "X X X" which, roughly translated, means coral.

Veteran Turner crewman Marty O'Meara pulls on his stogie, then says, "In time of peace, prepare for war," and runs the genoa sheets, checking the leads, to make sure the boat will be ready to tack instantly.

At the wheel, Turner feels that something is wrong and has come up ten degrees. He says, "Fools rush in where angels fear to tread."

The bow lookout sights coral but does not have time to relay the news before the boat is on it. A rumbling begins below, and the boat begins to shake as if in the grip of an earthquake. The growl grows into thunder, and it sounds as if the wood bottom is being torn out. Bowker checks his watch. It is 2216 hours.

Turner shouts, "I'm going to drive over it."

The boat grinds to a stop. The point man is nearly pitched overboard.

Turner: "Let's tack."

The boat won't budge.

Turner, now excited, yells, "Get the spinnaker poles over the side forward. Back the main. Back the genoa. All hands on deck." These commands are underscored with appropriate invective, since his speech has had a full day to recover from near atrophy after two weeks of sedate business life.

Flashlights stab the darkness, illuminating coral all around the boat and after 15 minutes of work the vessel continues to thump up and down on the heads. Everything the crew tries only seems to make *Tenacious* even more ensnarled. There is only 2½ feet of water forward.

Turner ashes his cigar and mutters, "I'd rather be in Philly." Then he strides around the deck issuing a torrent of contradictory orders. He loves it. He is Lord Nelson at Trafalgar. However, his crewmen are not English tars and more than one suggests that Lord Nelson return to the helm and shut up. Watch Captain Bunky Helfrich advises that a staysail should be flown off the backstay. Everyone seems in agreement and drops the futile tasks at hand. The main flops over on its own, the boat pivots, groans and slides off the coral head just as easy as you please—all by herself after 22 minutes aground. It is well known that God looks after children, drunks and yachtsmen.

Later, after successfully charging across the 12-foot shoal, Turner volunteers, "I was so mad at that coral that I wanted to jibe around and hit it again. I'd rather sink than lose." No one utters the thought that the best way to lose is sink.

Tenacious is like a floating stage with Dacron sails instead of a black curtain. The crew are both bit players and the audience. The man at the helm is the star of the show. He should have a straw hat.

Near midnight of the third evening, *Tenacious* is closing rapidly on Mira Por Vos, a giant dark rock that is 100 yards across and 20 feet high right in the middle of the race course ("Three strikes and we're out"). It is nearly invisible at night. The rock was probably discovered by Columbus and in Spanish Mira Por Vos means "watch out for yourself." It is good advice. At odd intervals throughout the race Turner breaks out with impromptu limericks and now he spouts:

"There was an old man who was morose / Because he had hit Mira Por Vos / It was the only way to win / He said with a grin / But unfortunately we came too close."

Listen: The next day it is discovered that the alternators are not working and the batteries are nearly dead. Emergency running lights are taped to the bow and stern. A flashlight is strapped to the backstay to illuminate the masthead fly at night. The anemometer and speedo needles fall limp. The Omega drops dead the following day for want of juice. But that is not all that is wrong with the boat. An improper mix of resin was applied to part of the deck which gives it the appearance and, worse, the feel of a terminal case of psoriasis. The keel bolts leak about ten gallons per watch while the boat is on the wind. A stern stanchion pulls out and new screws have to be machined and installed underway. *Tenacious* will finish the race without an engine, without instruments, without electronic aids to navigation and without ice. The crew will have second-degree bottom rash.

Perhaps here it is appropriate to mention that *Tenacious* is one of the hottest ocean racing boats in the world.

Listen: News is picked up on a portable radio that *Kialoa* has won the race while *Tenacious* is 150 miles from the finish line slatting in the doldrums. No one bats an eyelash. The "Windless Passage" had done to *Tenacious* what coral heads had failed to do. Crew morale continues high and Turner appears to still enjoy the race as much as if he were winning. He has lost before.

Turner: "Oh God, first you make us think we're going to win, then you squash us like a bug. Oh please don't punish us any more. Bring us some wind!"

Bowker: "Dem dat dies 'll be the lucky 'uns, Mister 'akins, dem dat dies."

Turner: "This is turning into a war of nerves, men."

Crewman John Potter says: "Your war and our nerves."

Rising from the galley Bowker pipes up, "I just found a penny in the sink. I'll throw it to the wind gods."

O'Meara deadpans, "Bowker, we just got a penny's worth of wind. Now how 'bout trying a dollar bill."

Bowker, with a pious countenance: "Those who can smile in the face of adversity are the blessed ones."

Turner: "What in God's name are we doing out here floating around? Why, if we had any ambition we'd be at our offices making money, providing for our families."

Anonymous crewman: "Who said we had any ambition?"

Bowker: "Ocean racing is crazy and the longer the race the crazier it is. The Transatlantic Race is craziest of all!"

Turner: "Why do we have to race across the ocean? I'd like to see a 3,600-mile race from Execution Rock to Stratford Shoals."

Bowker: "Everyone would come out and watch the crazies. It would take a year and a half to finish."

Later in the day the cruising-type ketch *Southerly* and current World Ocean Racing Champion Wally Stenhouse's *Aura* ghost by *Tenacious.*

Turner: "We've got to beat *Southerly.* They expect us to beat 'em. Now look at where *Aura* is. Wow, we're going through her like fat through a goose."

O'Meara takes a bearing and says: "We're lucky if we've picked up a degree on them in the last 15 minutes."

Turner: "Okay, crew, get to work! I'll buy 100 rum punches for you in Montego Bay if we beat *Aura.* If we don't beat her then I'm charging everyone $5 a night for sleeping on the boat."

The on-deck watch springs to mock action, trimming and tweaking and looking thoughtfully at the sails.

Turner hears someone cough loudly below. He immediately relinquishes the helm and dives down the hatch. The coughs were meant to cover up the sound of pop-tops being ripped off beer cans smuggled aboard and stashed in the eventuality of just such a hot afternoon. One of Turner's hard and fast rules is no alcoholic beverages consumed while racing. A minute later two full beer cans come flying out of the hatch and over the side as if they were two rotten apples. The captain scampers back to the helm as a breeze fills the spinnaker.

Turner shouts with glee, "Look at *Aura*'s chute collapse! The World Ocean Racing Champion can't even hold his chute."

And with that, there is a loud WHOMP on *Tenacious* as her chute also collapses. The crew falls into uncontrolled mirth.

Turner: "Well, that just goes to prove that the WORC champions are only human. . . . Look at us now. We're droppin' *Aura* like an empty no-deposit bottle."

Aura now slips to leeward in search of fresher winds.

Turner: "I never split with the competition unless they are going the wrong way; then I sail against the fleet. If you're slower you've just got to take your lumps and wait for the *chagos* (the word is really *"chavos,"* Spanish slang for "fellas") ahead to make a mistake like putting up the wrong sail. Of course, I try to have a faster boat."

Anonymous crewman: "Like *Mariner.*"

Turner: (Insert your favorite four-letter words.) ". . . You've got to have a proven winner. That's why I bought the Cal 40 *Vamp X* and we won the Circuit. Look at all the races we won in *American Eagle* when she was five years old. I bought *Lightnin'* only after she had won the One Ton North Americans. I wouldn't have bought this boat if *Recluta* (her near sister) hadn't done so well at Cowes. Now I've got *Stinger*, winner of the SORC. The best way to win is to buy a winner."

A crewman slings a bucket of bilge water from out of the hatch and says, "Why don't you buy a bilge pump."

Turner, oblivious to the suggestion, changes the subject, "Gee, I haven't farted much this race."

Potter: "That's because all of the gas has been coming out of your mouth."

Listen: As *Tenacious* approaches the high green mountains of Jamaica, Bowker comes on deck in the role of chief purser and passes out tourist cards that must be filled in. The diversity of occupations is typical of the make-up of Turner's crew as he sails around the world. Former Omega promoter Franz Schneider is now a successful producer of black Kung Fu movies and has enrolled Turner as the villain of a proposed new film titled *Black Commodore*. Jim Mattingly is a salesman for the Bob Derecktor boat yard. Bunky Helfrich is an architect and an IOR measurer (he did not measure *Tenacious*). Woody Cox is a former all-American football player. Marty O'Meara is part owner of a new dog track.

Turner: "What! No sailmakers aboard! No wonder we're losing this race. We need brown thread Ted from Marblehead! What are you going to put down, Bowker?"

Bowker: "*Mariner* . . . oops, I guess that's a dirty word around here."

Turner: "I tell you one of my life's ambitions is to take every nickel I've got to buy *Courageous* and *Mariner*. Then I'll invite the best skippers in the world to sail against me—and I'll take *Courageous*. I guarantee you that I'll win every time."

And so, as *Tenacious* sails into the brilliant orange glow of the Caribbean sunset and the crew settles down to watch for the green flash, R. E. "Ted" Turner, better known to some as the "mouth of the South," jabbers on about the next America's Cup. The smart money is betting that he will return to Newport in 1977 to the scene of last year's defeat. They are also wagering that he'll be racing in a proven winner. We'll see. In the meantime, Captain America rides again.

In Their Hour of Triumph

John Hersey

A Pulitzer-Prize-winning novelist's perceptive report on an America's Cup summer at Newport, with all its color, vivid personalities and tensions

On *Elan*'s signal halyard the narrow rectangular flag bearing the letters NYYC snaps straight out in a vector of boat speed plus a promising morning southerly that reaches its fingers up the East Passage. There should be a decent testing breeze outside for *Enterprise* and *Courageous*. Ted Hood and *Independence* have a lay day.

Elan, the Bertram 58 chartered by the America's Cup Committee for their summer's work, has rounded Fort Adams and is laying down a white road alongside Newport Neck. The wide lawns of Hammersmith shimmer in the haze; a committeeman's wife remarks that Mrs. Auchincloss has just put this remaining classic mansion up for sale—the last gasp of an era?

Formality wanes in the world. Below, in the carpeted and air-conditioned master cabin, dark blue uniform "sailing jackets" (Vanderbilt and his afterguard wore them while racing) are laid out, as if by the ghost of a club steward, on a bed. But the men above are dressed for comfort. The great assertive chin of Chairman George Hinman chops off his jocular remarks above an open-necked madras shirt. Bob Bavier has on red shorts. Briggs Cunningham is the only member of the committee in jacket—khaki and cool—and club tie. "Uniform" for all the men consists of nothing more than a Nassau straw hat with club colors on the band—blue ground, narrow red midstripe edged with white.

Someone points out Fort Wetherill off to the right, and the tall spars of *Sverige* and her workhorse *Columbia*. Cunningham, who won the Cup in *Columbia*, shakes his head over the Swede. A Twelve-Meter with a tiller? Leg-driven grinders? "We'll see," Briggs says. Three more Twelves, *Australia*, *Gretel II*, *France II*, under sail and aslant, make a superb sight cutting the two blues of this cloudless day. The wooden Frenchman lifts an azure flank to committee view. "Is Marcel aboard?" a committee wife asks. "Can you see if Marcel's aboard? Why, it looks like a Sunday picnic!"

Out at the starting area the committee go above to the flying bridge—enchanted platform of decision, absolutely no visitors allowed. Hinman radios to the race committee, already anchored on *Bobbara*: *"Let's have a full-length course without the reaches."* In other words, a four-and-one-half mile windward-leeward-windward-leeward-windward race. Up to now the beats have been short—two and a half miles. The committee knows what it wants to see. (Yesterday, Hood against North, the wind suddenly veered 30 degrees after the warning gun. Four minutes before start time the race committee radioed to *Elan* that they thought they should cancel and give the boats a new course. No, the committee answered, carry on. They wanted to see how the skippers would react to the changed conditions, and they also wanted to see a close reach on the third leg.) Today they look for a sustained trial of nerve, of tactics, and of boat speed between Lowell North on *Enterprise* and Ted Turner on *Courageous*. It's time North showed something; Turner has been hammering him. But more than that: This is a showdown of philosophies. North, the controlled perfectionist, who has designed his tight-leeched sails by computer and has tuned his boat by computer, versus Turner, the canny, aggressive sailor who believes in the human hunch.

No round-de-round at the start. North sits endlessly on Turner, sails shaking, in the covering tactic devised by Dennis Conner. But half a minute before the gun Turner trims and falls off on starboard tack and builds enough way to luff up and force North to tack. Thus they start at opposite ends of the line, Turner with a slight advantage. But on the long climb to windward—*Elan* stays within spitball distance of the two bevelled transoms—North slips out from under and gets a lead. Turner changes jibs to perfection, running the new one up in a headstay slot just before a tack and taking the old one down as the boat goes over. North's tacks are smooth, in ideal, programmed curves; Turner charges at the wind like a mastiff. North holds on and has 25 seconds at the outer mark.

There is heavy stamping on *Elan*'s flying bridge—a message to wives below. It has been a tense beat. The sun has crossed the yardarm. The wives jump to. Bloody Marys are passed up the ladder.

Downwind Turner attacks and attacks. Several jibes. Tight sailing. "O.K., boys, get your tape recorders ready," Hinman says—the idea being that there'll surely be an opportunity now, even at a distance, to pick up some colorful sounds from the titanium vocal chords (not standard equipment for America's Cup larynxes) of Ted Turner.

A luffing match. The lead changes hands. Turner covers North after they round.

Thirty seconds later the headstay rod on *Courageous* parts with a thwang, the jib sags. Turner bears off sharply to save the mast. He throws his hands toward the sky as he passes *Elan*. A point for Lowell North.

L. J. Edgecomb, mastman on *Courageous*, can be seen going aloft in a wildly swaying bosun's chair. An empty freighter, its high-riding bow bulb pushing hills of water aside, comes bulling down the sea. Turner, crippled, cannot change course. *Elan* runs interference for *Courageous*. The freighter turns away.

Courageous is taken in tow. From half a mile's distance, Turner radios that the spare part is in Marblehead; can't possibly repair and race again. When the radio has shut down, Cunningham cups his hand to his ear and says, "I can hear the cussing from here."

Elan runs far up peaceful Mackerel Cove, to get out of the swell, and anchors for a quiet lunch. Over a meat salad with artichoke hearts and Greek olives and *conchiglie* with diced apple, the committee discusses what they have seen. The three Twelve-Meter sailors do most of the valuable talking. Hinman asks Bavier what happened in the crucial moments on the second leg.

"Lowell carried him up too far," Bob says, "Luffing was all right, but the moment Ted jibed, Lowell should have gone, too."

After lunch, *Elan* runs in to Bannister's Wharf to check on the damage to *Courageous*. Standing by a piling, Turner, in his blue denim engineer's cap and green tennis shirt—also dressed up in his best manners—explains to Hinman that the rod parted at the foot, just where the threads begin for the fitting. "That's where they always go. We had three of them let go on *American Eagle*. When you slack off the backstay on a run, it thrashes around, and on the wind, when the jib is pulling hard" —he has one fist gyrating restlessly over the other— "it works and works. Fatigues the metal." Then Ted Turner is suddenly himself. Frustration comes to flower in him. The left fist opens and the right fist crashes into it. "Dad-dammit!" he shouts.

Ted Hood is taking *Independence* up Narragansett Bay in Wedgewood-blue air and rippling water to look at some recut sails under ideal conditions. He gives the leeward wheel (*Independence* has two, side by side, as on *Gretel II* and *Intrepid*) to his navigator, Peter Lawson, and the stocky skipper walks forward for a close look at the jenny.

Hood wears gray shorts, and from the rear he seems to consist mostly of a tanned pair of piston-powerful calves, which are just incidentally connected overhead to a square body. The jenny is trimmed hard. Hood raises a flat hand and places it against the cloth just forward of the leech. His head is canted back. For a long time the sailmaker-sailor touches the seven-and-one-half-ounce cloth that way, and it seems that some transmission of energy is taking place, not from the huge, taut foretriangle to the attentive man, but the other way around.

Then the tension breaks. Hood jots down a note on a spiral pad. Walks aft. He is a Yankee, given to trimmed speech that has less draft in it than his sails; but on his face there is a play of expressions that amounts to a vocabulary. His crew can read that fizz now; he's satisfied. With a couple of minor adjustments, that sail will do.

He sits down on the afterdeck. "I was the first to use a computer to cut sails," he says. "It was a disaster. We almost lost our shirt. Either the computer would crash or the human being would punch in a wrong number. I don't use the computer much now. I think you have to use your natural instincts and your observation of how a sail sets and drives a boat. The computer checks up on you, that's all."

A new age has come to the big boats. With respect to it, Hood stands somewhere in the middle, between North at one extreme, completely sold and dedicated, and Turner at the other, who uses a term describing a primitive form of fertilizer to sum it up. This is the age of the computerized Twelves.

The technology of big racing boats has moved for decades at a stately pace, then this quantum jump—or *is* it? Harold Vanderbilt had a stadimeter, duralumin mast, Park Avenue boom, shunt dynamometers to measure backstay tension, anemometer aboard the mother ship—those were about all; he writes of his navigator figuring out where they were, in one race, by taking a sun sight! *Ranger* in 1937 had only three new winches; the others were cannibalized from *Reliance* (1903), *Resolute* (1920), *Enterprise* (1930), *Rainbow* (1934), and his M-boat, *Prestige*; he used main sheet grips that Captain Nat Herreshoff had invented and made for him 34 years before. Vanderbilt thought that his *Enterprise* beat *Shamrock V* because of weight saved aloft, yet *Enterprise*'s mast weighed a ton (when it was made at Bath Iron Works a small boy lying on his back on a cable car running inside the mast held the inner end of the rivets); the boom weighed 2,330 pounds; the Egyptian duck mainsail weighed more than a ton. Three tons above decks.

Since then the technology has done all it could to marry delicacy and strength. A Hood main for *Independence* weighs 120 pounds.

Sails have gone from cotton to Cordura to nylon to Dacron to Kevlar—none of them absolutely ideal—and from 15-ounce to 5-ounce cloth. New weaves, like the triaxial, stiffen the lighter stuff. Microballoons—the tiny bubbles that make a rigid bulk—have enabled light yet strong underbody adaptations. Many of the improvements have been for efficiency as well as weight saving—cross-linked coffee grinders, so four men together can get in a jib in a jiffy; hydraulics; trim tabs; slot headstays; self-tailing winches. And electronic instruments—readouts labelled knotmeter, windpoint, rudder (tab) angle, windspeed (at both masthead and in the slot). . . . With all these changes, and many others, it has been calculated that since *Vim*, 38 years ago, there has been only a slight increase in speed-made-good to windward in a breeze.

But what is really different is the super-secret navigator's nest on each of these boats, off the main cockpit, where the little mind-box lives. And what makes the computer a true departure is that it has brought at least a potential change—at every stage, from the designer's first dream to the final gun of the final race—in the entire decision-making process.

Lowell North is a man who looks as if he is thinking about something else. He leans back on the blue sofa of Cunningham's *Chaperone*, which the *Enterprise* syndicate has chartered as tender. It is early morning. A long day's work lies ahead. North seems tired. He clips off short answers. He has been getting boat speed out of *Enterprise* but has been making tactical errors. It is a down time. But when he starts talking about computers, the mask of control dissolves, a radiant face comes out from the cover of caution, and the hands begin to move with the arcane logic of flow charts. This sailmaker-sailor's tongue seems to have levitated into a higher language.

"The greatest problem at present is the interface between your sensors and the computer. The wind-direction sensor will give you readings of two tenths of a degree eight times a second. The optical decoder has 1,800 slits—five slits for every compass degree. You're going back and forth two or three degrees in waves, and you have distortions from heeling, upwash—so with such sensitive devices there's gross overkill, when you're trying to get an absolutely accurate true wind direction. First you work it out theoretically. Fudge for the distorting factors. Calculate. Then tack. Average the two, and you have it.

"Once in a while you get mysterious malfunctions. The last few days the first digit has been left out of our wind direction numbers.

Let's say true wind is 180 degrees, multiply by eight (readings per second), then multiply by ten (you get an average every ten seconds)—so your readout is 144,000. But we'd get 44,000—a pretty funny number on that heading. But the nice thing is you can change the program. The instrument guy is sending us new chips—very simple: he's putting some zeroes in front of the readout number, so if a digit fades off, it's a zero and nothing's lost. . . .

"We have a special tacking program to tell us how we're doing coming about. It averages over ten seconds. You get five two-second boat speeds, and five two-second compass readings. It takes these ten readings"—the pairs of North's outspread fingertips approach each other—"and matches them up and plots your progress through the tack and gives you a delta of the amount lost in the tack. You can then compare with other tacks when you've turned sharper or slower and work out the most efficient tack in given conditions. . . .

"We use the computer to design our mains and jibs. We don't have the computer trained yet to design spinnakers. General Motors has programs for designing the curves on car bodies and they've given us some help on spinnakers. Heiner Meldner has developed a program, but it costs too much money right now. We gave GM drawings of shapes of spinnakers, and they ran them through their program and gave us back the shapes of cuts: mathematical curves; drawings plus offsets and tons and tons of numbers. We'll have a program ourselves eventually. . . ."

"I'd like to see the boats stick more to sailing," Briggs Cunningham says, "than to all the mechanical contraptions. All of this data comes out of the computer. Miles and miles of tape. At night they have to go over it all. VMG, wind speed, wind direction; one sail against another. But there's no machine that can anticipate. The wind can shift five degrees, and you're either going to lay the mark or overstand. I just hate to see it all get so darn mechanical."

Hood's navigator, Peter Lawson, standing by the crew shop on Bannister's Wharf, amid the bustle of getting ready to go out and race, talks about the box. His blond Coldstream-Guards mustache jumps with joy. "We're figuring in the fun details now. The entire science of instruments will have to be revamped. The instruments aren't up to these computers. We're dealing here with hundredths of a knot. In 24 miles a few hundredths of a knot will win a race. . . ."

"I'm not much on this electronic stuff," Ted Turner says. "It's not my style to run up a lot of statistics. I have a wife and five kids, a ball club, a basketball team, a television station—I don't intend to spend all my time fiddling around with numbers. North's sails are all supposed to be computer-designed. That's a lot of b.s. It's a big fizzle. We'll see how absurd it is before we're through."

George Hinman is sitting on a lounger in the air-conditioned saloon of *Elan*. "As a sailor I don't like it." he says. "Take tacking down wind. You used to do this strictly by the seat of the pants. It was a matter of a sailor's judgment. 'I've got a feeling this is the right moment to jibe.' But now the computer says, 'Jibe now. Steer 136 degrees,' Not 135. Maybe it's better. Maybe it'll win races. I just don't like it."

America's Cup heritage and the drift of all things toward numbers: Edward Burgess designed the defenders *Puritan*, *Mayflower*, *Volunteer*. Nathanael S. Herreshoff built *Vigilant*, *Defender*, *Columbia*, *Reliance*. Edward's son Starling Burgess designed *Enterprise*, *Rainbow*, and, with his inheritor Olin Stephens, *Ranger*. Stephens designed another *Columbia*, *Constellation*, *Courageous*, another *Enterprise*.

A symbolic moment, then, in the long summer of '77. Richard du Moulin, North's regular navigator, has hurt his back. Halsey Herreshoff, grandson of Captain Nat and a kind of math genius, is brought out from Newport in a whaler to navigate for North for the day. He is transferred to *Enterprise* via *Chaperone*. Aboard the tender he calls up to Stephens on the flying bridge: "Just a sec. I brought you a couple of books, Olin." He takes them from his duffel. These works of linear communication turn out to be: "Elementary Practical Statistics," by A. L. O'Toole and "Applied General Statistics," by Croxton, Cowden, and Klein. Stephens whiles away the afternoon on the flying bridge of *Chaperone*, while *Enterprise* drills, using a hand calculator to work out a tailor's problem from one of the books, on the correct cuts for a man's shirt.

Eight o'clock in the morning. A sweet hot blue day. Two splendid bimbos, whose curved surfaces even the versatile General Motors computers would have a hard time turning into numbers, are already up, swabbing the decks of Ted Turner's yacht *Tenacious*. From somewhere far beyond their chirping can be heard The Voice.

NO ADMITTANCE! At the gate in the white lattice-work fence on Bannister's Wharf, where *Independence* and *Courageous* are tied up, stands a young man named Randy Meyer, in the police-like uniform of Bonded Home Security, Inc., to keep out spies.

Ted Hood says: "I don't know an awful lot about the history of the Cup."

"Oh, I've looked at a couple of those books with all those pictures in 'em," Ted Turner says, "but hell, history doesn't interest me. I'm interested in winning races."

"Only what I've read in the brochures," Lowell North says.

"This is a New York Yacht Club cup," Briggs Cunningham says. "The press has blown it up. The *America*'s Cup. People across the country began to think of it as the country's cup—America's cup. But it isn't. This is strictly a New York Yacht Club affair."

The generations of skippers—modulations of the modern social era. Charles Francis Adams, Vanderbilt, Cunningham, Bavier, Mosbacher, Hood, sailmaker; North, sailmaker; Turner, owner of the Atlanta Braves.

Jay Gould was turned down for membership in the New York Yacht Club, according to its archives, because of "his notorious 'robber baron' tactics in finance." Was *Rainbow* chosen over the faster *Yankee* in 1934 because the Boston people weren't in the inner inner circle? It took two tries, and some tact, to get Ted Turner admitted to the club—a defending skipper must belong. But this brash competitor does not censor his own views on the old club's mug out of any feeling of being a crasher at the party.

"The primary purpose of the Cup," he says, "is to improve international understanding. The highest form of sportsmanship and good will is involved. We're ambassadors of the American way of life. That doesn't mean you don't race hard. You're respected when you're a hard driver or a winner. But many areas get warped. When I race abroad, I don't take any guys with me that aren't gentlemen. I always have a guy or two of the nationality we're racing against. We try to learn the customs of the country. The guys don't get drunk and tear up yacht clubs. Part of the deal, of course, is to make love to foreign girls. That is one of the best ways there is to improve international relations. But, you know, you can't pick your nose and wipe the boogers on the blazer of the host commodore. It isn't done."

Edward du Moulin, manager of the *Enterprise* syndicate, finds it good to explain that in their house, Seaview Terrace, at dinner, the

Enterprise gang wear open shirts—"in deference," du Moulin says, "to the California style of life."

The generations of syndicates: Morgan, Astor, Vanderbilt, Aldrich, Sears, Iselin, Forbes—patricians, men of great inherited wealth. The *Enterprise* "syndicate," officially speaking, is the Maritime College at Fort Schuyler Foundation. *Courageous* and *Independence* are owned by the King's Point fund of the U.S. Merchant Marine Academy. Contributions to both are 100 percent tax deductible.

Lee Loomis, the big committee chairman of the Hood-Turner campaign, sits host-like in a brightly printed shirt on the afterdeck of *Independence*. "In the old days," he is saying, "the money didn't mean that much to the syndicate members. Today you have to make it fun for the contributors. You don't have any benefit to offer them. It's not *pro bono publico*. There's no earthly reason to contribute anything unless you get some fun out of it. They've all had an opportunity to sail on one or the other of the boats. We take them out on the tender. . . . Contributors today are businessmen rather than men of inherited wealth. In those days the commodores were the owners, the sailors. There's no commodore supporting the effort now. . . ."

There is certainly a business flavor to things. Edward du Moulin slips naturally into corporate terminology as he speaks of his boat's downwind helmsman, John Marshall, who runs the North Sails east coast loft. "John," he says, "is our Vice President in Charge of Sails."

We are below in the cool cabin of Ted Turner's 61-foot ocean racer, *Tenacious*. Half stretched out on a berth, the skipper of *Courageous* talks along about this and that, with the rough, vibrating, immensely potential energy of an idling diesel engine.

A guest, knowing of the controversy over Lowell North's refusal to sell design-tested sails to Turner on a boat in Ted Hood's syndicate, presses a button. "Is the America's Cup," he asks, "a business or a sport?"

Turner leaps up from the bunk. "This is *most* disturbing." He begins to pace—into the galley, far forward, into the head. Cabinet doors slam. Turner's throat seems swollen with outrage. The engine image is dispelled in him; there is a huge cat in the man now. "For me, yachting is a game, not a business. With Hood and North this is a high point in their careers. Their primary interest is a chance to pommel their sailmaking rival. Their companies are on the line.

They'll go to no end to win. Millions of dollars of business worldwide hangs on this. The Cup committee is footing the bill for these guys' advertising campaigns. It's the big shoot-out. It has given me a great deal of happiness that so far"—he is speaking in midsummer—"I've been able to cream them, and I hope to continue to do so. It would be the best thing that could happen for the sport."

A finely geared governor controls the pace of Lowell North's candor. *Enterprise* is beginning to move in the trials. "If we win," he says, "it'll be sure to help business; if we lose, it will be sure to hurt. Hood has more to gain than we do. We're on top. He stands to gain first place. If we win, we stay first; if we lose, we'll have to work to come back."

Hood's laconic New England speech is screwed down tight. He has only 20 words to spend on the whole controversy: "When we were on *Nefertiti*," he says, "my crew seemed to think I was giving all the better sails to the competition." In the odd slant of throat down from Hood's smallish chin there seems to be a canary in the act of being swallowed.

Contributions in kind ("Used on the boat that won the America's Cup"?) to the *Enterprise* syndicate: International paint, Danforth anchors, a Robalo powerboat, Samson line, beer, soft drinks. For a good fee the New York Yacht Club America's Cup Committee will sell the right to use a Cup logo. Examples of takers: Sperry, Rolex ("Cup Defenders know that in timing, as in racing, performance is an art"). If you badly need an *Enterprise* money clip ("27 in 77," pewter finish), you can get one for $5.95. Each of the syndicates has been loaned by a Newport car dealer a Camino Classic, with boat numbers and the lender's name prominently displayed. The Cup races will continue after this message. . . .

Can these increasingly commercial campaigns, based on tax-exempt donations and clustered around expensive, computerized racing machines that are built for four to seven days of supreme contest and are not much use thereafter, survive in this world? Are we coming to the end of a great story?

"You do have a little bit the 1938 atmosphere," Lee Loomis says. "You don't have the Depression, but the future is doubtful. The Cup would collapse if the Europeans won it. Then it would be just like the Gold Cup. It wouldn't be America's to have and use and run any more."

PART III
The Thinking Cap—
Opinions and
Expertise

Advice from experts—the people who have won races, designed winners, developed new techniques, made historic passages and introduced innovations—has been a continuing staple in Yachting's *pages from the first issue on. While an article on how to install storage batteries in the years before World War I does not make for fascinating reading now, there remains a great store of information that is still pertinent, and, more to the point, still readable. As can be seen from the authors' names and subject matters, it is a diversified field that provides entertainment and instruction, often of lasting benefit.*

1907

Wanted: Wholesome Boats for the America's Cup

Sir Thomas Lipton

In our first issue, the gallant "Sir Tommie" had something to say about the America's Cup competition that still seems pertinent today

In my three efforts to lift the America's Cup, to take it back across the waters whence it came, consideration and courtesy have ever characterized the actions of those who were called upon to defend it, while the general public—naturally desiring that the Cup should remain here—gave me every hearty encouragement, born of a generous regard for true sport.

It is of this cup in its connection with the new rule of measurement that I desire particularly to speak. No more striking indication of the spirit of true sportsmanship actuating those who guide the sport in this country could have been given than the adoption of such a rule of rating as would eliminate the freak racing machine of past years. Under the uniform rule adopted in 1905 it was hoped that a more wholesome type of boat would appear, and the results of last season's racing in the United States have entirely justified that hope. It is what has been needed both here and abroad, a good, wholesome boat, a boat that cannot only go fast, but can give a good account of herself in heavy weather; a boat that can cross the ocean with no fears that it will succumb to wind and waves on the way over.

As I conceive, that clause in the rule regarding contests for the America's Cup made it incumbent for the challenging yacht to cross the ocean under sail, simply to insure a good, wholesome racer, and not a craft whose usefulness would be ended the minute the international event was over. I confess that in bringing my three *Shamrock*s to this side I did so not without misgivings that they could survive the passage, misgivings not solely inspired by the fear of the loss of the yachts themselves as of lives of the devoted men who crossed in them.

There is yet another point, and I think a strong one: What really is the use of racing with boats built under the old rules? True, there is the event in itself, and an exciting race, but little else. There is nothing learned; the educational side of the sport is neglected absolutely. Designers grasp little or nothing that is new in contemplating the models of these racing machines, but in yachts built for the America's Cup contest under the uniform rule there would be much learned. We would see, for one thing, if the rule as it stands produces an ideal racer, or whether more changes are needed, and by the same token designers could go on from these boats and design still more satisfactorily the boat qualified to stand rough weather, and yet at the same time break records.

I am satisfied that the trend of American yachting will be toward the production of this sort of boat. It is a plain call. It is certainly a grievous condition when a challenger must sail his boat across the Atlantic to race for the Cup, harassed, as I said before, by fears that perhaps the boat may not survive the passage. It is far from satisfactory both to the challenger, and I know to the designers, now they have seen the situation through the challenger's eyes.

With a challenger designed and built in accordance with the rules under which racing was conducted in this country last year I am certain that any fears for her safety in crossing the North Atlantic would be unwarranted. I am well aware that as yet this uniform rule has not been tried out as thoroughly as those most interested in yachting on this side would like, and I heartily concur in and appreciate their desire to study the workings of the rating throughout the coming season before giving themselves utterly to it. I have no desire to embarrass American yachtsmen by a challenge at a time like this when the practical test of the rule has little more than begun. But I am certain that this practical test carried out in full will leave no doubt in the mind of any yachtsman that the wholesome boat is the sane boat, the safe boat, the most sportsmanlike, and the most satisfactory boat all around.

And if events so shape themselves that in 1908 an international race for the America's Cup between two yachts built on these principles is practicable, why, no one need be surprised to find that one of them bears the name *Shamrock IV* on her stern. The achievement of Mr. J. Roger Maxwell's schooner *Queen* in the Atlantic Yacht Club's ocean race off Sandy Hook last September when she completed the America's Cup course triangle in very nearly record

Sir Thomas Lipton, who unsuccessfully challenged for the America's Cup five times—twice after this article first appeared. Standing to his left is New York greeter Grover Whalen.

time, shows that a race between boats built under the uniform rule need by no means result in a tortoiselike exhibition of footing; quite the contrary indeed.

I violate no confidence in saying that a great many of the members of the club that holds the America's Cup—of which club I am proud to belong—have expressed the utmost faith in the existing measurement rule, and the greatest desire to see all yachtsmen, all designers, bending their energies toward the production of yachts that are as much at home, and as safe for those sailing them, in a stiff blow off Sandy Hook as in a zephyr on Long Island Sound.

As the satisfaction of winning the Cup would be doubly gratifying to me were the winning craft an all-around wholesome craft, so, I have no doubt, would the defenders feel similar gratification in succeeding in keeping the trophy here with a racer no less seaworthy.

My various visits to the United States have been filled with naught but the pleasantest experiences, none more so than those associated with American yachtsmen, whom I have found, without a single exception, to be gentlemen actuated by high, sportsmanlike ideals, in which the spirit of fair play is by no means lacking, and good fellows as well. I have met them on the Great Lakes and on other inland waters of the country, and, as everyone knows, off Sandy Hook in the greatest events in the worldwide sport of yachting, the races for the historic America's Cup, and of them all I hold not a disagreeable memory.

I desire also to express my appreciation of the manner in which the yachtsmen of the Great Lakes conduct their racing. I saw the fall regatta held on Lake Michigan, off Chicago, and I never in all my experience saw a regatta better handled or more skillfully sailed. The salt breeze is not their portion, but they have all that the salt seas require of those who sail upon them—pluck, skill, endurance and daring.

While in the West I heard criticism of the tendency of Great Lakes yachtsmen toward freak craft, and in fact not all of their swiftest racers may be dignified by the term, wholesome. But that this will be rectified there is not the slightest doubt, and the movement in that direction may surely be said to be as well defined, as strong as the tendency toward the freak ever was. Throughout all the country, so far as I have been able to grasp prevailing opinion, the wholesome boat is the great idea. And just as it has come on the Atlantic Coast so will it come on the fresh water lakes where big seas and high winds are to be encountered. Without doubt there is as deep necessity for the seaworthy boat on such lakes as Michigan, Erie, and Ontario and Superior as there is on the deep salt sea.

Numbers of yachtsmen and others have spoken of the better understanding, the better feeling, which my attempts to lift the Cup and my various visits here have brought between the United States and the mother country. If that is so, and I sincerely hope that is so, it is more than adequate compensation for any disappointments I have felt in the failure of the three challengers which in the course of the past years I have brought to this country—that puts a star above the mere failure to win a cup.

1920

On Shipyards and Drawbridges

Catherine Drinker Bowen

The first published work by a young woman, already an ardent sailor, who was to become a prize-winning author

Some shipowners may really dislike being laid up in a yard for repairs. Anyway they all pretend to hate it. But I know now that this attitude is merely professional with them. I can't remember one skipper—from the salty owner of the seagoing barge *Belfast*, with his forty odd years at sea, to the high-salaried captain of the eighty-foot express cruiser *Nancy*, out of Marblehead—not one, who wasn't proud to stand with his hands in his pockets watching them scrape the barnacles off her keel. Not that they all keep their hands in their pockets; a good man, no matter how high his command, will climb the ladders himself on the job, for inspection or to lend a hand. But they are all proud to see the men working on her, and quick to tell you how many hundred dollars' worth of repairs she's getting. I won't vouch for those Olympians in charge of over a thousand tons. Perhaps when their *Mauretania*s are safe in drydock they go up town for a five-dollar dinner and leave the first officer in charge, returning next day to exercise a magnificent vocabulary upon their juniors. By the way, this same talent for forceful and highly colored word-combination is enormous and admirable in all skippers "on the ways."

Many times have I turned quaking at these rich sounds from the chest of some portly skipper, and watched the offender, wondering at what moment he would shrivel up and drop off the ladder. I know of one instance, though, when the tables were turned, and an over-zealous crew took up hammer and wrench without waiting for orders. I heard the story far from salt water, at my own cosy fireside.

Joe Dawson, familiarly known as "Babe," was in command of one of our hundred and ten foot "Mosquito boats" in 1917, and knew rather more about the water than most of the ex-college sophomores with similar commands in the Navy at that time. He and two other boats from his squadron had to run into port one time for gasolene. Being in strange waters, Babe took on a pilot and, acting on what he had every reason to believe expert advice, ran right up to the dock. However, he thought things looked a little funny and sent a man forward to sound. What was his horror to discover that the water just covered the lead! Well, he carried out his starboard anchor and started her up, and then he carried out his port anchor and heaved away on that side—nothing doing. Babe knew he was there to stay, so he went below to think things over and to get rid of the sight of his two sister vessels further out in the harbor slowly and peacefully filling their tanks by lighter. Imagine his feelings! A serious offence, running your boat aground. Nothing heroic about it either, just plain stupid; and here he was, with a good chance of losing his command. In the midst of these profitless ruminations a great commotion outside, hammer blows and banging of all descriptions, brought him on deck. Looking over the side—the boat was high and dry by this time, bilge strakes and propellers showing—he saw a gang of his own men, bossed by his faithful boatswain Jim, standing in the yawl boat and in the mud, working away on her rudder gear with much show of earnestness and concentration. Babe knew that the stern hadn't grounded at all, but it was with some alarm that he called Jim aboard for explanations. That gentleman was obviously embarrassed, but managed to stutter—with a jerk of his thumb toward the watching crowd on shore—"Aw, Cap'n Dawson, we don't want those loafers to know what's happened so we just thought we'd come down and do a little work on her so's they'd think we just ran her up on purpose for repairs!"

Well, she floated off the next tide, and the upshot was that Babe got his tanks filled at the dock in a hurry and raced right out of the harbor past his two sister boats still patiently lightering out their gas in five-gallon cans. When he reported to the flagship the commander told him it was the pilot's fault anyway, and that as long as he'd made better time filling up than the other two they'd let him off this time!

My introduction to the delights and trials of a shipyard was in Portland, Maine, when Mr. Bowen and I were fitting out for our first cruise in the auxiliary ketch *C. D. B.* The fact that we usually do most of our own repairs before setting out each summer is responsible for the joy I take in shipyards; for the fun of painting and fussing over the boat is one of the greatest satisfactions in the cruiser's holiday, from our point of view at any rate. The *C. D. B.* was new to us that year and had been laid up for eighteen months, so there was plenty of work to be done before we had her caulked and painted and had stepped the masts, set up the standing and rove the running rigging, and bent on the sails. We had eight hundred miles to go, and only our two selves as captain and crew, so we lingered in shippy, salty old Portland until we had everything shipshape and in prime working order.

One of the most efficient, and certainly the most sociable, shipyards I was ever in was at Rocky Neck in Gloucester, Massachusetts. Having dodged countless lobster pots from Portland to Cape Ann, we picked one up off Annisquam and trailed through the river with two yards of rope wound up on our propeller. Everyone in Gloucester recommended Sherman Tar, so round the point we went and I had my first ride on a real-sized marine railway. I have ridden down the Angel Trail in Arizona Canyon and up the Funicular at Hong Kong and round the Steeplechase at Coney, but they never gave me the thrill I felt at Rocky Neck when they got the wedges set under the *C. D. B.* and she began to roll ahead!

We lay three days in the yard, although the business which took us there was accomplished the first morning by "Cholly" the machinist and his right-hand man, known as "The Swede." "Cholly" was a wonder—quick, dexterous and always in complete control of the situation. He did in an hour what it had taken Noah, our machinist friend in Portland, three days to pronounce impossible. His short, sturdy frame and snappy black eyes held no suggestion of New England; he said he used to live in Philadelphia but came north because he didn't like the climate. His patience with The Swede was infinite. The latter was inclined toward dreaminess; when called sharply he would give a jump and run off anxiously in the wrong direction, usually dropping his tools en route. When his face expressed anything at all, it expressed worry, and a kind of anxious helpfulness—a desperate desire to do his best. I watched him with much sympathy because I felt sure that, employed in his place, I should have behaved in exactly the same way.

There was at all times upon the docks a swarm of what Sherman Tar called "Them summer artists." "Yes," he said, "sometimes you can count as many as forty. Shoot off a gun any direction and you're sure to hit one." Indeed, the outlook from Mr. Tar's yard was a fit subject for brush and canvas. The long spars of the fishing schooners rising above their crosstrees to a tapering topmast, slender and graceful against the blue sky; sails spread to dry flapping gently in the breeze; the weathered hulls of old schooners lying against the high piles of the docks—scarred old bodies, but sturdy still, their once bright colors beaten and faded into soft greys, with here and there a flash of the ancient glory—black and gold, red, blue; no wonder Gloucester is the Mecca of the art student.

To our right on the ways lay a small fishing sloop on which the captain and a young man, probably his son, were doing their own repairs. They were very friendly with us and, although our intercourse as far as words went was meagre, we parted feeling that we liked their style and they liked ours. On the other side of us was a ninety-foot express cruiser out of Newport. White, immaculate, glittering with brass and bright shining mahogany, she sat on her cradle like a queen on a throne. Any shyness which I felt at the sight of this resplendent stranger was soon dispelled by her captain, a garrulous, tough old seafarer well on the far side of sixty. He was born with a tiller in his hand, he said, and had no use for these new-fangled gasolene boats. "Look at this one, dazzles your eyes at first, don't she? Well. I got to keep her shined up like that so's you don't notice what's underneath, light, flimsy planking, careless workmanship all over. Just like all of 'em, built for style and nothin' else. All these folks" (meaning the owners) "care for is gettin' 'round on the water as quick as you can on land." I had seen "these folks" one afternoon, a man and woman, somewhere around the forties, faultlessly turned out in the newest creations in "sporting costumes," alight at the yard from a gorgeous limousine, stroll languidly over to the yacht, glance at her, nod to the captain, and depart. My husband being in the college professor business, it follows that we are not, as yet, to be numbered among those who pay the income super-tax; yet I owe no allegiance to the Red and bear no grudge against those fortunates who step from their motors to their yachts. Nevertheless I could not withhold a chuckle at the Captain's next sally: "Come on aboard, young woman," he said, "Here, wait till I put over this landing-stage—look out there! . . . say, you're pretty spry, ain't you? Wish the boss's old woman was like that. I have to git a derrick to haul *her* aboard!"

It was our pride that the *C. D. B.* was often mistaken for a Gloucesterman—and by fishermen, too. Thirty-six feet over all, painted black, she had the lines of a Provincetown ketch and looked twice her inches. In any port, the comment of seafaring men lounging on the dock or sitting on overturned barrels in critical contemplation of our craft, was; "H'm; decked over—built pretty heavy—you can go round the world in her." Or, "Good solid timbers you've got there—well, she'll stay, she'll stay." And stay she did—good old *C. D. B.* With only one experienced seaman on board she stood up under some pretty stiff weather before she covered her eight hundred miles of Atlantic coast that summer. She balked at nothing, head tides, gale or heavy sea, except—drawbridges. To windward or leeward she could scent one a mile ahead. She would kick along under engine innocently enough even after the draw was in sight and we had blown our fog horn for the keeper. Then, when she had a trolley at one end of the bridge and ten automobiles at the other, when the gap for our passage was beginning slowly to widen; then, with a snort of derision and triumph, the engine would simply—quit! After this had happened in the Cape Cod Canal, in the Annisquam River—where we had hung in a veritable mill-race of tide for an hour—and in the Sakonnet River at Tiverton, my superstition concerning drawbridges and gas engines amounted to a cowardly fatalism. Happily the captain, who was also chief engineer, was made of sterner stuff. While I sat at the wheel trying to appear unconcerned under the glowering scorn of the bridge-keeper, with the shriek of automobile klaxons burning my ears, my only hope was to keep my gaze riveted upon the khaki-shirted back of Cap'n Ez. below cranking her up. I shall not dwell upon these painful incidents nor upon the temper and disposition of drawbridge keepers in general; of how they, evilly taking advantage of the yachtsman possessing neither clutch nor reverse, waited, before appearing at their posts, until the *C. D. B.* had thrown three wide circles to kill time and tide near the bridge. I suppose they required this encircling performance as a sort of obeisance before them. Nor shall I linger to tell of keepers who would gingerly open the bridge a crack big enough to see through, beckon us to come on, and then leer over the side to see if we would get safely past! Once at Louis Steele's yard up the Delaware, Louis himself, after watching us do the usual pirouette before the old keeper on the Delanco bridge, told us how he got his money's worth out of this drawbridge nuisance. He said he was taking some spur-piles up Rancocas Creek to build a wharf for a sand-pit. . . . Well, he came to the draw and they opened for him all right, but his barge was too wide by half a foot to squeeze through. Louis told the keeper he'd have to take out one of the piles in his bridge and give him room; offered to pull out two and then replace them himself. No, the man wouldn't do it. Louis went up town and called up the district commissioner at Wilmington and told him the situation. The officer asked Louis how much beam he had.

"Sixteen and a half feet," Steele told him, "and the draw was sixteen feet wide." Then they got the gate-keeper on the phone and told him the law required a forty-two foot opening at that place and that he'd have to do what Louis wanted. It ended by Steele sitting peacefully in his barge while the piles were pulled out—and the county had to pay him twelve dollars for every hour he was held up!

The *C. D. B.* is ours no longer. The *H. C. L.* was too much for us, and we sold her. The new owner writes us soothing letters about what a good boat she is and how much he enjoys cruising in her. He hasn't said a word about drawbridges yet, but he will soon. I hope he will understand her feelings and not force her at them, or get mad and whip her up and try to take bridge and keeper in one jump. His letters are so agreeable that I am sure he must be nice himself, and he will probably treat the *C. D. B.* better than we did, but—Oh well, Ezra reminds me that Sherman Tar, the proprietor of our Gloucester shipyard, sold his old Georgeman sloop *four* times, and bought her back every time. There is much comfort in precedent.

1937

Designing an America's Cup Defender

W. Starling Burgess

"Tricks of the trade" from the designer of Enterprise *and* Ranger

In the early eighties, the narrow, deep and heavily ballasted English cutter was in full flower. Fostered by a curious tonnage rule which made beam a heavy penalty, the English yachts of that period had developed into a uniform and distinctive type. "Planks on edge," we called them. Their stems were plumb with a deep forefoot; their keels swept aft to a raking stern post; and their sterns, ending in a narrow transom, were carried out with a long and graceful overhang. Despite their generous freeboard, they were wet and uncomfortable at sea. Their sharp bows, without any supporting shoulder of overhang, combined with low and heavy ballasting, caused them to pitch deeply and dive under, rather than ride the seas. Their long bowsprits, carried to one side of the stem head and arranged to reef inboard, were often buried in green water. However, so strongly were these vessels constructed that they had the reputation of being able to live through any stress of weather. That this reputation was no idle boast has been amply attested by many a long and perilous voyage carried out in their old age by survivors of that time.

In America, a totally opposite design was in vogue. With long reaches of protected water, with shallow harbors numerous and close together, with comparatively lighter weather, and few tidal currents to contend with, we had developed, to a high degree of individuality, the wide, shallow draft centerboarder with inside ballast. Like the English craft, our boats were plumb-stemmed; on the other hand, their sterns were short and chunky. Their freeboard was low and so shallow were their hulls that flush decks were impossible and ungainly cabin trunks were almost universal even in the largest yachts. The term "skimming dish" was used to describe them.

My father, Edward Burgess, having spent the summer of 1884 sailing in English waters, was thoroughly familiar with the characteristics, especially the greater seaworthiness, of the English cutters when, in the fall of that year, he was given the order to build the *Puritan* for a Boston syndicate as a candidate for the defense of the America's Cup.

The *Puritan* was a fast, able, and thoroughly wholesome vessel of great beauty. She was a cross between the extremes of the American and English types; of deeper body than the American, of greater beam than the English. The outside lead keel was the major part of her ballast, but she retained the customary American centerboard.

She and her successor, the *Mayflower* of 1886, both of which were built at the Lawley yard in South Boston, and the *Volunteer* of 1887, built on the Delaware, both designed by my father, changed not only the whole trend of American yacht designing but that of the great American fishing fleet as well.

The work expected of the yacht designer of fifty years ago was very different from that of the present day. The model and the cabin arrangement, the sail plan and the superintendence of the construction were about all he was concerned with. Designing in those days was an intuitive art, not an intricate engineering problem.

Most yacht designers of his time, as did Nathanael Herreshoff who succeeded him, shaped a wooden model by hand, but my father (who was a superb draftsman) preferred the drawn line. The preparation of the board and paper was a serious affair, almost like a religious rite. Cotton cloth was stretched over the six-foot board and secured at the edge by innumerable tiny tacks. Meanwhile, my mother cooked the flour paste while the rough white paper was asoak in the bathtub. When mounted and dried on the cloth, the paper shrank to a drumlike tightness. Then, with many grades of sandpaper, a surface was attained quite as smooth and much sweeter to draw on than the glass and marble boards of today which are used for big ship work.

An important design was always begun on Sunday morning when my father had the whole uninterrupted day before him. It was always my privilege to spend Sundays with him at the office. We arrived at an early hour, my father, his draftsmen, Waterhouse and Arthur Binney, and myself. There being no steam heat week-ends, we were kept warm by an enormous pot-bellied iron stove which it was my duty to stoke.

Having drawn the sheer and deck plan, my father ran in approximate sections by eye, checked the stability with an Amsler integrator (of which he was very proud) and then began serious work by filling or cutting with great exactness to a predetermined displacement curve. Just how or from what he evolved this displacement curve, I have often wondered in vain. He set great store by it. When a section, diagonal, or buttock line finally satisfied him, he immediately inked it in with whatever color of ink (and there were bottles of many colors) came handiest. Neither draftsman was ever allowed to touch the lines until they were faired and ready to trace.

The construction was a matter of neither calculation nor invention; it was simply a duplication, with changes on a linear ratio, of what had gone before and proved sufficient. The sail plan was the conventional cutter rig; gaff-headed mainsail, club topsail, forestaysail, jib and jib topsail. Little or no change seems to have been made in the shape or proportionate area in going from an older to a newer vessel. All spars, of course, were solid. The masts were big sticks of Oregon pine in a single piece from heel to topmast band. Topmasts were housing. Details of iron work and fittings were stereotyped. Sheaves and bitts were usually of lignumvitae. I can remember how the bitts used to smoke with heat when the long main sheets were eased off "on the run." Except for the centerboard, there were no winches.

The size of spars was settled in a few words between designer and sparmaker. Rigging details were left entirely to the professional rigger. Those of the yacht differed but little from coaster and fisherman practice.

Puritan won two of the three trial races, defeating the new New York sloop *Priscilla* and the older yachts *Gracie* and *Bedouin*. On September 14th and 16th, she met and defeated the fine cutter *Genesta*, challenger for the America's Cup, owned by Sir Richard Sutton and designed by J. Beavor Webb.

Mayflower, built the following year, was much like *Puritan* save that her deadrise was higher and that the turn of her bilges was almost at the water line. She was defeated in the early trials by *Puritan* but in the end was selected to meet *Galatea*, whom she easily defeated. I can remember *Galatea*'s arrival at Marblehead after a prolonged ocean passage. Her sailors were a picturesque lot, with loose red caps and brass earrings like ancient pirates. *Galatea*, owned by Lieut. Henn and like *Genesta* designed by J. Beavor Webb, was not as fast as her predecessor.

In '87 came the *Volunteer*, the last of my father's Cup defenders and the last of the line which might be called racing and cruising vessels in contradistinction to the out and out "racing machines" which have defended the Cup ever since.

In the *Volunteer*, my father departed from the plumb stem and drew a clipper bow of moderate overhang, his object being the increase of deck room and the decrease of length of bowsprit rather than taking advantage of the water line length rule. The *Thistle*, challenger of that year, was owned by a Scotch syndicate, and designed by the famous Scotch designer, George L. Watson. She, too, had a clipper bow and much greater beam than the two previous English challengers. She was a ship of rare beauty and excellence of design. Looking at her model now, one wonders why she lost.

Not long after *Volunteer*'s victory, Nathanael Greene Herreshoff, of Bristol, who had been devoting his genius for many years to the design of hulls and machinery of high speed steam-driven craft, reentered the sailing yacht field and, when the next challenge came from England, his *Vigilant* was selected to defend the Cup in 1893. From then on until 1920, his boats were the defenders. They were *Defender*, *Columbia*, *Reliance* and *Resolute*, and each one was selected after a series of trial races.

In the summer of '29, came to me the fruition of an ambition nearly fifty years old. The New York Yacht Club flag officer's syndicate ordered me to prepare the design of a Cup defender to meet Sir Thomas Lipton's last challenge with *Shamrock V*. Harold S. Vanderbilt had been selected to sail the new yacht and it was between Vanderbilt and myself that her proportions, rig and characteristics were decided.

For the first time, challenger and defender were to meet on equal terms. That is, both were to be built in accordance with Lloyd's scantling rules, at the top of Class J and to sail without time allowance.

No longer would the challenger, necessarily strong enough to cross the Atlantic on her own bottom, have to meet a vessel of lighter scantlings sufficient merely to sail off the coast in summer weather. The yachts were to be designed under our Universal Rule. Many years of building under this rule had proved that it never paid to make bow and stern full enough to incur a "quarter-beam length" penalty nor to take a penalty for less than rule displacement. Without these penalties, sail area becomes a function of water line length, slowly diminishing as length is increased. Water line length, however, is limited to 108 per cent of the yacht's rating measurement plus the constant five. The largest sloop-rigged vessel that can be built in Class J has a water line length of 87.08 feet with a displacement not less than 164.3 long tons. An 80-foot water line vessel of this class has a minimum displacement of 128.3 tons, which is but 78 per cent of that of the yacht built to the limit.

Vanderbilt and I first made a study of average wind velocities as reported by the Government Weather Bureau at Block Island over a twenty-year period for the summer season. This study led us to believe that an 80-foot boat, carrying 7,580 square feet of sail, was as large a boat as it would pay to build. It must be remembered that we were designing for a triple headsail rig and that such effective sails as the present four-sided "Greta" jibs and parachute spinnakers were unknown in such sizes as would be required; so to 80 feet we designed *Enterprise*. She was the smallest of the four American boats built for the 1930 Cup series. In the many races of that summer, the speeds of the American yachts were definitely proved to be in the exact reverse order of their length and weight, the shortest and lightest being the fastest, and the largest and heaviest limitations on weight and size of mast other than length. Therefore, I asked my brother, Charles P. Burgess, a naval engineer who had had great experience in light aluminum structures, to design the lightest possible aluminum alloy mast. It was a 24-sided spar of two skins without interior framework of any kind except at the deck and the points of rigging attachment. As our nearest rival, Clinton Crane, said of it, it was a marvel and it was also a marvel that we succeeded in keeping it in the boat. It had the delicacy of a fly rod and its staying had to be adjusted with every change of headsail or main sheet tension.

As the season progressed and our nearest rival, the *Weetamoe*, pressed us harder and harder, Vanderbilt's indomitable will to win pushed me to many inventions. The most outstanding was the "Park Avenue" boom with a four-foot-wide top surface on which were mounted cross tracks allowing the sail to slide to leeward in whatever curve we chose; then came spreaders of extraordinary lightness; and a battery of winches and gadgets, both above and below decks, which caused our boat to be nicknamed the "mechanical ship." *Shamrock V*, although of excellent design, was so poorly rigged that we beat her with great ease.

When it came to designing *Rainbow*, in '34, to meet *Endeavour I*, Vanderbilt and I found ourselves up against two radical changes in rule. First, the boats had to have cabin accommodations with no gear except the headstay below decks; and, second, the mast could not be below a minimum weight, center of gravity, or width of cross section. Feeling that *Enterprise* was about the right size for the conditions under which she was built, we figured that but two feet increased length in the new boat would be enough to take care of the added weight of cabin and heavier mast. In the trial races, *Rainbow* met a rebuilt and much faster *Yankee*. For the first part of the season, the *Yankee* had the better of us and it was not until we had ballasted *Rainbow* down to the limit of her flotation marks that she really began to go. She was selected, but the margin over *Yankee* was a narrow one. So, during the season, we learned that our boat was too small. The double head rig, as compared with the triple head rig of *Enterprise*, allowed much larger sails to be hung on the same framework of spars. *Rainbow* lacked the power and size to carry these sails to the best advantage. Then, too, Clinton Crane, in *Weetamoe*, had proved the vast possibilities of enormous parachute spinnakers, which also called for a larger boat.

The final victory of *Rainbow* over *Endeavour I* was due to Vanderbilt's consummate strategy and helmsmanship, his power of organization, and, above all, his never lagging attention to detail.

Vanderbilt ordered the design of *Ranger* from Sparkman & Stephens and myself last fall. *Endeavour II* was already built, to the 87-foot upper limit of the class, and had made a creditable showing against *Endeavour I*. Olin Stephens and I found at our disposal the new towing tank of the Stevens Institute of Technology in which Professor Kenneth S. M. Davidson had worked out a most extraordinarily ingenious method of testing sailing models in which the useful driving force of the wind, its heeling force, and its component of leeway were closely resolved by the mechanical resistance of springs and balance weights. For testing a model's ability to go to windward, we were enabled to plot speed made good to windward directly against wind speed.

Nicholson had given me the lines of *Endeavour I* so our first step was to try out, as measuring sticks for the new model, the models of *Endeavour I*, *Rainbow* and *Weetamoe*. We were encouraged to find that the models of these three boats gave results strictly in accordance with the observed performance of the full-sized vessels.

Vanderbilt, Stephens, and myself were fully agreed that we must go to the 87-foot hull. Four parent models were constructed and departures in the shape of overhangs, position of the rudder post, and so forth, were tested in most of the parent forms. The model selected for *Ranger* was so unusual that I do not think any one of us would have dared to pick her had we not had the tank results and Kenneth Davidson's analysis to back her. However, not only did the dial readings indicate her as the best of the lot but her photographs showed a wave formation much smoother than that of the others.

Aeroplane design, the development of high tensile strength, corrosion resisting aluminum alloys, and the progress of metallurgy in general, have had a profound effect on the spar and rigging design of the modern America's Cup defender.

Ranger has not only an aluminum alloy mast but a main boom and two spinnaker booms of aluminum as well. So resistant are the new aluminum alloys to corrosion that *Ranger*'s mast is left bare of paint or protective coverings of any nature. With steel, this would be quite impossible.

Tank Tests in Yacht Designing

Olin J. Stephens II

The young designer who had worked with Burgess on Ranger *tells of the then innovative practice that radically changed the art, and science, of yacht design*

Probably *Ranger* will be remembered in yachting history as the boat that proved the value of testing yacht models in the towing tank. At least her success has done more than anything else to call attention to the usefulness of the towing tank to the yachtsman and the designer. Until the middle of this summer there has been a great deal of skepticism and the opinion was often expressed that models were more likely to be misleading than helpful; now there is complete acceptance of the fact that model testing is an important part of the design of any racing yacht.

This wide interest makes it worth while to review what has been done and to explain the *how* and *why* of yacht model testing as carried out under the direction of Professor Kenneth S. M. Davidson at the Stevens Institute of Technology. For it is he who has developed the method and the equipment used in the work on *Ranger* and other yachts that, after testing, have by their performance shown the value of the tank.

When the first model towing work was started at Stevens Institute in the fall of 1931, it was not surprising that there was a good deal of doubt as to whether anything worth while could be worked out; the testing of yacht models was not new and the performance of yachts built after model tests had not been noticeably above the average. Also, on account of the high cost of towing models, such work had been done only on large and important boats. It is said that G. L. Watson designed *Shamrock II* after testing her model

Olin J. Stephens II

against others, and that, following her defeat by *Columbia* in 1901, he expressed the wish that "Nat" Herreshoff might also have had a towing tank. Although model tests were used in the design of other America's Cup boats, among them *Vanitie*, Watson's expression was typical of the general opinion of towing tank tests. On the other hand, the general method of model testing had played an important part in the development of the steamship and the airplane, and to Professor Davidson there seemed to be a good chance of success in new methods of applying well-known principles to yacht testing.

When the work at Stevens first started, there was little money available. This in the long run has helped, at least from the yachting standpoint. The first testing was done in the swimming pool, when it was necessary to use much smaller models than those made for the usual steamship tests. Twenty-foot water line models were being used in Washington because, though smaller models had been tried, the predicted resistances had been pretty far away from the actual resistances found in practice. So, in the older tanks, large models were used as a matter of course. The expense of using them was not a severe drawback when working on the plans of a naval vessel, a merchant ship or a large power yacht.

Many full sized yachts, such as Six-Metres, are not much larger than these models, therefore the relatively high cost of working with models put tests out of the question in the case of ordinary design. The opportunity of using a small model with its low cost made the whole problem practical and interesting to the yacht designer and I have done everything I could to cooperate with Professor Davidson since he first talked with me about the work.

This problem of getting accurate predictions with a small model was the first one which had to be solved. To obtain the resistance of the full scale boat from the model, it is not possible to multiply by a single factor. The model resistance must be divided into two parts, one representing principally frictional resistance (that caused by the friction of the water against the hull surface) and the other, residual or wave making resistance. At speeds high enough to cause waves, it is impossible to separate these two factors by a direct test of the model. However, because they must be multiplied by different amounts before they can be added together to give the final resistance of the full sized boat, the division must be made fairly accurately. To do this, it is necessary to calculate one or the other part. The success of resistance predictions based on large models has lain in the accuracy with which the frictional resistance could be calculated, both for the large model and the ship. When the model was small, this calculation for frictional resistance seemed to become unreliable.

However, at about the time this question came up at Stevens, new developments in the theory of frictional resistance had been worked out and, although they were at that time connected chiefly with aeronautical research, it was possible to apply them to small yacht models. It is unnecessary to go into these theories, but it was discovered that, by roughening the forward edge of the keel and then applying the right correction factor, accurate correlation could be made between models as small as three feet on the water line and the full sized boat.

This ability to work with small models cut down the cost of experimental work to a point where it could be carried on with real hope of success.

The purpose of earlier tests with large models of sailing yachts had been, as in the case of power driven vessels, to determine the resistance to forward motion with the boat in an upright position and moving along her own center line. Perhaps in some cases the models had been heeled and possibly even skewed a little to simulate leeway, but if this had been done it was evidently done with small models and without any knowledge of how to deduce their full sized resistances accurately. With the question of the small model cleared up, the next step was to determine the forces actually applied to a full sized boat by the wind acting on her sails and to scale these down properly from ship to model and up again from model to ship. To do this, sailing tests were made on the 23-foot water line *Gimcrack*, a small boat with a fairly conventional rig. These tests consisted of taking simultaneous readings of wind speed, boat speed and heel angle, while *Gimcrack* was being sailed close hauled in winds of various strengths. *Gimcrack's* resistance was checked, both by towing the actual boat and by towing a model. Her stability was also checked both ways. From these tests curves of the driving and heeling forces exerted by the sails at various heel angles and wind strengths were determined. Appropriate values taken from these curves can be applied to other boats, making it possible to calculate the probable speed for a boat built to a model that has been tried out.

For a given design which has a certain characteristic sail area, height of rig and height of center of gravity, we can determine what the heel angle will be for a wind of any given strength and, at that heel angle, what the driving and heeling forces applied by the sails to the hull must be. From a model test of the hull the speed through the water and the number of points away from the wind the boat should be at her best can be determined. From this, her speed made good to windward can be easily calculated.

The emphasis has been placed on speed made good to windward because that is generally considered the most important point of sailing and is probably the most difficult to determine from tests. At the same time, other valuable data can be obtained from the model test. Running and reaching speeds can be worked out and leeway determined as well as the position of the true center of lateral resistance and the stability of the hull in motion which usually differs from the stability at rest.

This has all been worked out over a period of six or seven years. I have not dwelt on the technical features of the work but those who are interested are referred to a recent paper by Professor Davidson.*

We took photographs showing the carriage in the Stevens Institute Tank with a model in position for a test run at a heel angle of 30 degrees. Sensitive scales on this carriage measure the resistance of the model as well as the 'thwartships force at each end of the model. Actually, this total 'thwartships force must be just sufficient to support the opposing force of the rig as scaled down in magnitude. As the pictures showed, the model was slightly twisted from the direction of its motion and its motion through the water in that position creates the necessary force.

The accuracy of these tests is really amazing. Their value has been indicated not only by the success of *Ranger* but also by the outstanding success of boats designed after model tests in classes which, through the building of a great number of boats, have been built up close to their peak. I think it is generally recognized that this type of model testing has earned its place as an important step in the design of many yachts. It should be emphasized, however, that a great deal of care and thought must be used to get the greatest advantage from these tests and to avoid being led astray by the results. The speed predictions are remarkably close, but our racing boats are close as well, and small differences in design data will throw points across the probable range of speed.

The tank will not design a boat; it will answer a question. To get a useful answer, the right question must be asked and, to have the answer mean much, there must be some basis of comparison. In the actual practice of using the tank to work out a new design, there must be considerable flexibility. Sometimes only one model is made while at other times several are needed. This, of course, depends on the speed of the model which has to be beaten and on the designer's ability to produce a faster model.

However, while successive improvements in design in a class or type of boat make it gradually more difficult to beat any particular

*Some Experimental Studies of the Sailing Yacht. Transactions of Society of Naval Architects and Marine Engineers, 1936, Vol. 44.

boat, the definite quantitative information supplied by model tests can build up a background of understanding of the influence of various shapes, and changes in shape, which distinctly help the designer in attempting to improve an existing design. The method of calculating speed also emphasizes the relationship of the various factors such as resistance, stability, leeway, sail area, etc., and helps to give the designer a clear picture.

So far, with racing boats, a number of models, perhaps two or three, sometimes more, each with variations in shape, have been made before settling on a final design. However, even when the last bit of speed is not important, the model test is valuable for the information it gives about stability and balance under sail, and the action of the model in waves. The relation of these data to the speed curve is extremely important and may well affect a decision between boats fairly close in speed.

It is too early to predict just what the effect of the tank will be on the yacht designer and his design. I have heard some people express the fear, others the hope, that the element of chance has been eliminated from yacht design. I am sure that is not the case. It will be a long time before all the possible variations in yacht form, great enough to make a real difference in performance, have been tried out. In the meantime, the ability to turn out an easily driven, stable, well balanced hull will be as important as ever and, to take full advantage of the tank, the ability to work out the hull and rig structure and their weights accurately and efficiently will be even more so.

From "Golwobblers" to "Mae Wests"

C. Sherman Hoyt

The legendary racing sailor tells of the origin of some of the unusual terms used in sailing

Recently rereading the *Traditions and Memories of American Yachting* of my life-long friend W. P. Stephens, I was amused, if somewhat sympathetic, with his irritation at the common usage of rather new words and terms applied to yachts and yachting.

Old age does not always mean tolerance and oldsters are prone to resent the application of new and often slangy terms to something they feel should have a different terminology. We are too apt to forget that for ages seamen as well as yachtsmen have invariably abbreviated all nautical terms whenever possible. The shorter forms, if arrived at years ago, have become so familiar that we use them without thought and more than often misapply them. When new rigs or devices are developed we frequently coin new descriptive terms to identify them.

"W. P." was particularly irked at references to yachts of the 76-foot rating measurement class, as "J" yachts, and to the general usage in this country of "marconi" as descriptive of yachts rigged with pole masts and triangular sails attached to and on the after side of such spars. To my mind, designation of classes by letters instead of by measurement ratings is logical and in conformity with the general nautical desire for brevity. As to the application of "marconi" to the normal rig of these days, its origin is easily explicable. When Charles Nicholson designed *Istria* (15-Metre Class of those days in Europe) in 1912, he lengthened the topmast so that the jack yarder could be dispensed with and the luff of the topsail set on a track on the topmast. The result eliminated much weight aloft but gave the

131

yacht at anchor an abnormally high mast for those days and it was promptly dubbed a "marconi mast." For some years in England, and to this day in this country, the rig as subsequently developed when the gaff on the mainsail and the yard on the club topsail were eliminated and a triangular sail substituted, has been designated by the slangy name of the mast. Possibly this was quite illogical, but its usage has become so common that I doubt if a much better term will supplant it. As a boy, such triangular sails were known to me as "leg o' mutton." The British prefer "Bermudian lug." Why not "bugeye" or "Chesapeake Bay" or "Long Island Sound sharpie"; all such craft and many others had gaffless triangular sails, at least on the mainmast. Why should we call it a "jib-headed rig"? It certainly is not on schooners. As I remember it, *Ethelwyn* in 1895, *Bogie* in 1896 and *Akista* in 1899, and some others of that period were called leg o' mutton-rigged on account of their triangular gaffless mainsails.

It was not until after the appearance of *Istria* in 1912 with her "marconi" mast that that term was applied to rigs as subsequently developed in experimental stages in smaller yachts, both abroad and here. In 1917, *Varuna*, one of the Larchmont one-design "O" Class, was so rigged and did well against her gaff-rigged classmates. The NYYC "50" *Carolina* experimented with the "marconi" rig in 1919 against one of her sisters in the event that the America's Cup match (postponed from 1914, to be resumed in 1920) would permit such contraptions. The usage of "marconi" as descriptive of such rigs had become universal until 1921, when *Nyria*, the first really big cutter so equipped, appeared on the Solent and British yachtsmen suddenly bethought themselves of Bermuda native craft. Admittedly such have triangular mainsails, but of vastly different proportions and in most other respects quite at variance with the newer rig's development, yet the British dropped "marconi" for "Bermudian lug," or "jib-header." Somewhat illogically, in their measurement rule the rig—or at least the mainsail—is called a "triangular mainsail."

But enough of "J," "marconi" and "Bermudian." Mr. Stephens also sneered at such terms as "Mae West," "Annie Oakley," "Greta Garbo" and "Ginny." Many such were born either for the sake of brevity or to give a distinctive name to new sails developed in racing competition and differing from the normal. I think I am responsible for some. As a small boy on an uncle's schooner, I allowed that a "balloon maintopmast staysail" was too much of a mouthful, why not call it a "golwobbler"? This was laughingly agreed to and the terminology was generally adopted in the racing schooner fleet of the early nineties. Alas for an inventor's feelings, "golwobbler" was soon shortened to just plain "golly." "Mae West" was born on board *Enterprise* when in drying on deck an over-size balloon jib, two large deck winches made certain protuberances in the sail suggestive to one of our hands of certain physical characteristics for which Miss West was famous. "Annie Oakley" I think also came from *Enterprise* when *Shamrock V* broke out a spinnaker full of holes. A "Genoa" or "Ginny" jib was so christened at Oyster Bay when Sven Salen astounded us by carrying to windward on *Maybe* what we have termed a balloon jib. Admittedly it was cut differently but we referred to it as a "Maybe" or "Swedish" jib and were promptly corrected by Sven, who assured us that he took no credit for it. He had run across such sails when racing in Italian waters the previous winter and he called his a "Genoa" jib. A "quad" is of course short for a "quadrilateral" jib. A "Yankee" to the British is what we still rather lengthily term a "No. 1 jib topsail." A "chute" in turn is short for a "parachute spinnaker" and so on along the line.

Nautical language, its origin, abbreviations and applications, is to me most fascinating. Origin is frequently difficult to trace. To know why marine toilet facilities are referred to as the "head" is simple, for in the earlier days of sail the forecastle head was utilized for such purposes, at least for seamen or foremast hands. Then the forecastle head, in turn abbreviated to focsul-head, was basically a grating under the bowsprit and forward of the forecastle proper. Plumbing in those days even on shore was at best most primitive, even if not entirely lacking, and the grating was the place to do it. The long cumbersome term of forecastle-head was soon dropped and nowadays, no matter where located on shipboard or how modernized and sanitated, one simply goes to the head.

The English language, as that of a seafaring people, has often quite unconsciously absorbed certain terms. Few know where the "devil" is on shipboard. In the early days of wooden ships the deck seam between the covering board and the deck planking which nibbed into it was apt to give trouble and was called the "devil." Hence the expression "between the devil and the deep blue sea" meant a somewhat precarious position at the deck's outboard edge. Similarly we are in a predicament when "the devil to pave (pronounced for no valid reason by our British forebears as pay) and no pitch hot." This is frequently misquoted and even meticulous authors like Kenneth Roberts will have a nautical hero say "hell to pay and no pitch hot," which makes no sense at all. Why want to pay hell with hot pitch? Nobody has ever been able to give me a satisfactory explanation of why in British naval and merchant service a white flare is always called a "blue light." The nearest sensible answer was given by an Irish friend who said: "Damned if I know but they are always wrapped in blue paper!"

One hears many and various explanations for such everyday words as "yacht," "schooner," "cutter," "sloop" and "ketch." Certainly they are now applied to rigs greatly at variance with those earliest on record, to say nothing of their derivation. No, those with a nautical bent will continue to invent slang terms for new and strange gadgets (by the way, how did that term originate?) and will shorten to the limit all long winded nomenclature. Look what has happened to capstern, forecastle, boatswain, cockswain, larboard, and many other words that are pronounced quite differently than spelled. Even yachting experts slip in new ones now and then. How about turning the noun "barge" into a verb as has recently been done by our experts on racing rules? I can find no dictionary with a definition of "barging" yet its interpretation, through misapplied use for only a few years, is quite well understood, if more often ignored, by all racing yachtsmen.

A yacht and a ship are such beautiful things that they become objects of love or even idolatry to those associated with them. It is therefore more than reasonable that we should give them and their gear pet names of endearment even if such at times border on the vulgar or even the obscene. We shorten mother to mom and father to pop or dad with no intent of disrespect, so we will continue to go to the head, refer to the captain as cap and call our dearly beloved ship a fine old bitch.

"Do You Anchor At Night?"

Ann Davison

The first woman to have sailed the Atlantic single-handed answers what she calls her most frequently asked question with a report of how she does it

Believe it or not, that is one of the first questions invariably greeting a single-handed ocean crosser on arriving at a strange port. Having pointed out the grave inconvenience of stowing several miles of chain, the inevitable come-back is, "Then I suppose you *lash the helm* and leave her to herself?" This quasi-casual piece of nautical talk is expected to throw me, which it does, because I know from experience the utter impossibility of explaining the problem to the uninitiated. For problem it is. They don't want to know how to stop a ship at sea, but how you manage to sleep alone on an ocean. Which question I am still trying to solve.

So far I either go on sailing until I fall asleep and drive round in circles so that after the fifth jibe I heave to, bleary-eyed, crawl below and couldn't care less if we *are* run down. Or else I keep weary watch 'til dawn and then snatch a couple of hours with the hope that at least we are visible in daylight. If anyone looks. This applies to sailing in the shipping lanes, which one so often does. There is no doubt whatever that the big ships can't see the little ones at night. The navigation lights of a sailboat are too close to the water, and are only the feeblest of glims anyway, and I think you can take it that small boats don't show up to any impressive degree on the radar screen. Be that as it may, I have too often been too nearly run down not to be pretty concerned about the matter. One might keep out of the shipping lanes but since the big ships take the shortest way between two points and little ones are slow enough without having the voyage made even longer, I regard that as simply evading the issue.

The solution would seem to be to organize so that one's ship is visible at night and arrange for some sort of self-steering device so that one does not have to sleep at the expense of progress. This is an important psychological factor for I find I *begrudge* sleeping, so that I don't get nearly enough at sea, which impairs efficiency and in turn makes one slower than ever so that the whole thing winds round in an increasingly vicious circle. For Trade Wind sailing *Felicity Ann* has a pair of those excellent twin staysails under which she will steer herself without fuss for days and weeks on end as long as the winds blow and she is required to run only dead before them. This happy state of affairs does not apply too often and unless closehauled *FA* has to be shown the way and sailed every inch of it. I have tried all sorts of trick lash ups, but she won't have any of them. The moment I go below she sneaks up into wind and lies there, waiting. I have been told by experts that this is simply a matter of trim, and if I remove some of the ballast and general gunk forward and lighten her head she will be much more amenable. Conversely I am assured by other experts that her lines being what they are she will never be any better. Well, this so far as I am concerned is a matter for experiment but whatever the outcome I am determined that *FA* is going to learn to sail herself in future and let me sleep in peace.

Electrical devices, whilst not entirely out of the question, are not very practical in such a small ship. A dynamo and batteries would add weight where least desired and the general management and maintenance of electrickery in very small yachts is invariably a nightmare for anyone not an electromagician, and I am not, which washes out a patent "George" for self steering. But I hear rumors of a gimmick that works off a towed spinner that I am going to look into very searchingly for future cruises.

This reluctance of mine to install electrical equipment also washes out a nice all round white electric light on top of the mast which seems to be the most satisfactory way of calling attention to one's presence at night. I haul up a kerosene lantern, which always seems too heavy for the halyard and does its best to dash its brains out against the mast. And I have yet to discover a kerosene lamp that is proof against the sudden drop inseparable from certain sailing conditions (which, so far as I am concerned, seem to prevail), but hope dies hard. One day I will find one or else some method of protecting flashlight batteries so that they won't go prematurely flat through heat and humidity. Edward Allcard has on board his *Wanderer* a dry cell brass riding light reputed to have a continuous burning life of 10 days which he seemed to be swearing by, so something like that might be the answer. For the purposes of this argument I have in mind cruising in the Pacific where it is not possible to pop into a handy port for battery renewals.

Before leaving this vital question of sleep there is one other point to be mentioned. Comfort. I don't hold with the rugged Before the Mast and Round the Horn attitude. It may have been good enough for my grandfather but it ain't good enough for me. When I sleep I like to wake feeling refreshed and not as though I had been left hanging on the clothesline all night. Which up to now has been the case. True, there is a bunk aboard *FA*, a settee job with a foam rubber mattress enclosed in some sort of iron casing. It is supposed to be washable. It probably is, but it is also convex longitudinally, so that one rolls to and fro up and over the peak. It is cold and unyielding in winter, and molten and sticky in summer. It sweats inordinately and is permanently damp. It is all in one piece and like fighting a giant python to get out of the hatch on deck (where there is no room for it anyway) to air. There is a canvas leeboard with lashings to make fast to eyebolts in the deckbeams to prevent one being decanted on to the cabin sole, but it also precludes one from getting out in a hurry without doing oneself grievous bodily harm. At sea I always sleep on the cabin sole, which is the only stowage place for a large fisherman type anchor, a couple of coils of rope, some sail bags and, frequently, wet sails.

It is inconceivable that I have suffered these conditions for nearly two years when the answer is so simple. Three foam rubber cushions on the settee without the iron casing . . . and what a joy it will be to get at the settee lockers without the python fight everytime . . . and snap fastenings for quick release on the leeboard lashings. Don't ask me why I haven't done this before. Frankly, I don't know.

Incidentally, for future cruising the fisherman anchor is to be exchanged for a Danforth which, it is hoped (you will note I am an incurable hoper), will stow neatly on deck. Experience has shown that the heavy canvas spare mainsail and trysail, both of extraordinary bulk and awkwardness, are just so much supercargo. The trysail can be omitted altogether. If there is too much wind for the tiny triangle the main can be rolled down to, it will just be too much. If I take a spare main into the Pacific it will be of the same light weight as the present one, which makes a jolly little bundle one can tuck under one's arm. This is going to leave loads of room in the sail locker, so there shouldn't be any odd sail bags cluttering up the cabin sole, which will then be relatively clear if I feel I must sleep on it.

But all one tells the bright eyed quayside questioner is, "Oh, you just heave to and sleep."

This foxes them so they change the subject and ask how you eat. Resisting the impulse to say by raising the fork in the usual manner, you remember what a bore it is to fix a meal for yourself at sea. How all the canned goods which looked so delicious when you bought them lost their appeal at sea. How you longed for fresh foods, red rare meat, green green salads, vegetables, fruit, and a genie to prepare them. So you mutter something about eggs. Scrambled, or an omelet. One meal a day. "Is that all?" they cry. *All*, you—meaning me—cry back. All? It is a veritable feast. If you can get it.

You think of how you sit on the settee because there is no room to stand up, one foot hard against the table locker opposite, poising a bottle of alcohol in one hand to prime the pressure stove. I ran through a succession of little can things with spouts for this caper, but they rusted through in no time so I gave them up and returned as you might say to the bottle. The drill is to hold the uncorked bottle at just the right angle so that as the ship rolls the alcohol is tipped into the priming cup. It needs only a small amount so this is quite a feat. It becomes a game to see if you can fill it just the right amount in one go without flooding the cabin, and gives a satisfactory glow with which to start the day, if you can. When the alcohol flame dies down and the pilot light casts its pale gleam you pump like mad and the burner lights, with luck. Then on to the stove goes the frying pan with some butter, and in due course two eggs to be fried. This is a big day. This, you think, is going to be a Good Breakfast, and dwell on the coffee (instant) to follow. But the eggs are barely set when the stove fades out, hissing a stream of blinding black smoke. The jet is choked, and of course, the pricker has inexplicably decapitated itself since last used, and the spares, *of course*, are in a sealed tin in the starboard locker, forward.

After moving the dozen or so large and bulky objects that bar your way, the locker door is found to be swollen from damp and quite immovable. A screwdriver or something is needed to pry it open, meaning an obstacle journey aft over the dozen or so large and bulky objects to the tool kit. And back again to the locker. All this, mind you, taking place in a cabin behaving like one of those trick things they have at Fairs to make you lose your balance. Once the locker door is open all the items therein hurl themselves at you with unaccountable affection. You find the tin of spares, break the seal, extract a spare pricker, reseal the tin, and return it together with all the other oddments to the locker, hurriedly shutting the door before they can burst it open again. And crawl back to the galley. There, the two congealed eggs stare up at you with the jaundiced glare of a hangover. Saying whatever you say on these occasions you climb out into the cockpit to Get Away From It All.

I might abandon my old-fashioned steam model cooker and invest in one of those modern deals that don't have to be pumped and clear their own throats automatically. But as genii are hard to come by these days I don't see any way of developing a sea going appetite. Which is just as well really. I get so nice and thin on a long voyage.

And so, you simply smile at the eager questioners and repeat vaguely, "Eggs. And flying fish. Oh, and er, onions. They sprout you know, and you eat the tops." As a bright afterthought you add, "And vitamin pills."

It all sounds quite revolting.

You look healthy enough, they say doubtfully, and then with a ghoulish gleam in their eye, ask if you are ever seasick.

It is very strange, but for some quaint reason seasickness comes into the category of low comedy. Though if there is anything so unfunny as seasickness in ordinary everyday life I have yet to come across it. The snigger quality apparently inseparable from this unhappy state possibly explains why so few mariners will ever admit to being victims, and then only as to something pretty shameful and best not talked about. Keep your mind above it and get plenty of fresh air. But Heaven knows you can't get any *more* fresh air than you do at sea. Oh yes, I get seasick. For the first 24 hours out I could wish I had never been born, or that ships had never been invented, were it not for Dramamine, which for this particular mariner is a very powerful ju-ju indeed. The only thing is that it puts me to sleep. So I take a benzedrine as well. Which keeps me awake. And I feel perfectly normal until the little balance jobs in my ears have adjusted themselves to the motion, after which there is nothing the ship and the sea can cook up between them to make me ill.

But I tell the indefatigable enquirers, no, I am not seasick. Which is sadly disappointing, so they cast about for something else. It must be pretty lonely, they say, on your own on the ocean. Haven't you a radio or something to call up other ships? They have only a hazy notion of this sort of operation and visualize one lifting a receiver and dialing QE for the *Queen Elizabeth*.

I have a radio. In fact I have two radios, both dry battery sorts, one short wave for time signals and the other for fun close inshore. It is one endless battle to protect them from the ravages of damp and salt and humidity. Next time I shall try plastic and/or rubber bags and silica salts. But communicating from me to you, that is the outside world, has been strictly limited to cries of "Hi" when close enough to another ship and a cheerful wave of the hand when not. I do carry a few signal flags of the International Code such as V for use in emergency, apart of course from the Q and *FA*'s own letters. But small yacht flags are so small I doubt very much whether they can be seen by other vessels.

I did try calling up a freighter one night by Morse, with a flashlight, one of those five cell deals with a blip switch. We were on our way to Nassau and as usual taking rather a long time about it, and it occurred to me it might be a kind gesture to my friends if I asked a passing ship to report me to Lloyds. Also I wanted to try out the Morse I had been practicing so assiduously.

All went well until the freighter started talking back. I could read her one letter signals, but this was conversation and just a blur of stuff. You know, as though I really *knew* Morse. It was most embarrassing. I was holding the flashlight in one hand, trying to keep the beam directed on the bridge, a notebook in the other, a pencil in my teeth, and was steering with a foot. Meantime, *FA* being of an experimental turn of mind was trying to row herself with the boom. The freighter showed a keen interest and talked faster and faster. You start these things easily enough, but it is not so easy to stop them. You can't say, oh skip it, we'll sit this one out.

Then she hove to, and I was terrified she was going to lower a boat or something awful, so very firmly signalled END and went below and shut the hatch and made a cup of coffee. There didn't seem anything else to do. Before I start on another long distance passage I shall really try and get this Morse signalling taped. It could, I believe, be an invaluable ace if played properly.

Yes, I tell those questioners, I do have a radio. Receiving only.

"Then you aren't *quite* cut off." They are disappointed again. It all seems so dull. "Don't you have any frightful storms?" they ask hopefully, "Aren't you ever frightened?"

The winds never blew for me more than 60 m.p.h. The seas were never higher than 30 feet. I never experienced the full force of a hurricane. And I never want to. What I saw was enough for me. I used to let *FA* ride with a warp over her stern, and go below, quite unable to bear even looking at the fury of the ocean. Those great gray hurrying seas. The way they hissed. The paralyzing, maddening scream of the wind. A scream that grew higher and higher as if the agony was too great to be borne. Which was how I felt about it.

I fix the questioners with a stern eye. "Anyone," I say, "who goes to sea and says he is never frightened is either a fool or a liar."

"Oh," they say, and look at one another uneasily and quietly move away.

If the questions people ask cause one to do a little secret soul searching, the statements they make when they think you are not there are even more illuminating. I was in Belhaven lying on my shoulder blades with my feet on the deckhead (the most comfortable way of sitting but only for us of the pint size boats) thinking beautiful constructive thoughts like—if the watertank is removed from under the cockpit then I could get at the stuffing box without shifting 300 lbs. of water and a tank first, and there would be room for batteries either side of the shaft, and a dynamo could be driven off the engine and lo, there would be light (this is always a dream of mine whatever I may say against it), and shaped watertanks could be fitted in those bilge lockers that are always so wet—when a voice obviously belonging to someone who could read said, "*Felicity Ann*, Plymouth, eh. Fancy coming down to North Carolina from Plymouth in *that*."

And another voice said, "Brother, I've news for you, Plymouth, *England*." It was a good thing they could not see me; I was all smug.

Then a third voice chipped in, "Yeah, but she followed the coast all the way." "She *did*?"

"No," said I coming out of the hatch, my honor being at stake, "she did not. Three thousand miles, long time *all* sea."

"Whaddaya know." They looked properly impressed, then, "How did you navigate?"

"Sextant," I said, casual like, "with the 'Air Navigation Tables,' similar to your 'HO 214.'"

That threw them. What I did not say was that I cannot imagine why this incredible mumbo jumbo ever works. Could it be that a small slow boat just can't get far off course? It can't be my workings, that's for sure. But the guy I overheard in Antigua, he had all the answers: "She is only one of thousands," he said. "You know what they do, these people? They work like slaves until they make a bit of money, then they buy one of these skiffs, and away they go. . . ."

Simple, isn't it?

1959

Racing Starts & Rounding Buoys

Bus Mosbacher

The two-time America's Cup winner and longtime top one-design skipper offers his thoughts on a key element in racing

The best start in a sailing race does not guarantee the best finish, and it is possible to give away an advantage rounding marks and still make a comeback, but the skipper who loses time at those points is saddling himself with an unnecessary handicap. More often, victory goes to the boat that can squeeze out those extra advantages that a good start or a good rounding of a mark can give you in a tight race.

Much of the success of these maneuvers comes with practice and experience. A sense of feel and timing can be developed through repeated exposure to situations, but it is still a smart idea to do some advance thinking and analyzing on these two vital facets of sailboat racing. When you have gone over the various possibilities that you might encounter ahead of time in your mind, it can be a lot easier to make that split-second decision that means you are off and flying, instead of wallowing around in a quicker-thinking opponent's backwind.

We are talking here of fleet starts in one-design racing. In the past year, a lot has been written and discussed on the match race starts that were a big part of the America's Cup competition, but the considerations are very different in fleet racing. In a match race your only concern is to put yourself in a position to command a single adversary. You can be late at the line, on the wrong tack for the way the wind is blowing, and at the wrong end of the line, as long as you have the other boat covered. But in fleet racing, putting

Bus Mosbacher, skipper of *Intrepid*

yourself in any one or a combination of these situations would probably be fatal.

In fleet racing, the object is to beat a number of boats, and it is a rare situation where just one of them concerns you, as it could in the final race of a series, in which one boat must beat a certain other one to win. In a fleet, the idea is to get around the course in the fastest elapsed time possible, and any such time-wasting maneuvers as tacking duels, luffing matches or special coverage of one boat at the start, work against that main purpose. There are times, of course, when certain of these maneuvers will have to be used, but it is generally best to sail your whole race as fast as possible. Sometimes, when certain boats concern you more than others, a "loose cover," staying in the same general area of a course and not letting the worrisome boat get off by herself on a flyer, should be used.

Many times an obsession with beating a certain boat has worked harm to a skipper. Often newcomers to a class concentrate on covering the maneuvers of the more highly-publicized skippers, forgetting that almost any boat can win on a given day in an evenly-contested fleet. If they had sailed their own race, rather than worrying solely about beating an "expert," they often would have done much better in individual races and overall standings.

Thinking, therefore, in terms of doing well against a sizable fleet of boats in your own class, what are the special considerations for getting a good start, and then for coming out on top in rounding buoys?

Preparation

Preparing for the start, leading up to getting away in the best possible situation to sail the rest of the race, begins long before the vital few minutes just preceding gun time. There are a number of things to check that seem obvious when you spell them out, yet it is amazing how many sailors, even good ones, fail to do them. First of all is being on time. The crew should know when the skipper wants them to show up and they should not keep him waiting or vice versa. There should be plenty of time to check over all gear and sails before starting out, and the condition of the boat should of course be the constant concern of the skipper. If he has let her bottom get dirty or some gear deteriorate, the race is probably lost already.

If you are cutting it close on time, a long ride in the launch if your boat is on the mooring may put you desperately late, or dry-sailed boats may all jam up at the hoist at the same time, causing confusion and short tempers. Then you have to rig in haste and probably won't do the job well. How many times have you seen a boat in a desperate hurry to make her starting time end up with battens sticking out of the pockets or a slide or two off the sail track?

You should have checked that the stop watch and race circular are aboard, and you should know the tide and current timetables for the day, as well as the weather forecast. And need I mention that you should have long since become thoroughly familiar with the rules? All this is obvious, yes, but still ignored by a surprising number of sailors, who usually end up in the losing boats.

In the Starting Area

Once out in the starting area, there are some additional things to consider. Take some tacks onto the course if it is possible to do this without interfering with the start of other classes. Check the current to see that it jibes with your paperwork estimate. Most important of all, get the feel of the wind. Is it steady from the same direction, or does it have holes and slants in it? Will you be able to plan your start well ahead, or will a last minute puff or slant change the picture?

A compass is a very handy piece of equipment to have on the starting line. It is fairly rare in most small boats, but I know dinghy sailors who use the compass to great advantage. With it you can check accurately on the way the line is slanted in relation to the wind, and whether the first mark is dead to windward or slightly off to one side, thereby making one tack or another the favored, distance-gaining one. This is as important as the angle of the line, as it affects your long range plans. If you carry one, you will know what side the spinnaker will be on on the downwind legs. All this helps you to organize the race ahead of time, although you must always be alert to changes in the situation.

A lot can be learned from the boats around you before the start. Choice of sails for the day by the other skippers can be interesting, and vital information can be gained from the classes that go off ahead of you. If you are well down on the schedule, it can be quite a help to see whether starting conditions remain constant or whether the wind is shifting back and forth in a pattern. One class may go booming across a squared line with everyone on starboard tack, and then in a following one the starboard tack boats may have trouble laying the line at all. This is when you must be specially alert and ready to change your own maneuvers right up to the last second.

You should be checking your stop watch (is it wound?) against the committee signals and keeping an eye out for any last-minute information from the committee boat such as course changes or postponements. This is no time to socialize with the people on the committee boat.

By the time the signals are up for your own class, whether you have ten or five minutes left to go, you should have established a clear picture of wind, current, angle of line and a general pattern for the most favorable start. An obvious sin, indulged in by the unwary, is to get too far from the starting area in any direction, especially to leeward.

The Starting Period

As soon as you can do so without interfering with other classes, run the line and time it. This should be done late enough so that conditions are not likely to change radically, but with plenty of time to get back to the other end of the line. You may not have to run the whole line to get enough of a time sense to govern the rest of your actions.

In every start, there will be a favored position. The more the line is cocked at an angle to the wind, the more this will be true, and the harder it will be to hit that favored position moving well with your wind free. You must also consider the pattern of the whole windward leg, with special emphasis on the tack you want to be on soon after the start. If the port tack is going to be the money-maker, but is not favored at the start, it may pay you to come through late at the windward end of the line, after the jumble of boats trying for the favored spot has cleared on by. Then you can drop over onto port tack as soon as you cross the line and be off and winging in free air on the favored tack to the mark.

Speaking of the port tack at starting time, I'm against trying it, even if it should be favored by a cocked line, and this becomes more important the bigger the fleet involved. Unless there is an absolutely clear advantage and you see an opportunity to slip through a safe spot, which is a very rare combination of events, the port tack is an unnecessary risk, just as barging is. To try to fight through on port tack, or to plan a barging start in hopes of getting away with it, is asking for trouble unnecessarily.

It is better to concentrate on keeping your boat moving well and free of entanglements with other boats, with freedom to tack. With way on, you can make adjustments better, get out of developing tight spots more quickly and shoot for last minute openings with better control. The type and weight of your boat makes a big difference in the amount of way needed to keep in control. A heavy keel boat such as an International takes longer to accelerate once her way is stopped, and it is better to kill time by zigzagging than luffing. A lighter boat can luff and stop quickly and pick up again right away when her sail fills. In either case it is vital to have your crew trained on what is expected of them so that they can automatically help the helmsman slow his boat and pick her up again, staying alert and anticipating his next moves. This was the tremendous advantage *Vim* had in her match race starts in the America's Cup trials. The crew was so good in making the adjustments needed to slow or drive her that I feel we had more flexibility and maneuverability than some of the competition.

Hitting the Line

We are now up to the point where the butterflies are swooping around the stomach, the boats are making their final jibes or tacks to square away for the line, and everything is beginning to get tense. In that last rush, with boats closing in from all sides, the watch ticking away and the line looming up ahead, it is very easy to forget all the cool, calm planning you had worked out in your head just a few minutes before.

I'm not in favor of a rigid pattern and an attempt to adhere to it strictly in situations like this. If you go through the same maneuver several times before the start and time it exactly, hoping to do it again when the gun goes off, you are tipping your hand to the other skippers. You are also setting up a schedule that will probably be impossible to keep when the time comes.

By now you have determined what is the favored postion, and it is safe to assume that a mess of boats will be fighting for it. This will make confused air that can kill your way and make maneuvering almost impossible. You should be close enough to the favored position so that you can shoot into it should an opening appear by

Everybody charging for the line—a tense moment

some miracle, but you should be paying more attention to keeping your wind free for the tack you want to take after the start, from as near the favored position as it is safe to get.

A common error is to look back and see a group of boats coming down from the windward end of the line, and to panic and flee before them like a rabbit before hounds. This can drive you too far down the line, sometimes all the way over it too soon (see frontispiece) or into a jibe away from it that will put you far back of the line as the gun goes off. There may be room to kill way and wait for the gun, but by then the boats behind will harden up. By the time you have way back on you are hopelessly blanketed and to leeward. Avoid such sitting-duck positions at all costs.

It is also wise to look for known peculiarities and special abilities of certain competitors. In the International Class we knew it was suicide to end up on the weather quarter of one outstanding skipper. Some skippers who drive off would not bother you in a spot like this, but this sailor is famous for his ability to point higher than almost anyone else and he could make things mighty difficult for someone unwise enough to be back there. Other skippers have favorite patterns they try to follow invariably, and you can pretty well tell where they will be at a given time in the starting period.

To sum up, then, it is better to avoid patterns and schedules, but to concentrate on keeping way on and your wind free as close to the favored spot as possible, assuming that there will be a battle for it, and ready to improvise right up to the crack of the gun. Think of the windward leg as a whole, and the position of the mark, in deciding where you want to be.

I am in favor of windward starts at all times when possible. Sending a fleet off on a run or reach in a round-the-buoys race makes for jams at the first mark. A properly run race should have a windward start, but there are courses where local conditions make this impossible, and every once in a while a skipper may have to start off-the-wind. For this reason, race committees of clubs where windward starts are the standard procedure might occasionally throw in an off-the-wind start as experience for local skippers who may have to compete someday on waters where local custom is to start the race in the same direction every time, no matter what the wind direction.

This is especially important in junior racing, as youngsters engaging in team races or sectional eliminations for championships at another club may be completely confused if they have only had experience in windward starts.

In an off-the-wind start, it is again of paramount importance to have your wind clear, and a slightly trailing position can sometimes be an advantage. If the first leg is short, it is wise to be on the side of the course corresponding to the side on which you leave the first mark. If the leg is long enough, it might be profitable to look for the best sailing angle.

Approaching Marks

Now that we are on the course, the next close-in maneuvering will take place rounding marks. Often a skipper with the skill to get speed out of his boat in the clear on open waters, and who is right in the fight as marks are being approached, will let the boats near him slip by in the mark-rounding process.

Here again it is vital to know your rules and to be sure of them in split-second decisions. Situations can develop with great rapidity as boats converge on a mark. It is also important to think ahead to the mark while you are on the leg of a course. Your approach to a mark can make a great difference in how you come out of rounding it. Your crew, again, should know exactly what is expected of them in the maneuver so that the skipper can concentrate on helmsmanship in close quarters. If a lot of boats are converging from different directions, it can be helpful to have one crew member clue the skipper on the situation. This information should be relayed quietly and factually, *not* by shouting something like "Gosh, look at him come!" or "Look out for this guy!"

In approaching the weather mark it is smart to plan to be on the starboard tack on the final approach. The advantages of this are obvious, but it sometimes takes some doing when you are in a tight battle with a group of boats, or the wind slants fail to cooperate. If you discover that your approach will not be in tight quarters, with right of way no problem, you might plan the last tack so that your crew can have the spinnaker all set and ready to go upon rounding.

Crisp, sharp maneuvers with way on the boat are important, and you are taking a chance to pinch up to a mark or to shoot it at the last minute. If you miscalculate and your way has dropped so that the boat is mushy, she may go out of control in irons and drift down on the mark or into another boat. Keep her moving.

Many boats waste distance in rounding marks by overstanding the lay-line. It is usually better to err on the side of underestimating and make on extra, controlled tack, than to waste distance sailing away from the mark by overstanding.

You should be considering the next leg and how to hold your

advantage over pursuing boats—a hard thing to do in swinging from windward to leeward legs in close competition—or, if you are trailing, figure how you can get on the wind of the boat rounding first.

Incidentally, if the race committee can set up a course with "port" turns it makes for less likelihood of jams and fouls at crowded marks.

On a leeward leg the inside position at the mark, if you are close enough to worry about overlaps, is of course the one to shoot for, and you sometimes have to think of this well back on the leg. It is here that exact helmsmanship and good crew work really pay off, as the ability to keep a spinnaker drawing until the last minute, or to delay preparations for going on the wind in a boat without spinnaker as long as possible, can mean those inches that gain or hold the overlap. When to put the board down, when to make a jibe if one is necessary, and steering on the actual approach to the mark are the things that make the little differences.

If you have the room and the right to do it, a leeward mark should be approached with a wide turn on the approach side so that you are close to it after coming around. A wide turn allows you to keep more way on for rounding up on the wind, while a sharp, abrupt rounding will tend to stall the boat. If you fail to sharpen up quickly and close to the mark as you round it, you may leave a hole for a boat close behind to slip into and get above your backwind. If you are the pursuer, you can sometimes gain a quick advantage by a smarter rounding, and it is important to look right away for the better tack on the new leg.

Very often a crew rounding a mark will be so preoccupied with trimming sails and squaring away the mechanics of a windward leg that they fail to check the wind slants. A boat may stand into a header without realizing it for quite a while.

If you get beaten badly enough and often enough you learn something. The thoughts just expressed represent a few things that I think I've learned. Very likely before we put *Susan* away after next weekend's racing someone will have made it more then obvious that I've learned very little. But, after all, that's what keeps us coming back to this wonderful sport of ours.

Single-Handed Passages

Francis Chichester

After his first success in single-handed racing, the famous solo voyager gives his thoughts on this very special field

(The author has sailed across the North Atlantic four times in *Gipsy Moth III*, twice east-to-west alone and twice west-to-east with his family:

1960—Plymouth, England, to New York (Ambrose Lightship). Alone. 40 days, 12 hours, 30 minutes.

1960—New York to Plymouth, England, via Azores. Cruise with his wife, Sheila. 42 days sailing.

1962—Plymouth, England, to New York (Ambrose Lightship). Alone. 33 days, 15 hours, 7 minutes.

1962—Pollock's Rip to Plymouth, England. Cruise with his wife and son Giles, 16 years old. 26 days, 12 hours, 40 minutes.

In the 1960 single-handed race from Plymouth, England, to New York, five yachts took part and finished as follows:

1. *Gipsy Moth III*, 39'7" x 10'1¾" x 6'5". 40 days, 12 hours, 30 minutes.

   Designed to Francis Chichester's specifications by Robert Clark, built by Jon Tyrrell of Arklow, Eire.

2. *Jester*, Colonel H. G. Hasler, a Folkboat with Chinese lug sail on an unstayed mast. Rig and wind vane steering both designed by Colonel Hasler. 48 days, 12 hours.

3. *Cardinal Vertue*, Dr. David Lewis, a standard Vertue. This was generally considered before the race to be the most suitable boat for a single-handed passage. Dismasted at the start of the race and started afresh two days late. 56 days.

4. *Eira*, Valentine Howells, a Folkboat with increased sail area. 63 days.

5. *Cap Horn*, Jean Lacombe (owner, Boname of New York). 74 days (started 5 days late).

Sir Francis Chichester at the helm

When in the USA Francis Chichester, who was recently given the Blue Water Medal of the Cruising Club of America, was asked by *Yachting* to tell how a single-handed ocean racer ticks, and how he was able to cut down his 1960 record time.—EDS.)

In America I was often asked how I had managed to cut 6 days, 21 hours off my 1960 time of 40½ days in the Single-handed Trans-Atlantic Race. In order to do this, I go back to the race itself: 3,000 miles on a great circle course from Plymouth, England, to New York. Because it is one of the most grueling courses to be found, the Atlantic had only once before been raced from east to west and that was in 1875 between *Dauntless* and *Cambria*, 120-foot schooners with large crews.

Before the race I had hoped to cross in 30 days but the truth is that I badly misjudged the Atlantic. I was far longer—26 days—on the wind than expected; the Atlantic seas were much rougher and for longer periods of time than I expected. I sailed through 1400 miles of fog instead of the 300 miles which I had expected. The fog did not slow me directly because I charged into it, awake or asleep, but I did find it difficult to drop off when stretched out on my bunk and so was indirectly slowed by fatigue. I think the threat of ice slowed me up. I admit being scared of ice when single-handed—the skippers of those bergs don't know that a sailing ship has the right of way! In the 1960 race I had no frequency on which to pick up ice reports. "Damn bad management for a navigator," you say. Indeed it was. In extenuation I should point out that the radio set I carried did not arrive till the afternoon before we sailed.

I also misjudged the constancy of the wind. I expected it to be steady for days at a time, but it was as fickle as in the English Channel or even the Solent. Frequent sail changes were required—sometimes several during the night—a lot of work for a single-hander in a 13-ton boat.

Last, I misjudged the capabilities of my self-steering wind vane. Before the 1960 race I imagined that with this device I would be able to race single-handed against a fully-crewed yacht. Miranda, my self-steering vane, could maintain a heading relative to the wind more or less constantly, but she could not sail the boat as close to the wind as a helmsman because of the danger of being caught aback when hit by a big wave or a brief puff from a different direction. And, as I said before, the wind was always shifting. Miranda could not trim the sails for wind shifts, to say nothing of changing them while I was asleep.

Gipsy Moth III was very new when I started on the 1960 race. By the time I had sailed her 8,000 miles over and back to England I was beginning to know her capabilities, and to appreciate what changes could be made to speed her up and make her easier to handle. Perhaps I should also add that I had learned a lot more about ocean racing. I set about making changes to rigging, gear and methods and then looked 'round for a good sail to test out my theories. I believe that herein lies the greatest incentive to adventure; a man gets an idea that some improvement will enable him to sail faster, fly higher, or dive deeper, and then a terrific driving force within him to prove that he is right takes over.

I thought to myself, "How splendid a sail if I could slip across the Atlantic again." Then I thought, "Why not try to break my 1960 record?" Air pilots and racing motor drivers go out for records, why shouldn't a yacht helmsman? I would see if I could break my 1960 record, and try to get across in 30 days.

First I had to speed up the boat. The architect for *Gipsy Moth III* was Robert Clark, and he designed a sweet hull. However, I had specified a boat to cross the Pacific, with no thoughts of an Atlantic race at that time. She had a 4¼ ton iron keel (I reckoned lead would be ripped off) for bumping coral. This hull is too slow and too big for solo racing. I imagine that, single-handed, I could get much more speed out of a 9-tonner than out of a 13-tonner like *Gipsy Moth*.

I could not change the hull, but I set to work on the rig. Captain John Illingworth designed the changes. I consider him the greatest ocean racer in the world, and as he is a naval engineer, I had great confidence in the new metal mast and rigging he designed for me. These are some of the things I asked for:

1. The backstays had to go to the counter because it prevented Miranda from swinging freely through 360°. John gave me twin backstays, 7½ feet forward of the stern at deck level.
2. The running backstays had to go. I cannot think of anything worse for a single-hander in a gale than a lee runner with blocks flying around and a weather runner which had to be winched taut for tacking.
3. I wanted a cutter rig instead of sloop, and I needed a staysail for control when a big genoa was suddenly dropped in a squall. As a result the after lower shrouds had to be taken well aft of the mast. The boom was prevented from being squared off, but as I prefer not to do this when racing, it was not a hardship. I found the staysail was a great success; it could be hoisted or dropped in a few seconds, increased speed on the wind in a light breeze, and gave good speed with a minimum of heel in a gale when set with a trysail and a spitfire jib.
4. My 360-square-foot mainsail in 1960 had not balanced the fore triangle, so I wanted it cut down. With a boom sheeted to the counter, it was a devilish thing to control in an Atlantic storm and I was grateful to have it shortened by about 4½ feet and sheeted at the forward end of the cockpit.
5. Without runners, a masthead rig was necessary. I preferred this because it enabled me to set a genoa of 420 sq. ft.—40 ft. more than the old one. This rig and the added staysail more than compensated for the loss of 80 feet in the mainsail.

6. I left my spinnaker in England this time. Even with a crew I consider it an unseamanlike sail—for a single-hander to find a snarled spinnaker upon awakening would be awful. Yet I like plenty of sail for running, so I got John to design me two telescoping spinnaker booms. The limit allowed by the R.O.R.C. rule—14 feet—was not sufficient for me. The new poles extended 21 feet each. I could set 1,100 feet of genoa in this manner when sailing alone and sleep fairly well. John suggested I should fit these poles well forward to lugs welded on the samson post, but this wasn't a success. I injured a hand in the dark when a pole slipped, and the clews of the sails used to sky. The poles did very well fitted to the mast in the usual way.

The next item I had to spruce up was Miranda, my self-steering vane. For the 1960 race I had a wonderful new design, but it needed too much wind to make it work. A short while before the 1962 crossing, I redesigned Miranda.

Miranda Mark One was a 14-foot mast rotating in a sheave. It had sails to weathercock and two arms which could spin 'round the mast or be locked to it if required. All one had to do, in theory, was to get the yacht sailing to one's satisfaction; Miranda's vane would always weathercock. One now locked the movable arms to the Miranda mast. A tiller line from the end of each arm led to the tiller. As these lines would not stretch, if the yacht's head fell off to leeward the tiller would be pulled to one side and it would stay over until the ship's head came back to the original heading.

Firstly, with the shortened main boom, and new back-stay arrangement, Miranda Two could swing freely through 360°. So now I could use it to control the yacht when headed downwind. Miranda Two has a gaff of 10½ feet and a boom of 8 feet, giving it the necessary power. (It is powerful enough to knock you overboard if it catches you when not harnessed.) The new Miranda is a tube which rotates 'round a fixed 8-foot mast, which reduces friction to a minimum. Although I designed her, all the drawings, as well as the construction, were excellently done by Ian Proctor. For a prototype it worked extremely well.

Miranda's sail area had to be cut down in a gale, and the original reefing arrangements were bad. The difficulty was in bringing forward the 10½-foot gaff (which was weather-cocking aft of the stern) and bracing myself on the counter to reef the sail, the boom being head high. This was one of the hardest tasks I have experienced at sea and it took up to two hours. Now I have a reefing arrangement which can be worked in a minute or two by simply pulling a cord at the Miranda mast without having to bring the whole contraption inboard. The resultant reef can be so neat that it is hardly noticeable and I believe this arrangement might be valuable for all small yachts.

To cut my time from 40½ to 30 days, I had to find means of combating fatigue, the well-known enemy of ocean racers. I had to figure out how I could accomplish gear handling and sail-trimming easily.

Bagging big foresails of heavy terylene alone was an awful labor. I had a net made for each side of the foredeck, enabling me to keep the sail inboard in a rough sea while I handled it. With twin headstays, I was able to keep a big genoa and a working jib hanked on at the same time. When I lowered a sail, I folded it into a sausage shape and lashed it down really well to the foredeck and pulpit. The spitfire, when required, was set above the genoa hanks. The staysail was always hanked on and could be lashed down in a few seconds. Other sails were kept lashed to the cabin top with ringbolts.

My trysail remained the same. It had a separate track and was kept rigged permanently, lashed down to the cabin top. I also kept a two-fold tackle rigged permanently on each side of the cockpit. Both these tackles were clipped to the trysail clew and used simultaneously in a gale to control the sail. With these arrangements sail handling was kept to a minimum.

All my sheets were of a straight-fibre minimum-stretch nylon, contained in a braided nylon sheath. My mainsheet of this rope has made four Atlantic crossings with hardly a blemish. I kept separate sheets rigged at all times for a genoa, a working jib, a staysail and the spitfire jib, besides the trysail tackles. If all this gear is not ready it is really hard on the willpower of a single-hander to rig it in a gale.

Tactics I regard as part of navigation—in fact the most important part. I think my tactics in 1962 were very much better than in the 1960 race, but I did make one serious mistake. Not far from Newfoundland I had a two-day head-on gale up to Force 9. The port tack heading, roughly northwest, was slightly the better tack and naturally enough I took it. After 24 hours of this leg I realized that I had made a tactical mistake; I was being pushed too far to the northeast of Newfoundland. I not only might have to pass through the iceberg area as a result, but also might have to stick to an unfavorable tack to get around Newfoundland. For the next 30 hours I sailed south on the starboard tack. I averaged three knots through the night with only the spitfire jib (65 sq. ft.) and that was sheeted aback to try and slow the boat up. At one time, because of the terrific bashing *Gipsy* was taking in the heavy seas, I lashed the helm to leeward, which headed the yacht very close to the wind and slowed her to 1½ knots. Later, when a west-by-north leg was favoring I could not lay it for about a day because I still wasn't far enough south. The tactical blunder had been made.

The more single-handed sailing I do, the more value I place on judgment in sailing tactics. To illustrate what I mean: If, racing with a full crew, you decide that you would go faster with a genoa instead of a working jib, you promptly set the genoa. But single-handed, you must consider what the effects will be over the next four hours if you set the genoa, or even over the next 24 hours. You must lose some time changing and if you get caught in a gale while you are asleep, you may lose considerable time shortening down, whereas with a crew you might only lose a few minutes. Therefore, it might have been wise to have kept the working jib and never changed to the big genoa. This is a simple illustration to the need for sound judgment in single-handed racing.

I should mention the radiotelephone. This was the first of a new model by Marconi, fitted with suitable frequencies for my crossing. Through this phone I talked a story every day to London. The story went through even when there was a gale. My last installment was sent half-an-hour before crossing the finishing line at Ambrose Lightship. In mid-Atlantic, London said they heard me better than the *Queen Mary*, and once I had to warn the man I was speaking to that I could hear what two people were saying to each other behind his back. This set made marine communications history. This was not due to me, of course, I merely twiddled the knobs, swore at having to interrupt my deck work, and uttered verbiage. It spoiled some of the romance of crossing the Atlantic alone, but so many people had said they would like to follow a trans-Atlantic race day by day that I felt I should attempt it.

PART IV
Wartime

Yachting *survived through the two major World Wars, when so many yachtsmen turned the expertise of their recreational hobby to military use, manning, especially, the hundreds of small craft, like subchasers, PTs, patrol craft and the off-shore antisubmarine sailing patrol, that were so well suited to their skills. Out of these experiences came many articles of interest to readers of a yachting magazine, some comic, some bloodily tragic, and all evoking the trials and tribulations of civilian yachtsmen suddenly thrust into new and frightening challenges.*

1916

A Western Ocean Cruise in Wartime

George H. Dillenback

An unusual Atlantic round trip by Wakiva *in the early days of World War I to bring back some of the owner's friends marooned abroad*

1. The Hurried Fitting-Out of the *Wakiva* and an Eventful Trip Across the Atlantic

Shortly after two o'clock on the afternoon of August 17, 1914, a toast was drunk to the *Wakiva* and we all felt that we were "under way," notwithstanding the fact that we still sat in the Plaza grill and looked out through an open window to the park beyond. There was something intimate about that toast—a sense of close association, a prediction of the future. I believe we all felt it, to a degree, because for several moments we were silent and thoughtful.

"Well, are you ready?" Harkness asked. We were, and jumped up eagerly; the spell was broken and each hurried over some half forgotten task, a belated purchase, a final telegram or telephone call. Small packages were stowed away in the Mercedes waiting opposite.

The trip to Sea Gate and the Atlantic Yacht Club was jovial, hilarious; we found names, ranks for each other. Harkness was dubbed the Commodore; Reed, the "Pilot of the River of Doubt"; McHose, "Admiral of the Irish Navy," and I was "Admiral of the Swiss Navy," and so we remained throughout the cruise.

At Sea Gate we experienced our first disappointment. There were many yachts in the offing, but the *Wakiva* was not there. Captain Grant, however, was, and explained that there was some trivial trouble with the plumbing, which could undoubtedly be repaired in a few hours. This was not surprising, as the big yacht had been put in commission from dry dock in exactly one week—a record, we believe, for a boat of her size and importance.

We spent the afternoon and evening and a part of the night between Brighton, The Witching Waves at Coney Island, and the yacht club. But that is neither here nor there. The *Wakiva* did not come to us, so we went to her in the club launch about 2 A.M.

It was good to be there, in the reflected lights and shadows of the Narrows. We sang a little, and talked a little, but not very much. There was something bigger than talk and song. A nearly spent crescent moon stood above us and marked our path to Tompkinsville, where the *Wakiva* rode at anchor near the battleship *Florida*.

There was little sleep for any of us that morning. A crew of coal passers came aboard, and then the water boat made fast alongside. At dawn the starboard gangway was taken up and housed; soon after that a bell jingled in the engine room. Slowly the *Wakiva* gathered headway and turned in a graceful circle as she dipped her flag to the *Florida* in parting salute and pointed her nose to the open sea and the road to Europe, three thousand miles away.

Other bells jingled, and gradually we gathered speed ahead, plowing the green waters between Hamilton and Wadsworth, past little Lafayette and the Islands to starboard, and Sea Gate to port. We watched the yacht club fade from view, and wondered who of those we cared for had seen us pass. At 10:45 A.M. we cleared the Ambrose Channel Lightship and passed three small steamers inward bound. Salutes were exchanged with flags and whistles; and very shortly we were alone upon the sea—no land, no smoke, no sail in sight. Somehow the day slipped from us at lightning speed and the sun went down smothered in rose mist.

There was so much to do, to see, that first day, that in retrospect it seems that we neither did nor saw anything tangible. It was all so new to us—the rhythmic hum of the engines, the stinging whip of spray, the gentle motion, the freedom of the bridge. All must seep into our consciousness, so that all too soon a boatswain's whistle sounded and the flags came tumbling down. The sun had set and night shadows gathered in the hollows of the white-capped waves.

That first dinner was memorable, too; just we four seated about an oval board in the center of the spacious saloon, and healths were drunk, and those left behind were not forgotten. Coffee and cigars in the smoking room on the boatdeck filled our cup of contentment to overflowing. After reading the wireless reports of the war and the baseball scores, someone suggested auction bridge and a rubber was started. I glanced at my watch; it was nearly twelve, but no one would believe me.

Suddenly we were startled by a brilliant light shining in through the windows of the cabin. We hurried on deck. A short distance off we could see the running lights and the searchlight of a steamer. For some time she held us and searched us, bow and stern. The First Officer ran up the Stars and Stripes and flashed a light upon the flag. Suddenly all lights were extinguished aboard her and she disappeared as completely as though swallowed by the sea. It was very still—nothing to be heard but the snap of the wireless, "Who are you?" "The American steam yacht *Wakiva* bound for Liverpool. Who are you?" "The British cruiser *Essex*." "Good luck, good-bye!" It seemed like some sea phantom. It was all so sudden, so unexpected, so quickly over. Where the lights had been there was the black ocean, no blacker, no lighter than the sea all around us. We considered this an impressive and fitting ending of our first day at sea and turned in shortly after eight bells.

The *Wakiva*, in which we were making the trip, was a steel steam yacht, 195 feet on the water, 239 feet over all, with 30 feet beam and drawing 14 feet of water. While the *Wakiva*'s bunker capacity was sufficient to carry her across the Atlantic, fearing an embargo in England, and so as to be prepared against an emergency, we carried an extra supply of 183 tons sacked on deck. This was stored in the bunkers as soon as sufficient had been used from them to accommodate the extra supply.

Our crew consisted of 46 men all told, viz.: captain, 3 mates, 3 quartermasters, 1 bo'sun, 8 sailors, chief engineer and 17 men in the engine-room department, with 10 in the steward's department and 2 launchmen. Quite a sizable crew!

August 19th

Lat. Obs. 40° 20′ N.	Lat. Acct. 40° 10′ N.
Long. Obs. 67° 56′ W.	Long. Acct. 68° 00′ W.
Var. 14° W.	Barom. 30.04
Dev. 3° E.	Thermo. 79°

Distance, 288 miles from Battery, New York City.

We, that is three of us, breakfasted together and hurried upon deck. No sail showed upon the horizon, but white-topped, tumbling waves played joyously in the sunlight and we were glad. We hastened from port to starboard, up on the bridge and down again, forward and aft, seeking nothing and finding much pleasure in an intangible immensity. A flock of stormy petrels followed us—darting, fluttering, as quick almost as the eye. The wireless operator reported that he was in communication with Siasconsett. At first there is always something shocking in the thought when you fancy yourself alone—a little world tossed about, willynilly, beyond help, beyond recall, and someone says, "I am in communication with such and such." Your little world is lost. You are but an atom in a huge fabric. However, there is a reassuring sense in it, too, so we flashed "Good morning" to some of those left behind.

At 11:30 Reed awakened Bush with a fly swatter. It did not seem right that on such a morning time should be wasted in sleep.

All day, while the sun was bright, there was great activity amongst the camera fiends, including Goodwin, the moving picture operator. This and that were snapped, and each of us many times.

Reed Vail had a happy thought; there were many papers, magazines and periodicals aboard, and he hit upon the plan of giving us a few each day, and from then on we had our daily publications. In our gratitude we dubbed him the Librarian, but he still remained the Pilot of the River of Doubt.

That evening after dinner we lounged about and swapped lies and told stories of every country of the globe, for we had traveled much between us. In due course the wireless report was handed Harkness and he read it to us, but it was all of war and fallen cities and murdered men, and—baseball scores. Then we settled the destinies of Europe, each to his own fancy, but then, as there was some difference of opinion, we soon found ourselves talking of ants and bees and their habits, and unanimously agreeing that ants and bees and men had many characteristics in common. We turned in—the exact time I have forgotten.

August 20th

Lat. Obs. 40° 27′ N.	Lat. Acct. 40° 19′ N.
Long. Obs. 62° 21′ W.	Long. Acct. 62° 15′ W.
T. Course N. 88° E.	Barom. 30.14
Distance., 257 miles in	Thermo. 78°
23 hrs. 36 min.	Water 80°
Dist. per log, 260 miles	Var. 16° W. Dev. 3° E.

Bush in his cabin from 5:30 A.M. to 7:30 A.M. killing flies with a fly swatter!!! This disturbed Reed and led to an early breakfast for us all. In mid-morning we picked up the steamship *Philadelphia* by wireless and relayed messages home.

There are shoals of flying fish around us. Sometimes they rise and skim the surface for several moments at a time. One flew aboard and was nicely fried for luncheon. However, there were other things for luncheon, too.

Toward sunset we discovered a steamer to port and almost at the same time another to starboard. We steamed midway between them and tried to raise them by wireless, but neither replied. They were a long way off, and through the glass appeared to be freighters.

August 21st

To-day we are having typical Gulf Stream weather—one moment the sun shines in balmy lassitude, and the next the rain comes down in torrents. It is fun staying on the bridge to the last moment of sunshine, then racing for the smoke room aft before the downpour; sometimes you get wet. Heavy wind squalls and calm weather alternate; even the sea changes quickly. For a little it is quite rough, and then again for a time quite calm. A steamer passed, hull down, upon the horizon. We held a faint line of smoke for a long time, but could distinguish nothing of her. She failed to answer our call. These westward-bound vessels are either quite secretive or very stingy.

Later we raised up the steamship *Philadelphia* again. She reported herself as 803 miles from New York at noon. We figured (without official verification) that she was within about 40 miles of us. We talked with her for some time. It is nice to have someone to talk with when you are alone at sea.

August 22d

Lat. Obs. 39° 52' N.	Lat. Acct. 39° 51' N.
Long. Obs. 51° 33' W.	Long. Acct. 51° 20' N.
T. Course S. 86° E.	Barom. 30.10
Distance, 260 miles	Thermo. 76°
Dist. per Log, 261 miles	Var. 22° W. Dev. 2° W.

Distance from Battery, New York, 1,042 miles.

August 21st merged into August 22d with no perceptible change. No one of us knew when or how it happened; suddenly we realized that night had come and gone and that it was August 22d. That was all, there was not even the slightest jar, and so we went upon the bridge to see the sunrise. The dawn was very beautiful, the entire circle of the horizon was massed with heavy clouds, like huge mountains rising from the sea, and gradually, as daylight grew, they took shape and revealed ugly chasms and deep ravines. Some seemed tipped with white snow clouds, which slowly turned to pink. The

Swiss Alps seemed spread before us like some glorious panorama of the gods. Suddenly a rain squall broke upon us and all hope of seeing the sun rise was abandoned for that day.

During the morning two more flying fish came aboard. I did not see them, but they were served for luncheon, and I had my share. This daily gift from the ocean seems providential, as all of our fresh fish supply was left ashore. It arrived at the dock too late to be put aboard and we sailed without it.

The last of the coal was removed from deck this A.M. and the decks were swabbed down preparatory to stretching awnings. We are rather a saddened crowd this afternoon—Harry asleep, Vail looking for something to snap, while Bush is on the bridge looking for a German battleship.

Captain Grant gave us our first lesson with the sextant to-day, and we each in turn "pulled down" the sun. It is quite a trick, but when you try it be sure that you have your sextant.

The night was brilliant, with a stiff, cool wind which kicked up quite a sea. When I went to my cabin I found that a chair had been overturned. That night we knew that we were well out to sea.

August 23d

Lat. Obs. 41° 27′ N.	Lat. Acct. 41° 2′ N.
Long. Obs. 45° 33′ W.	Long. Acct. 45° 49′
T. Course N. 71° E.	30″ W.
Distance, 200 miles	Barom. 29.82
Dist. per Log, 272 miles	

Distance from Battery, 1,332 miles.

The *Wakiva* rolled and tossed and repeated both operations many times during the night, and we learned many things in the morning. It was raining heavily, the sea was very high (this we had suspicioned), waves climbed aboard, and Bush's cabin began to leak from overhead.

Poor Bush! You were rather funny and a very busy man with your pail in one hand and your bed in the other, looking at once for a trickle of water to fill your pail and a dry spot to lay your bed. But never mind, there are oil bags slung over the starboard side and any moment the sea may calm down. Be of good cheer, the worst is yet to come.

The wireless is constantly aware of ships all along the line, but they will not answer when called; we believe them to be British battleships or cruisers. The *Wakiva* carries trisails fore and aft to keep her steady, but heavy seas continue to break on the starboard quarter and wash the after deck. The wind has shifted from S.W. to N.W.

After dinner we stood on the starboard bridge and tried to determine the roll of the ship as indicated by the rise and fall of the second officer standing to the port side. At the lowest point his head was level with our eyes, at the highest his feet, and so he went up and down against the sky line. We tried to figure that if he were five feet ten and a half inches tall, and the height of the bridge fifty feet from the water line on an even keel, and the width of the bridge forty feet six inches, and the starboard roll two-thirds of the total radius, and the port roll one-third, how many degrees was the *Wakiva* rolling? Harry looked at the indicator in the chart room and found that the maximum was 32 to port and 18 to starboard, but that if she rolled more it would be much greater.

August 24th

Lat. Obs. 42° 53′ N.	Lat. Acct. 42° 37′ N.
Long. Obs. 40° 14′ W.	Long. Acct. 40° 00′
T. Course N. 70° E.	Barom. 29.86
Distance, 250 miles	Var. 25° W.
Dist. per Log, 271 miles.	Dev. 2° W.

Distance from Battery, 1,582 miles.
Distance from Liverpool, 1,638 miles.
Half distance 2:30 P. M. to-day.

The first man who noticed that it is darkest before the dawn noted a very obvious fact. It is dark, dark as Tophet, and perhaps a shade darker in mid-ocean, and weird—very weird. The sky seemed a great black semi-globe, clamped tight upon a great black circular plane. The running lights reflected on the surface seemed but to emphasize the gloom beyond. Overhead were the masthead lights, but no stars. On the bridge the binnacle seemed to smolder and crackle as it glimmered through a crevice here and there. A faint glow illumined the compass card with a grim, intangible lustre. The wind moaned through the rigging and slapped a halyard now and then against the foremast with a sharp, vicious sound. Again a wave broke on the bow and sent a swish of stinging spray the length of the ship. We rolled and tossed and pitched, and there seemed no safe beacon to guide us. For a moment we could see a dim shape at the bow (or was it fancy?), a deeper bit of gloom across the bridge moved, or seemed to move. A dim awesome figure draped in so'wester and greatcoat, crouched half over, turned and turned back and returned a wheel. And those three shades, those three scarcely human figures, working in accord, but in grim silence, control the destinies of fifty men.

But there, you see them all now, one after the other, at the wheel, at the bow, on the bridge, and they all look ahead to a streak of fainter black. It is the east! They take shape now—the lookout, the helmsman and the officer on watch. Suddenly there is a gruff growl forward, "Sail on the starboard bow, sir." It is beyond our sight. Another growl, "Aye," from the bridge. For a time the light seems to grow from the sea, then from the horizon all around, and the dawn is breaking. At last you see the sail, too. The officer crosses to your side of the bridge and holds out a binocular. "Headed this way, sir." You wish that you too could growl "Aye," for, although a landlubber, you are dressed in so'wester and oilers, and feel a veritable dog of the sea. But you can't, because all that you can see is a little black speck bobbing up and down, down and up, upon the horizon. The light grows and the speck takes shape. Even to you this little schooner appears to be very small to be so far at sea. Off the starboard bow you see that she is under double reefed mainsail, brailed foresail, jib and staysail—stripped right down to next to nothing. She makes heavy weather of it, and you are very glad that you ride where you do. She carries a foreyard, has an elliptical stern, and is evidently a French fishing boat bound for the Grand Banks. You shiver a little and ruminate upon the unequal fortunes of men, then turn again to the east with a prayer for the fisherman's luck. The dawn spreads and the binnacle light is doused. The lookout bobs up and down, now clear against the sky, now dim against the sea. The misty, burning daylight fades, and the little wind clouds overhead are pink. The night is past, another day has dawned.

August 28th

Lat. Obs. 50° 5′	Lat. Acct. 49° 52′ N.
Long. Obs. 16° 33′ W.	Long. Acct. 16° 50′ W.
T. Course N. 71° E.	Barom. 30.22
Distance, 258 miles	Thermo. 60°
Dist. per Log, 279 miles	Water 61°
	Maximum roll Pt. 17°
	St. 13°

Distance from Battery, 2,659 miles.
Distance from Liverpool, 571 miles.
Distance from Fastnet, 271 miles.

The last three days have been very much alike—fair weather, smooth sea, and the *Wakiva* steaming about twelve knots, so that we made good about 280 miles per day. We amused ourselves as best we could, finally resorting to practical jokes on each other to keep up spirits and while the days away.

A large school of porpoises kept abreast of us to-day and quite near for a long time, then suddenly disappeared. I wonder if they enjoy life as much as they seem to. They appear always to be playing at some tumbling game, and one cannot help believing it must be great sport.

There are many sea gulls astern now, and the pleasant little stormy petrels or Mother Carey's chickens have deserted or been driven off. Late in the afternoon we passed a steamer outward bound, without a wireless rig, for which we were thankful, for there was no chance of her refusing our call as so many other ships have done. After coffee and Grand Opera a la Victrola, we played a rubber of auction, but eventually found our various ways to the bridge to watch falling stars. The night was very black all about, but brilliant overhead. Suddenly a signal light flashed very near us from the sea. As we did not reply at once and were not prepared to answer as she fell astern, she circled and followed, flashing her impatient call for attention all the while. We tried to raise her by wireless without result. Captain Grant ordered the flag hoisted and a light thrown upon it. It looked very pretty, our flag at the masthead, whipping in the light, with the dark night and a British cruiser astern. We at last explained our identity and business by the code, and in turn asked who she was, but the only answer we received was a rather fretful and snappy "Good-night." She doused her lights and disappeared. It was rather weird standing there at the after rail and wondering whether she had turned and resumed her course or whether she still followed with watchful eyes.

We tried auction again, but when Bush bid three clubs and was doubled, and Reed, his partner, bid four clubs to take him out, as he said, and was doubled, the game was abandoned for the night.

August 29th

During the morning we sighted a British cruiser with two stacks, but she ignored us. Kept grimly on her way, probably under orders.

At 1:45 P.M. we passed Fastnet and asked the lighthouse keeper, via wireless, as to weather conditions in the Irish Sea in general and about harbor mines in particular. He told us to "ask further up," which is undoubtedly better than telling us to "go below." Later he said he might tell us for five shillings, but he didn't. At four or five we passed Galley Head Light. It was getting rather thick in the Irish Sea. Some say the Irish Sea is always thick, but Bush says that this is not so. About this time we set our proper flags—the New York Yacht Club burgee and the panther on the red field, our private signal, and the Stars and Stripes, brand new and sassy, in honor of the Emerald Isle—also to dress ourselves a little, and rigged signal halyards. Passed many fishing dories and whaleboats, gulls and longbeaks.

The fog which had long threatened shut down upon us then and we lost all trace of land. We went along for some time at slow speed, when the bells signaled stop, then full speed astern. A rocky shore loomed cruel and threatening dead ahead. "Hard a port," the order floated to us from the bridge; slowly we stopped and backed away. The watch reported eleven fathoms, and the double guns of Daunt's Rock boomed regularly two by two. Straight upon our course again we proceeded cautiously until the fog lifted. Then we boomed along at full speed for old Kinsale and Cork Harbor. There was plenty to see now—the rocky coast and light house, here and there a trawler to port or a full rigged ship to starboard. We plied merrily between starboard and port, port and starboard, eager to see everything, particularly the square rigged *Russian* under our lee, going light into Queenstown for orders. She was a beautiful sight; her square sails towering tier on tier, her rugged crew at the stern. We saluted and she replied. The signal "pilot wanted" fluttered at the truck, and a little red-sailed clipper yawl bore down upon us, a small boat fell away and brought our pilot to us. He was a comely lad and jolly, with a bright eye and a ragged beard, a pleasant smile, which was most contagious when he talked—for he had a brogue thicker than the fog off Kinsale.

He gave us papers—Cork papers—the latest he had, but they were four days old. The pilot had hardly warmed the bridge with his sunny presence when a dapper little black side-wheeler came flying at us with all kinds of signals and harbor patrol flags set and a frantic "stop" waving from her signal halyards. We stopped. She was called the *Flying Fox*, but looked more like a flying fish—her wheel boxes like ill-developed wings.

There was some talk through megaphones from bridge to bridge. "Lower your hoist," from the *Flying Fox*. "Lower your hoist," from the bridge. The crew started to lower the wireless aerial hoist. "Hoist E X," from the *Flying Fox*. "Hoist E X," from the bridge. The crew looked for "E X" amongst the signal flags. "Make haste with the signals," from the *Flying Fox*. "Hurry up with those signals," from the bridge. The crew made haste, and the flags soon went up and the hoist came down.

"All right, *Wakiva*," from the *Flying Fox*. "Aye, aye," from the bridge. A bell jingled and we gathered speed and slipped in between two miniature Gibraltars and dropped anchor in the outer harbor of Queenstown or Cork Harbor. We could go no further, for the sun had set and there were regulations and great guns on the cliffs, showing black against the crimson sky.

Later, when it was quite dark, searchlights swept the harbor all night long, while other lights shone straight and steady, opposing a bar of light to entrance and exit alike. During the night a steamer slipped in and anchored beside us, as we knew by the rattle of her cable and the new red and white lights between the shore and us. The lights of Queenstown twinkled and winked in mockery, for they seemed to know that we were marooned upon our ship.

August 30th

Shortly after sunrise the *Wakiva* moved up Cork Harbor and anchored off Queenstown, so that when we came on deck we were very near the little houses bordering the quay, and the glass was hardly needed to read the names above the doors of the various shops and "publics." There were many O's and Mc's, but no McHose for, as we afterwards learned, the McHoses are from the north of Ireland, which fact added nothing to our popularity with the barmaids.

We loafed around the decks waiting for the customs people impatiently, eager to be off. The little town was so near, and beckoned to us so charmingly, that we resented the delay. However, the pilot volunteered the information that as it was Sunday and all the Irish are a deeply religious people, they were probably all at church, and the customs people no doubt along with them.

Nevertheless the town and harbor were well worth the attention we were forced to bestow upon them from the water side. In spots it was almost Italian in its picturesque disorder; tiny pitched-roofed houses seemed to crawl one upon the other, built as they were, terrace upon terrace, with broken chimney pots and with flowers and wicker cages in the windows; some houses were red or blue, while others were pink or green or yellow, like flowers splashed over an emerald hill. To the left the town proper was more imposing, with its substantial buildings and paved streets, the most important of which is called the Beach, and is a pleasant promenade, where there is a band stand and a yacht club.

At last the customs' tug put out and slowly came alongside, and in due course we were granted permission to go ashore. But the launch would not work and there was further delay. Eventually we went ashore in the four-oared gig commanded by the second officer. We walked about the little streets for a while, while Harry arranged for a motor to come to us from Cork. And then to pass the time we all clambered into a jaunting car and drove through the town and over the hills.

At last our car arrived and we were off. All the way to Cork the road follows the River Lee, beginning at a point opposite the Naval Station. It is a lovely ride of ten miles through parks and meadows, the silver thread of the river flashing upon us from unexpected places. The railroads and bridges were all guarded by troops, and Ireland held quite a martial look. The men tolerated us, but the girls all smiled at us. It seems that every woman in Ireland wears a smile along with her bonnet and tailored suit and flat-heeled shoes.

Harry arranged in Cork that we should motor to Dublin, so we made the run back to Queenstown at good speed. We were eager to be off and scarcely glanced at the huts and colleens, the pigs and chickens as we passed, but as it turned out our haste was wasted. We were refused permission from the authorities, and as they said we would very likely be shot by an over-zealous sentry and would certainly be arrested and put in quod upon our arrival in Dublin, we decided to stick to the ship.

As we weighed anchor the sun slowly made its way nearer and nearer to the horizon, and the bells pealed their clangerous notes from many belfries; but to us the various sounds floated gently and more gently as the white line gathered at our bow and we set our course for England.

August 31st

We are nearing Liverpool, our objective as far as the yacht is concerned, and the Irish Sea is full of traffic. Everywhere are important little patrols, flying their flags jauntily and crossing close under our bows. Some signal us and then wig-wag the others. We are permitted to continue for a time without other hindrance than frequent hails and repeated questions shouted through megaphones.

The steamship *Aquitania* passed quite close, with her bow stove in from a recent collision. Then followed the *Finland* and *Warwickshire* in quick succession before we slowed up to take a pilot aboard. This did not take long, and again we gathered speed and slipped by the Northwest Lightship, Holyhead Light and Scarry-Light-Bar Lightship in rapid succession. The Irish Sea is well dotted with steam trawlers and fishing smacks, with here and there a larger craft.

This must be a treacherous coast in fog or storm, as the channel is tortuous and marked here and there with the skeletons of weather-worn ships, piled and broken on the frequent bars. A little beyond Mona's Isle another patrol crossed our bows and signaled that she wished to board us. As other fussy little fellows panted up from all quarters, in a few minutes we were surrounded by patrols—one quite picturesque, with two red-sailed fishermen in tow, with huge Union Jacks flying from their mastheads. We were instructed to go abreast Buoy No. 5 and stop. We did so, and after some maneuvering the little steamer came alongside and an officer scrambled aboard. He went at once to the captain's cabin and soon came out looking a bit sheepish. He had failed to find that which he had expected to find, and for a little while we did not know what he was looking for. We went on, the signal flags flashing in the sunlight from bridge to bridge. We continued on up the Mersey and found much of interest on all sides.

Two men in a row boat came alongside. We passed them a line, which they carried to the dock. We were soon made fast and warped into a canal, where we became two sticks and a funnel in a forest of sticks and funnels reaching mile upon mile each side of the Mersey. The engines had long ceased their thrum and we tied up for the night.

We looked at each other with a question in our eyes, "Well, we are here; what then?"

2. Homeward Bound and an Equinoctial Gale

On September 8, after an all-night ride from London, we were "back to the ship," and glad of it. We had learned to love the *Wakiva* and preferred our more or less quiet smoke-room to all the grills and supper clubs in London. Then, too, it was Monday, and a new excise regulation went into effect in London that night, closing the public houses and restaurants at eleven; but there were no excise regulations on the *Wakiva*.

We slept a good deal that day and that night.

All night we plied merrily along the Irish Coast and passed the Island of Rathlin in a mist which toward dawn shut down in a thick fog, and then we went on at reduced speed and, tide-driven, lost our way. Capt. Grant could not reconcile the lights with his charts, and after going many miles up a Scotch loch we turned and went back and made a fresh start.

Last night the sunset was opalescent; this morning the sunrise was crimson and all above the Scotch coast was a faint glow of heather painted by the newly-risen sun and the half-spent moon.

Each sunrise sees a newly-awakened world, and it was good there upon the bridge to watch the coast unfold and the shadows disappear.

It rained all afternoon, but toward evening we saw rainbow after rainbow, some small, some large. One seemed a complete circle and reached almost to the ship herself.

Then there were three at one time, two together and a smaller one above. We repeated the sailor's doggerel:

> "Rainbow in the morning,
> Sailors, take warning;
> Rainbow at night,
> Sailors' delight,"

and confidently looked for fair weather on the morrow.

That night we were hailed again and questioned by the code. We answered in kind and then tried the wireless. For once we raised a response. It was the British cruiser *Pelorus*.

September 10, 1914

Lat. Obs. 55° 30′ N.   Dist., 259 miles
Long. Obs. 14° 24′ W.   Dist. per Log, 267 miles
T. Course N. 89° W.
    Distance from Liverpool, 459 miles.
Fresh S. S. W. to W.   Gale
    N.W.   Short, high sea

We have lost all faith in doggerels.

In the early morning, before dawn, the wind freshened, and at sunrise it blew a gale, which, in turn, kicked up a short, nasty sea. We rolled 36 deg. to starboard and 17 deg. to port. About noon it cleared and the sun came out, but the sea continued high and we had luncheon in the smoke room, in hand.

Waves break continuously over the bow and sweep the length of the deck with swishing, stinging spray. The sacked coal on the after deck has shifted and gives us a bad list to starboard. Wild-cat waves pile aboard on the beam now and then. The sea is running two or three ways at once.

At 2 P.M. the sun was put out by black rain clouds, and squall followed squall.

We dined in the smoke room, as it was uncomfortable below. Bush did not dine with us. Harry and I played rum after dinner and improvised a system of elastics to keep our cards on the table. From time to time one or the other of us slides the width of the cabin in his chair. Reed is trying to read. Speed has been reduced and we are making heavy weather of it.

About 11:30 Bush joined us in his pajamas and with bare feet. He said his cabin was flooded out, but nobody paid any attention to this. We put his feet in the sleeves of his sweater and covered him up with overcoats. Bush curled up on the couch opposite Reed and tried to stay there. Once he dozed and we all thought he had broken his collar-bone, if not his neck, as he shot from his perch as though hurled by a catapult.

About midnight one of the stewards stuck his head in at the door. "Commodore, one of the after bathrooms is flooded," he said.

"Well, bail it out then," Harry said.

He went below. We finished our game.

When it was finished, Harry and I went below. As we stood at the companionway we looked upon a surprising scene. Six or eight men, trousers rolled up, were working knee-deep in water, as it seemed for their lives. There was a door leading to the main deck on my left. As I watched, a wave crashed against it and the water poured in from below and above and on the sides—green, angry water. We rushed to the boat deck and looked down to the deck below. Men worked waist deep in churning, angry water, heaving sacks of coal overboard, while the waves pounded upon us and climbed aboard. The engines had long since ceased to hum. Black clouds hurried overhead, now obscuring the moon, and again scurrying off in frenzy, and stars and moon looked down coldly from between the rifts. The wind roared and shrieked through the rigging, the waves beat us with a hollow, drum-like sound. Occasionally an officer gave a sharp word of command, in a calm, reassuring voice. They were splendid, these officers, and those men, too, and fit to serve with Captain Grant—the calmest, most courageous of them all.

September 11

About four o'clock Captain Grant called us to the bridge to see the storm, which was then at its highest. The *Wakiva* lay hove to in the trough and rolled first one way, then another, the waves breaking on the starboard side and sweeping clear across her decks. The men still worked waist deep on the after deck. About a third of the sacked coal had been thrown over and they were stowing the rest in the bunkers.

We left the smoke-room and, holding fast to the rail, ran forward between rolls, and finally won our way to the bridge. Overhead were the stars and now and then the moon, but always the black clouds. It was very dark when the clouds obscured the moon. The wind whistled and shrieked through the rigging, so that we must shout to be heard. Add to this the boom of the waves breaking upon us. Then a furious squall broke, the rain came down in sheets and the wind increased in velocity. It blew so hard that it held both the siren and steam whistle open. The one shrieked continuously, while the other was more annoying because of its unvaried roar. The wireless short-circuited aloft and added its crackle to the din. The wind blew 80 miles and we rolled 48 deg. to port and 25 deg. to starboard. Sometimes on the port roll it seemed as though the *Wakiva* never could right herself, and I for one held my breath. It was glorious there upon the bridge, with the wind and the rain, the black night and the pounding waves, but awesome; and we seemed very little there in midocean, with no answer to our wireless and no possibility of successfully launching the boats. Our only hope was the *Wakiva*, and she did not fail us. Relieved of the unaccustomed weight of coal and water, and on her natural lines again, she rose like a gull to each wave.

During all this time the gulls circled slowly about, craning their necks in curiosity and calling their shrill calls back and forth. One lighted and bobbed about on the waves under our lee, and seemed absolutely at a loss to understand our object in lying there hove-to so long. Several little stormy petrels came aboard and rested while our engines were idle.

At dawn, Captain Grant put her on her course again. It was a ticklish job to point her nose into those big waves, but slowly, patiently, he did it, ever watching the combers rushing down upon us from the northwest. There was some trouble with the steering gear on the bridge, and two men at the wheel aft kept her to her course.

During the afternoon we again lay to, while four men on the bowsprit, silhouetted against the sky, bobbed about perilously. The bobstay had parted in the terrible pounding we had undergone during the darkness.

The sunset that evening was dreadfully magnificent. The west was blue and gold and crimson, capped by black storm clouds. The largest of these gradually took shape and appeared to be a monstrous dragon, crouched and ready to spring, its jaws extended and open, and spitting fire and smoke and dripping blood.

September 13th, 1914

Lat. Obs. 53° 5′ N.	Dist., 243 miles
Long Obs. 29° 25′ W.	Dist. per Log, 246 miles
T. Course S. 82° W.	

Distance from Liverpool, 1,023 miles.

Barom., 29.50	Var., 32° W.
Thermo., 51°	

Varying winds and high seas 8 to 9 A. M. Kept away to the northward to secure the bowsprit for the third time.

After a few hours' respite the storm broke again with renewed fury. It was very dirty weather and we were continuously enveloped in a mist of driving rain and whirling spray and spume, while the wind howled through the creaking rigging with hurricane force. There was more trouble with the steering gear, and it took four men at the wheel aft to keep her to her course.

During the afternoon a wild-cat wave climbed aboard and submerged the boat deck with green water. This meant that the main deck was completely flooded. We have stopped twice to try and save the bowsprit, which is very shaky, when the wind was at its greatest velocity. Speed was first reduced to six knots and then reduced again, so that we barely had steerageway. Eight sailors struggled the greatest part of the afternoon with the trisails, which, although furled, were chafing badly.

We have quite a hospital list. One sailor was stabbed in Liverpool, another sprained his ankle while showing off at Brighton, and there are several strains and wrenched joints received in the effort to lighten ship. We watched the sun go down, eagerly seeking some sign of better weather, but there was little promise in it. It looked cold and hard and cast a long ray across the sea, which painted the crests of the huge waves a transparent green, surmounted by angry combers, while the surface of the sea seemed to boil and churn as the wind whipped the spray in whirling mist.

At noon we were a poor half way to Cape Race, and making very little headway.

We awoke next morning to find a nasty, choppy, criss-cross sea, which attacked us from every quarter. The wind was heavy and supplemented by heavy squalls, and we are again running at half speed. It is the seventh day of wind and storm, and we are growing a little peevish. Even the old saw:

"Long foretold, long last,
Short notice, soon past."

has failed us, for one rarely sees a more sudden drop of the glass
than that which we had on the thirteenth; but this storm is now two
days old and no sign of abatement.

We had more trouble with the bowsprit and four sailors were
ordered out to fix it. While they were bobbing perilously between
sea and sky, the helmsman went to sleep or, at any rate, forgot
himself long enough to allow a huge wave to completely submerge
them. They were buried in the swirling sea for a long time, as it
seemed, before they came to the surface. It was almost a miracle that
they were not washed away, but happily all held tight and were none
the worse for their wetting. But I am sorry for the helmsman.

September 17, 1914

Lat. Obs. 47° 15′ N.   T. Course S. 64° W.
Long. Obs. 50° 11′ W.   Dist., 270 miles
        Distance per Log, 281 miles.
        Distance from Liverpool, 1,894 miles.
        Distance to Cape Race, 117 miles.
        Light to strong N. E. winds.
        Moderate to high northerly swell.

The night was so lovely and we felt so well that we stayed up to
celebrate. It was a very quiet sort of a celebration, however, more
of a happy sense of good feeling that made us loath to say good
night, so we kept putting it off until dawn, and then it was too late
to say good night. We spent the early morning on the bridge taking
observations of the sun through the sextant, and we grew during that
time particularly fond of Captain Grant's favorite instrument—the
"Grand Daddy Glass"—as he called it.

We passed very near a little fisherman over a hundred miles from
shore, anchored and pitching and rolling in the sea. Everything
appeared to be battened down and there was no sign of life aboard.
We wondered how she rode the storm and soon left her far astern.
Then we passed a large tramp steamer going East, and as nothing
else appeared upon the horizon we went to bed.

About 4 P.M. we ran into a heavy northeast gale, previously
reported via wireless from Cape Race. At 7 P.M. waves were breaking
over our starboard quarter, the decks and bridge were enveloped in

a whirl of spray and mist, the wind howled and screeched again through the rigging and water seeped in through the smoke-room door, making everything wet and sodden. It was impossible to play cards there in comfort, so we adjourned to my cabin, where the roll seemed less.

Speed was reduced again about dark, and at 9 o'clock the engines barely turned enough to keep headway. We read aloud a little; then the others tried to sleep while Harry and I tried to while away the long hours between two and five at rum. We placed a pillow on a chair between us, tied strings about it criss-cross fashion, to hold the cards, and struggled through two games. It was tedious work, but it served to shorten those long hours before the dawn.

Bush lay across my bed (it was impossible to stay in it lengthwise). Each roll pitched him forward an inch or two. First his feet hung over the edge, then his knees, but the pressure woke him and he hitched back again to begin the sliding process all over. We watched him, thinking each roll would throw him out, but it did not. He always woke just in time to save himself, much to our disappointment.

September 18, 1914

Lat. Obs. 46° 55′ N.   Dist., 173 miles.
Long. Obs. 53° 33′ W.   Max. Roll, 45° Port
T. Course, Various
   Distance from Liverpool, 2,067 miles.
   9 P. M. 17th inst. Hove to account of dangerous sea caused by a heavy N. E. gale of equinocetial force.
   Beaufort scale 9–10.
   5 A. M. Proceeded cautiously.
   2 P. M. Anchored in St. Mary's Harbor to await fine weather.

At dawn we went upon the bridge, and it was ticklish work getting there. We still rolled 45 deg. to starboard and we lay practically hove-to. During the hours between nine last night and six this morning we made eight miles. Eight miles in nine hours, when tired and worn with the buffeting, every minute was agony to us.

At dawn the storm still raged and the horizon was black with hate, and there seemed no hope of respite, but Captain Grant stood there beside us on the bridge quiet and contained. We were greatly impressed by his resourcefulness and confidence. He seems to know the dangers of the sea; there is no blind flaunting of fate here, but a quiet sense of confidence and a serene trust in God.

After that we went to bed with our clothes on and, after a long time, a very long time, we fell asleep and awoke in a land-locked harbor. The *Wakiva* rode quietly, with the faintest motion which seemed reminiscent of childish lullabies, while overhead the wind still screamed through the rigging. We had found St. Marys and safety.

St. Marys harbor is a perfect shelter. Many fishermen, steam and sail, have anchored here, driven from the Grand Banks. Far out to sea one can see the white caps rushing over and upon each other. It looks like a rapids out there beyond the bar.

We have found shelter in a fiord-like bay, surrounded by rugged hills of granite, heavily timbered. There are a few patches of lighter green, where the tilled fields contrast pleasantly with the dark forests. In a sheltered valley a number of white houses cluster round a steeple, and there are a few boats and seines upon the beach. It is a poor fishing village, but a gay metropolis was never more welcome.

There was a Scotch mist all afternoon and at dark a heavy fog shut down upon us. We fished a little and caught two cod. We did not weigh them. Confidentially, it did not seem worth while. After dinner we fished again around a light reflected in the waters of the bay, but without result.

September 19

We had planned to breakfast in New London this morning, but we have ceased to plan and have taken Destiny by the hand. May she lead us there at her own good pleasure, but may the time be short.

We left St. Marys at 7:30 A.M., and for many miles paralleled the rugged coast line. Then we shot across an open stretch—out of sight of land, but under the lee of Newfoundland and in comparatively smooth water—to Grand and Little Miquelon and St. Pierre. It was rather cold and we had snow flurries during the morning.

We have quit our deep-sea work and are yachting again. Land is nearly always in sight and it is a picturesque coast, particularly between bald St. Pierre and pretty little Miquelon.

Here, between the islands, we had a famous brush with a fishing schooner. She held us for a long time, the water boiling at her bow; and, finally, to shake her off we must needs call for another pound of steam.

Toward dusk we had a rebel sky, all gray and gold, and a sunset like a thousand suns.

September 20, 1914

Lat. Obs. 46° 10′ N.   T. Course, Various
Long. Obs. 60° 12′ W.   Dist., 285 miles
    6:45 A. M., Sept. 19. Left St. Mary's, N. F.
    9:22 A. M., Sept. 20. Anchored at North Sydney,
Cape Breton Island, to receive pratique.
    10 A. M. Proceeded to South Sydney.
    10:55 A. M. Anchored near the Royal Cape
Breton Yacht Club. Fresh to moderate and light
N. N. E. to W. N. W. winds. Moderating sea and
fine, clear weather throughout.

Everything seemed good to us as we lay off North Sydney, Nova Scotia. The dirty colliers inshore and the battered tramps at anchor offshore, the steam whistles and the clanging trolley gongs and the songs of birds formed a colorful symphony to our ears, accustomed to the boom of waves and the shrieks of wind and gulls. The green fields and the trees beckoned us to come ashore and rest in the quiet shade, away from tumbling seas and storm and stress.

As we watched the bustling life on land, all sounds ceased or were drowned save one; the mellow church bells tolled their message to the devout. A thin line of little children, attended by two sisters in nuns' black livery, stopped and bowed their heads in prayer, then went on again a few steps, stopped and prayed again, until at last they disappeared into pleasant seminary grounds and were lost to our view. But as the bells still chimed we fancied them, although hidden, stopping every little way to bow their heads and pray again.

Next day, as both gangs were up for the coal barges alongside, we went ashore in the launch, getting into her by way of the jacob's ladder over the stern.

Sydney is a dry town and is famous for its joy rides, sheriffs and huckleberry bushes.

We left Sydney at 5 A.M. on the 22d, dropped down the river to North Sydney and stood for the fairway beyond. We passed many fishing boats, whale and sword fishermen, and a steamer piled high on a reef, with a wrecking tug standing by. She was too far off for us to make her out, but appeared to be a goodly tramp. After dinner we stood at the rail on the boat deck doing our regular twenty-minute shift after meals, when we heard a hail from the sea. It seemed very near, almost under the starboard bow. We all looked eagerly in the direction whence it seemed to come, but could see nothing, although our deck lights brightened the sea for a considerable distance. It was probably a fisherman in his dory, a long way from his ship, as there was but one light visible, and that a mile or more away on the landward side.

For a while we delayed upon the bridge and waved our searchlight, swinging it here and there, high and low. We picked up a small steamer outward bound and, finding nothing else, soon gave it up. Shortly afterward we were in turn picked up by another search, a red light crossed our bow and then turned to green—it was evidently a coast patrol—and beyond that was a brilliant headlight. These two talked to each other with the Morse, but they did not bother us and soon disappeared in the night. Once we caught the gleam of sails and fancied them fishermen converted for patrol duty. That night we had a most wonderful exhibition. The sky in the north seemed to reflect the lights of a huge city, while overhead the stars gleamed in cold serenity. Suddenly this glow resolved into huge streamers which seemed to come from the sea; they moved and changed and disappeared and reappeared in a bewildering fashion, as though the searchlights from a hundred ships played upon the sky. Captain Grant hurried from the bridge to tell us of this phenomenon of nature, the Aurora Borealis. For hours we watched its constant play, but at last it faded and disappeared. Bed and sleep were out of the question after this brilliant display, and we sat there on deck in the lee of a lifeboat, silent, subdued by the grandeur of it all, when suddenly someone discovered a star larger than the others and followed by a wide tail of misty light. We found it with the glasses and watched it for a long time, as it seemed to squirm and twist in the sky like a snake.

September 23 was a dreamy day when land and sea seemed kin. There was very little to do but loaf and doze and enjoy the quiet charm of it all. Late in the forenoon a little bird came aboard. It seemed quite tame and hopped and fluttered about and picked at the crumbs we threw it, drank a little water, obligingly posed for the movies and then flew off again. During the afternoon we sighted whale-spouts. The count varied considerably; there were certainly two, and we all agreed that there were not more than five whales in our immediate ocean.

Bush and I were compelled to stomach considerable chaffing about our comet, particularly regarding its method of squirming like a snake in the sky, therefore it gives us both quite a lot of pleasure to quote the following clipping from a newspaper of September 30, announcing the discovery of a new comet by Professor Clarence T. Haggerty. He said the comet was visible to the naked eye and gave its position. 'Nough said; we discovered the comet three nights before Haggerty.

September 24

We lay off Cape Cod in a thick blanket of fog from 3:30 A.M. until 1:30 P.M., and while the astronomers slept the Commodore and the Pilot of the River of Doubt caught forty fish. Some of them must have weighed at least 10 pounds; even we admitted that, although we were compelled to listen to much odious comparison between tangible fish and intangible comets. We, however, finally admitted the fish, their heft, and supplemented this by adding that they, the two mentioned above, were not half so much fishermen as they were dog catchers. The entire kennel, I mean catch, the entire forty (including the 10-pounder), were dog fish.

Under way again we passed Pollock Rip lightship, and one of our torpedoboat destroyers followed us. At the Shovelful we still led her by a few lengths, but at Handkerchief she forged ahead and soon left us far astern.

Near Shovelful lightship we passed two schooners outward bound, one a five-master and the other a six-master. Everything was set and they made a wonderful picture racing for the fairway within a few boat lengths of each other. The smaller one led. The sun was bright and painted their towering canvas in silver. It was a beautiful sight and one rarely to be met with. We were all inclined to turn and watch the struggle, but we were homeward bound and there were old landmarks to fill our eyes, Vineyard Haven, Woods Hole and Gay Head.

That night we rode at anchor off New London.

The Last Day

At New London we cleared the customs, passed the medical examination and then went ashore. We were rather stiff and a little dizzy on land, and we all seemed to step pretty high. Reed got a haircut, then we all did some telephoning, and had a couple of American cocktails (I must look that word "couple" up in a dictionary and find out what it really means). Late in the forenoon we went aboard again and made our way to Larchmont. As we bore away in the club launch and the lights of the good ship *Wakiva* slowly receded and finally lost their identity in a host of other lights—we were all silent and thoughtful. It was the end of our cruise, many happy days had slipped from us and would never again be repeated, except in pleasant dreams.

1942

San Pedro to Key West in Wartime

Charles Peterson

Following her duties in the movie Captains Courageous, *a Gloucester schooner makes an unusual passage under Capt. Sterling Hayden*

The "Admiral Benbow Inn" of this narrative was on 52nd Street, New York. It was there, on April 10th, 1942, that this sea-hungry writer met Sterling Hayden and, over lunch, discussed signing on with him for his forthcoming voyage from San Pedro, California, to the West Indies.

For many years I had dreamed, connived, annoyed yacht brokers, visited boatyards. I had tried to trade my farm for a ketch and had almost driven the good wife silly with my plans. Frustration had dogged every attempt to get away and now, in the tinkling of an 'ighball, the whole thing was arranged. What possessed this best of sailors to make me ten per cent of his crew—me, a sailor of 17-foot sneakboxes and 27-foot sloops—I cannot imagine unless it was that he saw in my eyes that fanatical glint which so often helps compensate for ignorance. Besides, I am a carpenter of sorts, and willing as hell.

My own problem was that, in order to make the voyage possible I must sell a magazine article and this I did that same afternoon—an article and color photographs on the new Caribbean Maritime Commission and the return to sail for wartime cargo work.

The ship was the 120-foot Gloucester schooner *Oretha F. Spinney* which had been lying in San Pedro Harbor since her part in *Captains Courageous* in 1936–37. Hayden had just bought her.

Just one week later, Sterling met me in Miami and we spent three dull days there waiting for the Bahamian crew to arrive from Nassau, where he had rounded them up. We visited the pawn shops, looking for binoculars and a chronometer, went swimming at the Bath Club, and finally got the crew off the plane and onto a bus for the cross-country trip to California. (Not a word about that nightmare of five-minute meals, constant changing of buses and rechecking of bags.) Finally, to arrive in San Pedro and set foot on the ship, grimy as she was from years of neglect, was like entering a cool theater in August and relaxing with a movie of the South Seas.

And now meet the crew as they emerge from the fo'c'sle for the first day's work, in dungarees in place of the store clothes of the last five days. They are all black but one. Their faces are interesting.

Granville Conolly, Mate, Grand Cayman, 46, 5' 10";
Cyril Jones, Engineer, Jamaica, 38, 5' 9";
James Lightbourne, A.B., Turk's Island, 39, 5' 9";
Richard Mitchell, A.B., Abaco, 23, 6' 2";
Bruce Green, A.B., Abaco, 32, 5' 8";
Bertram Bevans, A.B., Andros, 27, 6' 3";
Joe Williams, Cook, San Salvador, 41, 5' 7";
Wm. Grist, A.B., Nassau, 17, 5' 10", white.

The next thirteen days were spent at the endless jobs necessary in fitting out a schooner for sea. Bo's'n's chairs were rigged first and several of the crew worked for days until the spars were all scraped and greased, the standing rigging tarred, lanyards set up, blocks repaired and running gear rove. Decks were scrubbed, galley stove relined and polished, water tanks cleaned and refilled. Grist and I, working from a skiff, spaded off the barnacles. I went to work removing a rotted 18-foot section of covering board and refitting a new one around the bulwark stanchions. At this point, I would like to get in my little say with the opinion that the Gloucester shipbuilders, excellent as they are in their general design, gave no thought to ventilation of hull. They seemed to make a point of ceiling the hulls up tight, thus making them an easy prey to dry rot.

I sorted out bo's'n's stores and built parts cabinets and tool racks. The "Chief" overhauled the six-cylinder Bessemer Diesel. Sterling was busy at the chandler's, the port and Navy authorities, swinging ship for deviation, and untangling red tape. This finally unraveled enough, on May 9th, to allow the *Spinney* to sail for San Diego and hauling out.

We were soon jogging along to a light breeze and feeling the deck heave to the swells outside. The watches were arranged (four on and four off) and I found myself at sea at last and actually at the wheel, a thrill for this long-thwarted-land-bound-son-of-Norway. The first night shut down, and I do not think I went to sleep for watching the phosphorescent bow wave or listening to the water, separated from me by five inches of plank and ceiling, gurgling by my bunk. And I venture that Sterling himself must have been thrilled, seasoned old salt that he is, for this was his own ship, his own command.

Dawn found us off San Diego. By mid-morning we were started up the ways and were high and dripping by afternoon. All hands anxiously awaited a sight of the hull but they were hardly prepared for the perfect specimen of Gloucester fisherman they found in the 21-year-old *Spinney*. Every seam was smooth and even, every plank like rock. Word got around and we soon had a steady stream of admiring visitors, some of them native Californians come to scoff at something from the effete East, but knowing when they left that they had seen one of the sweetest sailing hull designs ever turned out.

One-third of the rudder was gone but that was an easy job for the yard. All she needed was scraping, painting and some seam cement here and there—or so we thought at the time. In two days, we finished her bottom work and she went down the ways again, ready for sea at last and waiting only the official sanction to be off.

Just as we were about to sail for Panama, the first misadventure occurred. I had gone to town for my supply of color film for the magazine story. Sterling greeted me on the dock with: "Got some bad news for you; the officials say positively no cameras allowed to enter the Canal Zone."

"Good Lord! What'll I do?" was my first reaction.

"We can leave your outfit with my mother and have her ship it to the next port after Panama and do the pictures then," Sterling volunteered.

And so the complete kit, except for meter and lens-shade, was deposited in Mrs. Hayden's car and we cast off. Only a photographer can feel the irony of my position: a cruise like this, in the saltiest of schooners, with nothing to record it. I thought of the scenes I had planned—close-ups of the crew's faces; their sweating bodies hauling on a halliard; the play of sunlight and shadow on rigging and sail; some mountainous seas and tropical sunsets—oh, well, write your own ticket. I hoped for the best but I went about like a robot.

By late afternoon we had the four lowers on her and were running before a northwest breeze which was to hold fairly steady for several days. There was a heavy ground swell, too, which gave the ship some motion, and, by early evening, a third of the crew, including myself, were acquiring that apathetic stare and clammy feeling that comes with the first day out. A few doses of medicine fixed us up, and there was no more of that for the rest of the voyage.

On the second morning came catastrophe number two. I had just turned in at eight o'clock when Sterling sent for me and told me to look in the lazarette. I crawled in and saw what every sailor dreads above all: sea water sloshing around, running down the horn timbers. The devilish part of it was that the leak was concealed under a ceiling of 2½″ oak securely spiked down by master shipbuilders. There was only one thing to do. After three hours of work with auger and chisel, in the reclining position enforced by three-foot headroom, I had a large pile of firewood ready for the galley and considerable stern planking exposed—but no gaping hole to plug. We drove oakum all around the sternpost and down the horn timbers. Two hours of prodigious labor and we emerged at two o'clock into the dazzling sunshine, proud as schoolboys of our success.

Now came a long succession of beautiful days, bringing most of the things I had always wanted to see and experience—flying fish (they really do fly), schools of porpoises, tropical clouds, and that complete detachment from the world that comes only after many days at sea, with no news, no radio, no passing ships. An occasional squall, presaged by a surpassingly ornate sky worthy of Homer, might vary the routine. The crew would don oilskins, ready for action should the disturbance be severe enough to require it. When the squall hit, the *Spinney* would heel over just so far and sail like a Cup boat, rail awash, the skipper at the helm nursing her along with a firm and practiced hand. The torrents of rain accompanying these squalls made a perfect shower bath (in which soap would lather!) and we always took advantage of the opportunity.

After a week of fair winds, we reached the Doldrums. Days of slatting and motor work netted about seven knots. We did not stream a log. Accustomed to judging speed by eye alone on his many long voyages, Sterling could estimate ours within half a knot. Sure enough, I found myself becoming accurate in the part of human speedometer. To test our estimates, I dropped a piece of paper off the bow, counting seconds until the helmsman signaled its arrival at the stern. I am sure we would be in the regions of the Doldrums still were it not for the Diesel, for that part of the world is the worst of the seven seas for sailing ships. Windjammers of old were becalmed there for months.

Every night a strict bow watch was kept even though we did not expect to see much of anything. A secret daily changed signal was laid out on deck for the air patrol to see, and a plane would appear out of nowhere, circle twice, and disappear.

Finally, on the evening of the fifteenth day, we sighted Cape Mala and in the succeeding dawn picked up a fine breeze for the sail up the Gulf of Panama. The passage through the Canal, thrilling as it is for the first time, was doubly so in wartime. I enjoyed a balcony seat in the fore crosstrees.

Though we may not speak of the Canal, of Cristobal we may speak, if of nothing else than the climate, the most atrocious I have experienced. It rains hard for a period every day and for the rest of the time it steams. An August scorcher in New York is equivalent to a cool evening there.

We were barely docked when Beverly Turner invited the skipper and me to the Cristobal Yacht Club where we were given the run of the place for the length of our stay. It was like a page out of Conrad to sit in a porch chair with a tall drink and listen to yarns about the endless stream of 'round the world navigators, their personalities, troubles and little ships. Turner, of course, deserves a paragraph himself; in his strategic station, not a ship could go through without his knowledge and he had made a hobby of meeting and playing host to all of them as well as vicariously taking part in their cruises.

He is an extremely likeable, soft-spoken chap, slight in build. I am sure many a single-hander has had his troubles ironed out by Turner. One of his yarns concerns a Polish yacht of about 35 feet, which had lost her keel just before reaching Curaçao. Her owner, penniless, showed ingenuity that is about tops. He got hauled out, did some scraping and painting and minor repairs, got his clearance papers in order and, during the night, slid off the ways—with a section of rail from a nearby railroad siding bolted on as a jury keel! He arrived in Cristobal about two weeks later, having lived on peanuts in every known culinary form. Turner's brother-in-law bought the yacht. The Dutch authorities in Curaçao do not know to this day what happened to their track system but they suspected sabotage.

We were docked in Cristobal next to the *La Plata*, an extremely dirty and unkempt little banana boat of about 80 feet. Later, I read in the New York papers of the part that she played in the big spy ring activities which were made public last summer. She had a powerful modern Diesel, and a two-way radio, under an appearance of something off the Jersey mudflats.

Another boat of interest was the *Bluejacket*, a salty little Casey-built 50-foot schooner whose owner, Bailey, just happened to be going through the Zone to the South Seas when war broke out. The Navy wanted the yacht for patrol work, so they took over, made him skipper, provided all maintenance and crew, and paid him $700 per month. Gentle reader, that's what I call the breaks! Anybody got a ketch they aren't using for a while?

As to the town of Colon, there is a picture never to be forgotten, a kaleidoscope of vice, dens, saloons, importuning "girls," blaring juke boxes and, just before crossing the tracks to Cristobal again, a clean, white, prophylactic station and the Y.M.C.A. Write home to mother and sweetheart, soldier!

As time for our departure on the northward leg drew near, I could detect a subtle change in the crew and in myself, too. Naval officers would come aboard and chat and make matter-of-fact references to our chances of getting through or say, in an off-hand manner, that "the subs sure were thick out there." Going to New Orleans they called "running the gauntlet."

The men went about their work, but with a manner of restraint, and they were silent more often than not. Bruce's guitar sang the blues at night instead of the usual stomps. You could see that there was anxiety in their eyes behind the attempts to laugh it off, and homesickness, an integral part of a Bahamian, was mixed with a silent wonder whether they would ever see their beloved Nassau again. I was reminded of the old story of the bear hunter who eagerly followed a grizzly's tracks all day while they got fresher and fresher until finally they got too damned fresh and he decided to go home. Here, however, there was no turning back. You were part of a ship and the ship was being drawn North as inexorably as a compass needle.

I think the atmosphere of the town bred morbidity for, as soon as we were outside and watched the Isthmus fade under its low hanging blanket of cloud, our spirits rose and we breathed deeply of the clean sea air that was like a tonic after an illness.

There was no wind but we knew that we would pick it up after getting up into about 11° or 12° N Lat., and so it happened. Sterling gave the order to hoist the main. We went forward to start the deck engine, a large one-cylinder stationary of the old wood-sawing type. It decided to be cranky and would stop again and again after a few chugs. It was decided to get the big main up by hand as the breeze was freshening by the minute. That 68-foot boom and its hundreds of feet of halliards never looked so formidable as in that hour of toil by a short-handed crew. Seven men where fifteen or twenty was normal for the job. It was a time for concerted effort and frequent breathing spells, when your arms ached so that you could not rest them either hanging by your side or held up high. The skipper himself lent his strength to the job and it was like adding two more men. The throat and peak were finally jigged up, the sheet trimmed and we were sailing again.

Here was the best sailing of the entire voyage and the miles slipped by at better than 200 per day. The Caribbean gave us of its best—cobalt blue water, tropical clouds and a sun that made you feel that you had never really lived before. I swore that I would return to these waters after the war. Sterling and I practiced our semaphore, wigwagging nonsensical messages back and forth between quarter-deck and waist, or we took salt water bucket baths, made this and that repair and enjoyed life in general.

One morning Sterling ordered the lifeboat made ready as we were due for the channel the next night. Joe, the cook, filled several gunny sacks with canned goods and I cleared the boat of an accumulation of odds and ends that shouldn't be in her, such as hatch covers, canvas, odd lines, buckets, spare lumber, etc. We made the spritsail next day out of some strips of spare canvas. The weather was hot off the "Banana Coast" and we sat in the shade of the bellying foresail. The mate superintended and we plied needle, palm and waxed thread throughout our watch. When, at last, the bolt rope was sewed on, it didn't look too bad, albeit dirty. After all, the canvas had once been relegated to its final service as chafing gear and had knocked about the bo's'n's locker for years.

There was a nice decision to make in the choice of personal belongings to take. It did not take much thought to rule out a suitcase but I did hate to leave my new gray flannel suit before I'd even broken it in. I resolved to use that as my getting away costume, under the imperative oilskins, instead of the dungarees.

The following morning would see us through the Yucatan Channel and into the infested waters of the Gulf. The channel is about 100 miles wide from Mexico to Cuba and one of the "U" boat packs lay just north. Another kept rendezvous with all comers just south of the Mississippi Delta with, no doubt, a shuttle between the two much like the Grand Central–Times Square subway shuttle. Another, more scattered one, was farther east, towards Florida.

To me, as I went below for some sleep at the end of the dog watch, it looked like suicide to try for New Orleans and I saw to it that my going-away costume was handy before stretching out. A few hours before, Sterling had said that he was debating whether to go to New

Orleans or to Nassau, since, if he could not haul out at New Orleans (except at rates probably prohibitive), he would have to go to Nassau anyway and thus add several hundred miles to the voyage.

I fell into a fitful sleep and was awakened at midnight by a hand shaking my shoulder. It was the mate I saw as I turned on the light back of the dim-out screen I had tacked up around it. I went up on deck.

The engine was not running but we were bowling along at nine knots with a fresh breeze, on the starboard tack instead of the port tack as on the evening before. Scanning the sky, I made out the Southern Cross on the weather beam and Polaris to port. It could mean but one thing—we were heading for Nassau! The good news was verified by the mate, who told the watch to keep a lookout for an 18-mile light on Cuba to starboard. Now, if we could slip silently through the waters to Key West, we would be safe. We strained our eyes through the gloom and picked it up two hours later. Dawn broke soon after. We could then see, dimly, Cuba's peaks—and they were a welcome sight.

During the day, we reached for Key West. After passing two or three freighters nearly hull down to the east, we picked up the tower and smoke of the town about seven o'clock. The patrol boats came out to meet and identify us. We were given instructions how to enter the harbor and where to anchor. The skipper stood on the bowsprit and gave the steering orders, which we relayed aft to the helmsman, as he took bearings on the range lights, since night had fallen. We threaded our way under power and by nine o'clock had dropped the hook near the dim, ghostly shapes of several freighters at anchor. We were eight days out of Cristobal.

Next morning we were told that one of the freighters, *Domino*, had sunk a U boat a few days before by shell fire after sweeping the gun crew off the deck with a machine gun when she had surfaced near by. I felt proud of her and of her exploit and couldn't resist saluting as she slid out of the harbor to join a new convoy.

Toward evening, we left Key West on the last leg of the cruise. It was heart warming to see the jubilation of the crew as they neared their beloved Nassau again. The following night we picked up Great Isaac Light and then their good humor was irrepressible.

Bevans told of his wife's psychic powers. He said she would know he was coming home the next day and would tell the neighbors, as she always did when he was at sea. I kept my tongue in my cheek but decided to check the story for the sake of Science, but in the excitement of getting home myself I forgot to do so. The mate told me he knew where treasure was buried and, if I would sail down later, in my own boat, with a gold-finding machine, we could be rich. Boo was planning to get a job in a store, Mike would get his store teeth, and Lightbourne would see a clinic about those kidney pains. As for me, I had to get home fast because of the family, but I would return to the West Indies as soon as possible. And that's a promise!

At dawn, we let go the anchor in five fathoms of the crystal water of Nassau Harbor and watched it bite into the pure white sand bottom. It was the end of a wondrous voyage for me, but not the last one—I knew that. Boo rowed me ashore as Sterling and I exchanged farewells across the water. The *Spinney* lay there like a duck, knowing that her small wounds would be healed in a day or so and that she would be off again, this time with a cargo to carry and a part to play in this war.

1943

Squadron "X"

Hugh B. Cave

The vital work of PT boats in the desperate days of the Solomons campaign in World War II

"You guys may like the idea of squatting around on cots for the next couple of years," said Chief Torpedoman Hobert Denzil Wisdom, emptying his dungaree pockets of nails which he had pilfered from the carpenter shop, "but me, I got to have comforts." Snorting disdainfully, he sawed a board in half and nailed the pieces into place. Under his capable hands, a sturdy chair was taking shape.

The men grinned. But Wisdom worked on. In front of his tent lay an assortment of lumber and tools, also "borrowed" from the shop. Wiz was busy building furniture. It was good furniture, too.

"The trouble with you guys," he growled, "you're not civilized."

"Maybe," said Gunner's Mate Teddy Kuharski, "you figure to be here forever, huh? Maybe you expect to settle down and raise a family here." With a wink at the others, he placed a hand delicately on his hip and cocked his nose in the air—a dowager at a lawn party. "These, my deah, are our South Sea cousins, the Tulagi Wisdoms. Ah, yes. So unfortunate."

Wisdom grinned back but his hammer banged away without interruption. He put the chair beside a table he had constructed, then hauled another slab of lumber from the pile and applied try-square and pencil. Something puzzled him. Scratching his chin, he sat in the newly finished chair and for a moment was deep in thought.

Some of the others were building furniture, too; inspired, perhaps, by Wisdom's energy and the undeniable need for a few crude comforts. Comforts were scarce on Tulagi. This particular group of PT men, members of a squadron commanded by then Lieutenant Commander Alan R. Montgomery, of Warrenton, Va., had moved into a section of the torpedo boat base located midway between the huddled shacks on the shore and the lookout post on the bluff. They referred to it as "Snob Hill" and considered it an exclusive suburb.

Radioman George Gilpin came up. He was a dark haired southern lad with a sly sense of humor and a grin that could be hidden when necessary behind a studied lack of expression. "I got an idea," he said. "We ought to have some street signs around here to keep you guys from getting lost."

"We ought to have some streets, too," said Chief Torpedoman Elvie O'Daniel, "to get lost on."

"Will you birds shut up?" groused Wisdom. "I'm concentrating."

"He's concentrating," said Gunner's Mate Roy Beckers. "Everybody stand back."

"We need a place to shoot the breeze," Wisdom said. "We need a bench. I'm going to build a bench."

"The Seat of Meditation," said O'Daniel.

"He don't mean that kind of bench," Gilpin argued. "Besides, where would we get any mail order catalogs in this place?"

"I mean a bench to sit on," said Wisdom. "So we can enjoy the view here and shoot the breeze. It gets too damn hot inside these tents and shacks, and there's too many bugs. Leave me alone, you guys. I got to dope out a bench."

He built one. It was finished a couple of days later and occupied a place of honor on "Main Street," where the boys could sit back and look out over the settlement below and the sea beyond. On clear days, the sea was a soft, translucent green, very pretty.

It was a different sea at night. Too often, under cover of darkness, Jap destroyers or cruisers came "down the Slot" from Bougainville to put troops ashore on Guadalcanal and to shell exhausted American Marines encamped around Henderson Field. The midget mosquito boats of Squadron "X" patrolled the bloody waters between Guadalcanal and Tulagi, to prevent enemy infiltration. That was their job.

It was grueling work, nerve-racking work, murderous on men and boats alike. For the PT men, those October–November nights of 1942 were long indeed. The fate of Guadalcanal still hung in the balance.

Ashore, the men made the best of what they had. Inspired by Wisdom's work, the occupants of Snob Hill shed their dungarees in the broiling heat of those long afternoons and pitched in to make their surroundings homelike. They swept out the native huts and constructed shelves and cupboards. They put up pictures of wives and sweethearts, built tables for red dog and poker, dug trenches to carry off the rain water which otherwise would have inundated them.

It was terribly hot. Though nearly naked, the men oozed perspiration which attracted swarms of insects. Behind them, Tulagi's gaudy hills rose tawny and green, flecked with flowers and streaked by the passage of brilliant red and snowy white parrots. It was an unhealthy gaudiness, dank and stifling. No one was eager to explore it.

Tables and chairs grew in abundance, and the "snobs" enjoyed unheard of comforts in their high suburb. On the Seat of Meditation, the problems of the war were solved in heated bull sessions. Chief Machinist's Mate Halward Peterson remembered the good times in Panama. Gunner's Mate Leon Nale, a tall, slender lad from Alabama, talked wistfully of the girls he knew. Gilpin and O'Daniel ribbed each other. John Legg taught other quartermasters the finer points of navigation. It was a little like a front porch at home.

"These islands," said one of the men one evening; "these lousy, stinking islands—what good are they? For all of me, the Japs can have 'em. Nobody but a goddam Jap would want 'em!"

Said Chief Torpedoman Marvin Crosson, a quiet, studious boy with a fine knowledge of history, "They're not islands. Guadalcanal is not an island. They're nothing more or less than little points on a map."

"So all right. Let the Japs have 'em."

"That's just it. The Japs did have them, and it was important for us to win them back. Look here." Crosson took a dog-eared map from his pocket and spread it on his knees. "Here we are, right here. North of us the enemy is solid, with a string of stepping stones all the way down from Japan. South are Australia and the sea lanes we must use to defend it. From Guadalcanal the Japs could cover those sea lanes with bombers. See?"

They had known it anyway. Grousing was merely an outlet for cramped emotions. But, when the war was over and the Japs were liquidated, Guadalcanal and Tulagi could turn turtle and sink into the sea, for all these men cared. They wouldn't shed a tear.

A poker game was in progress one afternoon—Ship's Cook Frank O'Malley red hot as always—when the glittering sun was engulfed suddenly by swift clouds that let loose a flood. The men scurried for shelter. When it rained on Tulagi, you took no chances.

They plucked their personal possessions from the floors of huts and tents, hung them on anything handy, and pulled up their feet in the manner of a plane retracting its landing gear. Then dolefully they watched the ground about them turn into a sticky sea of mud. Without the drains they had constructed, Snob Hill would have been a complete washout. Tulagi weather was savage.

The Marines on Guadalcanal knew all about this freakish weather. They had been living and dying in it from the beginning, and their airmen had found it a foe almost as treacherous as the Jap. So did the overworked pilots of a handful of SOC biplanes based on Tulagi.

Brave men flew these Navy planes. They were the eyes of the PT boats, tirelessly searching the seas for signs of enemy activity. The weather made little difference to them. They knew that bad weather was a favorite weapon of the Japs and, under or behind any advancing front of swollen clouds, enemy warships were likely to be on the prowl. Consequently, they went out in the worst of it, under impossible conditions. The day of the poker game, one of them did not come back.

At the base, work went steadily on. In charge of the torpedo shop was Ensign (now Lieutenant jg) Stanley C. Thomas, who could make a torpedo talk. He and Chief Torpedomen Shorty Long and Herbert Wing had little time to be concerned about Tulagi's weather. Sun or rain, they were everlastingly occupied with the boats. It was a six-hour job to get a tin fish ready for firing, and the fish were fired often.

"Ten thousand bucks it costs," said Shorty, "to send one of these babies on its way. We have to be sure they get what they're sent for."

Other men were transferred from boats to base whenever the squadron as a whole had need of their talents. Chief Machinist's Mate Arthur Stuffert left his PT to work in the engine shop. Ship's Cook Charlie May was coaxed against his will to slave in the shore galley. Some of the men liked the change; some didn't. Most of them preferred the boats. Typical was Ship's Cook Lloyd Hummer, who ducked his chores ashore and rode one particular boat at every opportunity, praying for action. "Just lemme at 'em," he begged. "We'll show those apes!"

The man who really ran the base force was Chief Boatswain's Mate Charlie Tufts. Nothing stumped Charlie. No job was too big or too pesky. When tools or parts were needed, he sometimes took a walk—usually to the Marine encampment.

One day, returning from such a stroll, Charlie ambled solemnly into the torpedo shop and began emptying his pockets. A wrench came out. A handful of nuts and bolts. A weird and varied assortment of odds and ends for which the PT men had been tearing their hair. Charlie blinked at his collection. He was a mild man, a little bumpy in places, running short of hair but never of energy or ingenuity. "Now how in the world," he said, "did I ever get all this stuff? My, my. Someone must have framed me."

Those were the lighter interludes. Some of the others were less happily remembered. Like the night of November 7th. Three of the boats were patrolling that night within shouting distance of one another. One was commanded by Lieutenant Hugh M. Robinson, the squadron executive officer. Another was in charge of Lieutenant (jg) James Brent Greene. The third was skippered by Lieutenant (jg) Leonard A. Nikoloric. Youngsters, all of them. Robbie, the oldest, was 27. The other PT skippers had an affectionate name for him. They called him "Poor Old Robbie."

About midnight, the Japs came in. Brent maneuvered for a shot and fired a spread of four torpedoes at the leading enemy ship, a destroyer. One of the fish jammed in its tube. A fountain of sparks leaped skyward and the quiet night was bedlam. Torpedoman Brenton Goddard cleared the tube with a blow of his mallet.

The torpedoes may have winged home or may not. No one was sure. At any rate, the Jap was still in action and the dazzling fireworks of the "hot run" had given him a point of aim for his searchlights. In a heart beat of time, Robbie and Brent were trapped in the lights while the Jap's guns roared their defiance. The enemy was on his toes that night, performing at peak efficiency. His shooting was good. Too good. A salvo of 4.7's screamed from his main battery and one of them exploded with an earthquake roar on Robbie's bow.

Happily, every man on the mosquito boat was at his battle station. All were tossed about like tenpins but none was forward when the shell struck and none was seriously hurt. Where the bow of the boat had been, however, was now only a jagged mass of plywood splinters. The PT opened fire with her .50 caliber machine guns and struggled to escape.

"We in our boat," Lieutenant Nikoloric recalls, "heard the explosion just after getting in a shot. We saw what happened. Robbie's boat was less than 100 yards abeam of us, and the glare of the shell burst lit up the night all around us. We thought it was all over for Robbie and his gang. If that shell hadn't finished them, the next hit certainly would. The Japs were sending everything they had at her."

Owen Pearle, Nick's radioman, sent out a yell over the radio to find out who was alive over there. Someone was, because Robbie's machine guns were crackling. But, after what had happened, there *had* to be casualties. "Are you okay?" Pearle begged. "Are you all right?"

It was Lieutenant Robinson himself who answered. "Hell, yes!" he barked. "We're heading for home!" Despite the loss of her bow, the crippled boat was running with all the speed she could manage, executing a series of wobbly maneuvers that kept the enemy's shells wide of the mark. Meanwhile, Gunner's Mate Ben Parrish, wedged in his turret, clung fast to the grips of his guns and coolly shot out the destroyer's searchlights. It was sweet shooting.

The boat churned on, throwing up fountains of spray. She was getting away. But the Japs had a perfect target. The smoke generator had jammed, and the Jap had the range. Chief Torpedoman Alfred Norwood, an old-timer with what was needed, started for the smoke pot. Soaking wet, half blinded, barely able to keep his feet on the twisting deck, he fell on the generator and tore at it with his hands. It *had* to work. Without smoke, the PT was doomed. There, on his knees, Norwood wrestled with the valves while enemy shells crackled overhead like whips.

The valves let go and smoke gushed out—but backward. Now the smoke used on the motor torpedo boats is a chemical mixture shot forth under pressure. It is thick and strangling. It burns cruelly, like acid, and can sear the skin off a man's face or hands quickly. Norwood was caught in the hissing stream and stumbled back out of it, his face and arms in torment. But he went back in. He got his hands on the balky generator and stayed there, pounding it, until the smoke poured out the way it was supposed to. In all this time, the enemy's fire had not diminished.

With the white screen swelling in her wake, the PT at last shook off pursuit and left the Jap astern. Then Norwood looked at his hands. They were bright red, covered with thin, bulging blisters that broke and peeled away. They were aflame to the elbows. Norwood walked forward on the heaving deck and sat down by the port turret and was sick. But, without question, his coolness and ability in a grave emergency had saved the lives of his shipmates.

It was that way often in the little thunder boats. Fate put the finger on some one man and challenged him: "Brother, it's your turn." The chosen individual might be the skipper, the second in command, a man at the guns or a machinist's mate in the engine room. Officers or enlisted men, it made no difference. Fate played no favorites. Suddenly for a brief, bright flash of time, the lives of all aboard would depend on one man's ability and courage. None knew when his turn might come.

The PT made port that night, limping through the dark with the sea growling in her vitals. It was incredible, but it happened. The Jap who had crippled her was less lucky. Too avid for the kill, he forgot the other PT and left himself unprotected. His searchlight beams and the bright light of his gunbursts were a tempting target. The PT, with Nick at the wheel, Lieutenant (jg) Bernie O'Neill and Chief Quartermaster John Legg spotting, had stalked him half way across the Slot. Now she slipped up on his silent side, away from the thunder of the guns, and loosed her torpedoes.

A few hours later, Chief Yeoman John Wicks stood on an up-turned box in front of the squadron office and, with red and white paint dripping brightly from his brush, added yet another Jap flag to the PT emblem over the doorway.

The Guadalcanal Marines were sleeping better. The Japs were learning, the hard way, that Sleepless Lagoon was an area of peril, patrolled by savage little thunder bugs whose sting was often fatal.

1945

In the Path of the Hurricane

R. F. Hainge

The terrifying ordeal of the crew of a Coast Guard cutter

A few days before the worst hurricane in fifty years to hit our east coast reached the area off Cape Hatteras, the two Coast Guard cutters *Jackson* and *Bedloe* were ordered to the aid of an American Liberty ship which was in distress off the coast to the south'ard of that North Carolina cape. An Army tug, the *ATR-6*, which had accompanied the cutters to the scene, took the Liberty in tow and, with the Coast Guard cutters acting as escorts, began the slow trip to Norfolk.

I was the Communications Officer aboard the *Jackson* and in that capacity had noted the increasing frequency with which the hurricane warnings were being received. But, outside of the usual precautions that were taken at the approach of any storm, the hurricane did not cause us much concern. Its path was charted and the approximate time at which it would hit the area that we would be in was noted. As nearly as we could estimate, Thursday morning, September 14th, about six o'clock, would find us on the outskirts of the storm and from then on we expected a pretty rough ride. Although our vessels were only 125 feet long, they were excellent sea boats, fully proven, so that we felt no alarm.

The days preceding the storm were uneventful; the seas were moderate and only a light breeze was blowing. On the night before the storm hit us, I was officer of the deck during the watch from eight to twelve. At this time, the sea was almost calm but the sky and barometer gave unmistakable signs of the approaching hurricane. At midnight, I was relieved and went below to get what sleep

I could. During the early morning hours the sea began to make up so that after 6:30 I found it impossible to stay in my bunk. As I was going topsides, I thought to myself that we had estimated the arrival of the hurricane quite accurately. At this time we were just north of Cape Hatteras, on a course for the Virginia Capes. The wind was blowing about 60 m.p.h. from the NE. We were now rolling so much that first one rail and then the other would go under and the *Jackson* would dive into a sea, shudder a bit, and then come up as if to throw the water off. By this time the seas were sweeping over the top of the flying bridge, almost swamping the ship, and it was raining hard. The wind, which had risen to whole gale force, caused the flying spray and rain to lash at us like hailstones so that it was impossible to face to windward. We had the tow in sight astern but the *Bedloe* was out of sight, hidden by the seas on our starboard beam.

A short time later, we received a message that the Liberty ship and the Army tug had parted the towing hawser. As they were then in about 16 fathoms of water, the Liberty let go both anchors with a full scope of chain and, with the partial steam that she was able to get up, was trying to keep from being driven on the beach, then approximately 20 miles distant. The tug headed for port.

The fury of the hurricane mounted with each minute. Course, speed or mission assigned meant nothing to us then; it was a question of fighting to keep the ship from broaching-to. The Captain was conning from the wing of the bridge; the executive officer was advising him of wind direction changes and I was on the engine order telegraphs, helping the helmsman to keep on the desired heading by use of the engines because the rudder alone did not have the power to maintain the heading of the ship against wind and sea.

We estimated at this time that the wind was blowing at 100 knots and the waves were mountainous. The ship was being tossed about like a cork; sometimes it would seem as if we were lifted clear out of the water, to come down with a crash that made us feel as though we were going right through the deck. This continued for a couple of hours while the storm grew in fury. Our barometer registered 28.04 inches.

About 10:30 A.M., the ship was borne to the top of a towering sea and was then struck on the starboard side by two other huge seas. She rolled over on her beam ends until her mast actually dipped into the water. We on the bridge were tossed in a heap to the lee side. As these seas passed, the ship slowly righted herself only to be struck by another sea and rolled over on her port beam. At that moment the full force of the wind caught us and, for the second time, our mast was in the water. In a few seconds, it was all over. There was no opportunity to use the radio to send an SOS as the radioman had been thrown from his chair against a bulkhead, breaking three ribs. The skipper, who was in the pilothouse at the time she went over, led his men to comparative safety through the door leading to the starboard wing of the bridge. They were forced to climb up as through a trap door using the binnacle and engine telegraph as steps.

At the time, I was on the starboard wing, having just come topsides after decoding a radio message. As we went over, I was tossed against the ladder leading to the flying bridge. By the time I had regained my balance, the watch below were already climbing out of the forecastle. There was no confusion nor much talking. The skipper ordered the rafts cast off but there were only the four starboard rafts available as the port rafts were buried deep under water.

All the men who were on watch at the time the *Jackson* capsized had on their life jackets but most of those who were below had been thrown out of their bunks when she went over and, as the lights went out, they were unable to find their life jackets. Indeed, the first thought in their minds was to get out of the ship and in this they all succeeded. Due to the ship being on her side, the rafts had to be lifted from their racks and several men were washed overboard by the huge seas in the time that it took to get them free. As the rafts were thrown into the water, men jumped into them and began the struggle to hang on while they were being turned over and over. Since we were able to get off only half our rafts and as they were of the small type, about six feet long by three feet wide, to some of which a dozen men were clinging, they were soon loaded far beyond their rated capacity.

As we got the last raft into the water the ship turned bottom up. Many men still were hanging on to her sides and some managed to climb up on the slippery bottom and cling to the keel. Apparently the ship appeared a more substantial refuge than the tossing rafts from which the men were wrenched by the cresting seas as fast as they caught the life lines.

A short time after the ship capsized, I was washed off by a sea and remained so long submerged that I feared I would never come up. I held my breath until my lungs almost burst and hoped that I would reach the surface in time. Eventually I surfaced but only after swallowing what seemed like gallons of salt water. I looked about and saw that the ship was awash with a few of the boys still clinging to her keel. I learned later that they could not swim.

There were no rafts in sight so I just floated around in my life jacket, trying to catch my breath between cresting seas that were breaking over my head. Finally, as I was carried to the top of a big sea, I saw two rafts in the distance and began swimming towards them. They were probably only a couple of hundred yards away but it seemed an eternity before I reached the nearer one. To that raft ten men were clinging. I made the eleventh. Presently we saw another raft going by with only four men on it, so four of our party swam over to the other to even up the load.

The best that the remaining seven of us could do was to hang on to our raft and try to keep it on the surface by treading water. With so many clinging to it, any attempts to climb into the raft only caused it to sink further and it seemed that every sea that came along rolled it over and over. After each such sea had passed, we would all scramble back to the raft again, as it proved impossible to hold on while it was rolling over. I found a piece of marline in my pocket and with this I lashed my hand to the raft's lifeline. As a result the flesh on my left hand was cut to the bone.

About 1:30 P.M., when we had been in the water some three hours, the center of the hurricane passed over; the wind stopped blowing and, although the seas did not diminish in size, it was a great relief to have the wind drop and the salt spray stop driving into our eyes. From time to time we had seen some of the other rafts, as we were all drifting in the same general direction. Once we managed to lash two of them together but the waves banged them against each other so hard we were afraid they might crack up, so we cast off the lashings.

All this time we had been hoping that either the *Bedloe* or the tug might spot us but, due to the high seas and limited visibility, they failed to do so. As we learned later, the *Bedloe*, too, had capsized. Soon after the center of the storm passed over us, we caught its full fury again. From then on until midnight that night, a period of perhaps ten hours, it was a terrific struggle to keep a hold on the raft. Each time a hold was lost it became harder to swim back again. These struggles consumed our remaining strength and we later learned that it was during this time that most of the men from our ship were lost.

The quantity of salt water that I had swallowed made me violently sick; as a result, I fortunately cleared my stomach of it. At the time it left me weak but later, talking to the doctors in the hospital where we recuperated, I learned that this was one of the best things that could have happened to me. The men who had failed to rid their stomachs of salt water were the first to become desperately thirsty and later they had the hardest time trying to remain rational. After our rescue, I talked to our Chief Boatswain's Mate, an old hand, about swallowing salt water and he told me that the first thing he had done when he reached a raft was to put his finger down his throat to get rid of all that he had swallowed. This trick he had learned from long experience at sea and I pass it along as a point worth remembering in an emergency.

By the following morning the seas had subsided enough so that we could take turns getting into the raft and resting for a little while. At some time during the previous day, when the raft had been turned over so many times, the water breaker was carried away. We had lost our flares and one of the paddles in the same manner. The container of rations, however, had not been lost but we found that they were much too dry to chew or swallow without water, accordingly they were quite useless to us.

We decided that by paddling westward we would hit shore, which we estimated to be about 20 miles away. We took turns at paddling and hanging on to the raft and kicking with our feet. But we made so little headway for the amount of energy expended that I've since concluded that it is best to conserve one's strength and resort to paddling only when land is in sight.

On the afternoon of the second day we saw two of the other rafts in the distance and slowly worked our way over to them. They, too, had lost their water breakers. We talked over the events of the night before and it was then that we first realized how many of our men had been lost. Up to that time, we had lost but one man from our raft, that one's loss being due to utter exhaustion. But the losses from the other rafts brought our total to twelve for the first day and night.

Soon we parted again, each raft trying to make the best possible speed toward shore. The day was warm but when nightfall came the drop in temperature made us all feel cold. Several got violent spells of shivering in which our teeth would chatter for ten minutes at a time. But worst of all were the stings from the Portuguese-men-of-war, a multi-tailed marine pest similar to the common jelly fish. There were many of them around the raft and every time any part of one of their jelly-like bodies came in contact with one of us, or even if we touched a part of the raft they previously had touched, it burned like strong acid. The pain from these contacts continued for hours.

Sharks were another annoyance. We could see their fins cutting through the water all about us and felt sure that they were only waiting for the next man to drop from the raft. They did not attack nor did they come too close but the thought of having them so near, especially at night when we could not see what they were up to or how close they were, was extremely disturbing.

During the second day the sun's heat was so intense that, in spite of repeated warnings, two of the men drank a considerable quantity of salt water in an effort to quench their thirst. That night they became irrational and soon after sundown dropped off the raft and were lost. That left only four of us, three in fairly good shape, and the fourth exhausted to the point where he could no longer speak. With only four left we were all able to get aboard the raft at one time, thus getting some much needed rest. The sea had now become smooth which also contributed to our meagre comfort. We rested for an hour or so until our shipmate who was so weak slipped from the raft. Three of us were able to get him back aboard twice after he had slipped off, but the third time he went overboard we were too exhausted to give him any further help as he sank before our eyes. We took turns staying awake for the remainder of the night to keep a lookout for possible flares from searching ships and also to watch the two who were resting, just in case one should start to slip overboard.

This worked well for the remainder of the night. As we were now too weak to paddle any longer we just drifted. Early the third morning we attempted to catch with our bare hands some of the small fish that were swimming close around the raft but we were unsuccessful. We tried desperately for we knew that the moisture contained in those fish would enable us to stick it out another day or so.

It was while we were trying to catch the fish that we heard the sound of the motors of approaching airplanes. This was the first ray of hope that we had had since being cast away and you can imagine our jubilation. The planes were sweeping right up the coast, flying five or six hundred feet off the water. I tied my handkerchief to the end of our paddle and waved it frantically but they had already seen our raft and zoomed right down over us. There were three planes, all Kingfishers operated by the Coast Guard from the Air Station at Elizabeth City, N.C. After flying around and locating the other rafts, one of the rescue planes landed near us and taxied close enough so that we could paddle over.

It is hard to express our feelings as we saw the planes coming towards us. We were almost overcome with joy for we knew that we were saved and in a short time would be in a hospital where we could have all the fresh water we wanted to drink. That was the main thing. The pilot and the radioman on the plane helped us to clamber from the raft on to the plane's wing. There we collapsed, for we knew our worries were over. A little water and brandy were given us and we were told that the other three rafts also had been sighted and the men picked up from them.

The two-seater plane which had rescued us was too small to take off with the extra load, so the radioman flashed his base for assistance. Presently a crash boat arrived in response to his call and we were transferred to her and rushed to the Air Station at Manteo, N.C. It was then but a matter of a few minutes till we were put aboard a PBM (Martin Mariner) and flown to the Naval Hospital at Norfolk. One of the first treatments that we received at the hospital was a blood plasma transfusion and it felt to me like new life running into my weary body. I now can appreciate what a tremendous boost it must give to men wounded in battle or suffering from shock.

The 19 survivors of the *Jackson's* 40-man complement soon responded to rest and food. In ten days we were well enough to be discharged. We were all given survivor leave and once more were restored to our worried families and solicitous friends.

We now heard that the Liberty ship had dragged her anchors slowly toward the beach so that, when the storm subsided, she was but a scant mile and a half from shore. If the wind had lasted much longer she surely would have been on the beach. It was here we learned that the *Bedloe* had capsized shortly after we did and her survivors likewise were brought into the Naval Hospital at Norfolk.

All the survivors suffered from nightmares and constantly recurring memories of the harrowing and heartrending hours on the rafts, when our shipmates, one by one, slipped overboard in the shark-infested waters and sank from sight. It is safe to say that, by those of us who lived to tell about it, those 58 hours will never be forgotten.

PART V
The Lighter Side

There was a grim humor in some of the wartime adventures of yachtsmen in uniform, and the joys of civilian yachting have also had a light side. In many cases, the humor has been topical and therefore quickly dated, and a reader of the latter part of the twentieth century might wonder just what was so funny about it. In the early days, with a circulation that started at 5,000, there was an insider sort of clubbiness that concentrated on personalities, and the columnists who wrote under such pseudonyms as "Cap Stan," "Spun Yarn," "Tell Tale," "Boatsteerer" and the like devoted much space to joshing their friends. Alf Loomis, with his long run column "Under the Lee of the Longboat" written under the byline "Cap Stan," invented and built on the foibles of a mythical group of sailors known as the "Lee Rail Vikings," which was a handy vehicle for poking fun at pomposities, poor sportsmanship and other human weaknesses. Though much of the humor has been topical and ephemeral, a few examples of it are typical of what has been carried.

Skippers We Can Live Without

William H. Taylor

A noted deflater of stuffed shirts, Bill Taylor sticks the pin in some skippers he had known

We hear a great deal of solemn nonsense tossed around when skippers get together, particularly long distance racing skippers, about crews. Each has his own fetishes about choosing and training the men who are going to sail his boat for him. One skipper is all out for a crew of rugged, enthusiastic young fellows with strong backs and weak minds, ready to start from scratch and learn the game the way the skipper, in his infinite wisdom, thinks they ought to learn it.

The next skipper admits that a few youngsters are handy to have aboard, in case any dishes need to be washed or any particularly nasty jobs done aloft or on the bowsprit, but he wants a bunch of mature, seagoing characters along to lend experience and judgment to the enterprise and to carry on after the boys have worn themselves all out standing double watches and dashing up and down the deck and rigging.

One wants a crew of keen small-boat racing men, accustomed to getting the last inch of speed out of the boat every minute. Another sets a higher value on seamanship and offshore experience. One expects his crew to be on their toes as near 24 hours a day as is humanly possible, while another insists the watch below spend as much time in their sacks as possible, against the time when all hands are needed on deck in emergencies.

And so it goes. The skippers really get into quite involved arguments on the subject. So what?

Just who do these skippers think they are, anyhow? Who cares what they want? Does it ever occur to them that they're lucky to have any crew at all? Do they suppose for one minute that their individual preferences carry any weight in a democratic world? What we say is, the skippers had better find out what their crews want, or else get used to sailing single-handed.

The problems of skippers who want to gather and train crews are of no interest to us. What we propose to do is to offer a few priceless words of advice to the young prospective crew member who is launching himself out on the perilous sea of going to sea—especially of going to sea with the kind of people who consider themselves skippers, and with whom he will probably find himself more at sea than he has any idea of until he tries it. In a few words, our advice would be: "Avoid all skippers." But, inasmuch as no author gets paid for writing just a few words, we will elaborate on the subject somewhat, taking in not only our idea of the requirements for an acceptable skipper but also thumbnail sketches of a few skippers we have met in our day—and "big ropes in small blocks to 'em," we say, "and on a lee shore at that."

One type of skipper of which the young crew member should beware is the chest-beating, bull-voiced, autocrat of the quarterdeck, who doesn't realize that he has no quarterdeck but is sitting in the cockpit with the rest of us most of the time. This variety of skipper fancies himself a throwback to the belaying-pin-in-the-boot, brass knuckle, shoot-'em-off-the-yardarm days. He has probably read too many novels about hard case masters and mates of the Western Ocean packets and Cape Horn clippers. He may or may not be a good seaman but is practically never as good a seaman as he sounds—to himself, anyhow.

Nothing in this skipper's boat is ever done in a normal manner or a normal tone of voice. Ashore, he may be the mousiest and most amiable of men, but let him set foot on a deck—any deck, not necessarily his own—and he becomes a rampaging, roaring maniac. The simplest command (even in a 10-foot dinghy) is issued in a fore-royal-yard-there voice that frightens beginners into immobility and causes old-timers to laugh, for the first day or so, and quietly cut the skipper's throat if it goes on too long. We know of more than one such skipper who has not only driven his family and friends to stay ashore, or sail with somebody else, but who has attained such a reputation that sailors who live 1000 miles away shudder and write polite notes of regret when invited to join him on a little overnight race, or even just a leisurely cruise.

The basic trouble with this type of skipper, aside from the racket he makes, is that he throws everything out of proportion. We would be the first to agree that a thunderous manner of giving orders, accompanied perhaps by a certain amount of Christian language used in unchristian sequence, is not only excusable but a help to getting things done suddenly in an emergency. But when the same technique is used just to get the brass polished or a small pull taken on the tack downhaul, it gets tiresome if not downright objectionable. Besides which, it engenders in the experienced shipmate a suspicion that the skipper is trying to convince either you or himself, or both, that he knows what he's doing, in the face of all evidence to the contrary.

At the other end of the scale is the skipper who can never make up his mind. He may have a pretty good idea of what should be done, but he is always mindful of the fact that other people have ideas, too, and he's never quite sure but what some one else aboard may have a better idea. Hence he calls a conference on the simplest matter, such as whether to trim the jib sheet an inch or two. Since this brings out from two to a dozen conflicting ideas (depending on the number of persons aboard) on whatever subject is under consideration, the skipper generally winds up by doing it his way anyhow, with the result that each member of the crew is hurt because his suggestion wasn't followed.

Some skippers suffer from the hallucination that only they, of all the people in the world, know how to steer a boat. Such a skipper plants his transom firmly on the wheelbox at the beginning of the day and keeps it there, issuing orders, calling for sandwiches, cigarettes and highballs, complaining bitterly about the way things are done up forward and in general acting as if he owned the blooming boat. He just sits there and steers hour after hour, until either the anchor is down again or, on a long passage, sheer exhaustion drives him below. When the latter happens he reluctantly turns the helm over to someone else and issues such a string of directives and advice on the subject of steering that whoever takes over wishes heartily that the honor hadn't been thrust upon him. A skipper like this can be forgiven when you're out for blood in a matinee race, but under any other circumstances it is good practice to slip a few knockout drops into his coffee or highball after a while. If you aren't foresighted enough to have knockout drops handy, use a winch handle.

Beware particularly of such a skipper when he suddenly gets big-hearted and insists that you must take her for a spell. If you look around carefully at such a time you will find that he has gotten the ship into a position from which he doesn't know how to extricate her. If you take over at that point and don't pull a miracle out of your sleeve and win the race or get her back into the channel, you'll never hear the end of how you got the ship into a jam the minute you got your hands on the helm.

Another skipper to watch is the one who, when the cruise starts, says "Now boys, she's your boat. Take her anywhere you like and sail her your own way. I'm just going along for the ride and leaving everything to you." Oh yeah? The first move you make he'll pop up with a counter-suggestion, and it'll go on like that hour after hour, even day after day. Whatever you do, he'll have a better idea and, it being his boat after all, you can't just ignore him. But of course if anything goes wrong it's all your fault—after all, he told you to take over the ship, didn't he?

Once in a while you find a skipper who really does relax and enjoy it when he has a competent crew on deck. But what does he do? Does he turn to and wash up the dishes, crack the ice, make the bunks, clean up the galley and engine room? Not a bit of it. He probably relaxes with a good book. Now this is manifestly unfair. Here you are doing all the hard work, like steering, trimming sails and piloting, and on top of that this sojer expects you to do other work besides. What good is such a man? Heave him over the side and be done with him.

One skipper we can't get along with is the old maid type. You can spot one the minute you step aboard, because he'll probably insist on your removing your shoes, unless they're just the brand he personally favors, and walking around barefoot. He follows you around all day long with a little dustpan and brush, just in case you should drop an ash on deck. He flutters like a hen with a brood of ducklings every time the club launch or a dinghy comes along side, for fear his precious topsides will be marked. If you set a glass down for a moment on his varnish, he utters a moan and leaps to grab it up and move it to some less convenient place. He insists on taking all kinds of bearings when you're making a ten-mile run in deep water and clear weather. In fact, he's a pipsqueak and a nuisance, almost as much of a nuisance as the seagoing slob.

The seagoing slob is not only a nuisance but a menace. His boat looks like hell and is a sort of floating hell. Everything is piled on top of everything else and when you finally dig up whatever you're looking for it doesn't work anyhow. His sails are mildewed, his running rigging chafed and cowtailed, his bottom foul and his engine, if it works, leaks oil and water. His galley is filthy and his dinghy always has six inches of water in her. He mixes his martinis in an unwashed coffee pot.

Somewhere between these two extremes is a middle ground. A boat ought to be clean and neat and well-found and her gear ought to be good. But, like a house, she ought to have a lived-in look, and as though she were used for pleasure and not for display. Find a skipper whose craft looks that way and maybe you've got something—provided, of course, he doesn't have any of the other undesirable qualities we describe here.

Such as being an ascetic in the matter of food, for instance. Any skipper has a right to subsist on dry cereal and lettuce sandwiches if he wants to—probably deserves nothing better—but if he doesn't put out the porterhouse steaks for his crew he's not worth sailing with. When you're picking a skipper, take a squint at his girth measurement; if his tummy bulges comfortably, his ship probably feeds well. Of course there's also the would-be Duncan Hines who drags all hands into some port where nobody wants to go just to get a special meal at some restaurant he had a wonderful chow in five years ago—only to find the restaurant closed and no place to eat.

These are only a few of the skippers we find it difficult to get along with. There are plenty of others; for instance, the skipper who always anchors a mile from shore, beyond the outermost fringes of the fleet; the skipper who blows up like a firecracker in the middle of every race, insults his whole crew, and then spends an hour apologizing afterward; the skipper who feels called upon to do things "Navy style," with great pomp, ceremony and inconvenience; the skipper who routs all hands out at the crack of dawn to swab decks and chamois down the brightwork while the dew is on; the skipper who doesn't get started until noon when you have a long run to make; the skipper who keeps his decks so beautifully varnished that you fall on your face every time you try to go forward; the skipper who sits all day in the companionway so you can't get below, if you're on deck, or vice versa; the skipper who goes to bed at dusk and insists on the ship being quiet; the skipper who invites the whole fleet aboard and whoops it up all night when *you* want to turn in; the skipper who embarrasses his crew by making poor landings and mooring pick-ups.

Also the skipper who insists on having bright little sayings written in the log by everybody aboard; the skipper who runs a dry ship; the skipper whose idea of a cruise is to get stewed the first morning and stay that way until he gets home; the skipper who is always poking into places where he shouldn't go and getting aground so you can heave her off again; the skipper who pilots his boat as though she drew 30 feet of water and wouldn't cut a corner to save a ten-mile roundabout trip in the steamer channel; the skipper who glories in going out and slugging it out in all kinds of bad weather; the skipper who stays in port just because the weather's a little nasty outside; the skipper who—oh shucks! just any skipper.

Come to think of it, I guess skippers are the antithesis of the old German waiter's dictum on the subject of beer; there are no good skippers but some skippers are worse than others.

(AUTHOR'S NOTE—*Any resemblance of the above characters to real persons, living or dead, is the fruit of your own bad conscience.*
W.H.T.)

1947

The Crew I Can Do Without

Alfred F. Loomis

With tongue somewhat to starboard in cheek, Yachting's resident humorist, Alf Loomis, a.k.a. "Spun Yarn," answers Bill Taylor's screed

I hope you all read that article entitled "Skippers We Can Live Without" in the May number, because I am taking that for my text in the present article. Said screed was written by that prominent seaman and cioman William Hornblower Taylor in elaboration of his subversive ideas on employer-employee relationships aboard yachts that go to sea for pleasure. It is regrettable that a man of literary talents as widely recognized as Mr. Taylor's should have lent himself to a campaign which goes contrary to the spirit of the times. We are told by all the propagandists in the Western Hemisphere that there can be no invidious distinctions drawn between blacks and whites, Gentiles and Jews, Californians and Texans, Republicans and Democrats, Truman and Wallace. The lion and the lamb were about to lie down together when into this harmonious symphony Mr. Taylor piped his sour note and claimed the existence of a gulf between capital and labor, master and man, owner and crew. I shall do everything within my power to bridge this gulf and to reaffirm the brotherhood of the sea. But not right now.

The trouble is, as Mr. Taylor himself pointed out in his introductory paragraphs, it is difficult to find good crews for seagoing yachts. The young ones who formed the backbone of the sport before the war have grown up and are facing one of two problems in the world of today. Either they want to skipper their own yachts, or they want to stay ashore and support the families which they carelessly acquired in the sad delusion that they would be on the Army or Navy pay roll all their lives. And the young ones of today are either too young to be of any use or have served time in the armed services where they picked up the fantastic idea that they should devote the present to rounding out their educations. It is bad enough to have them attend institutions of learning all winter—these ineffable young veterans feel that they should also go to summer school. Some of the G.I.'s who are satisfied with nine months of mental nourishment spend the summer in gainful employment, thus partially relieving their parents of a financial burden which they would have been only too happy to assume. Take it either way—the sordid lust for learning or the inordinate yen for earning—the manpower pool has been drained of its most promising material.

Then we have the old duffers who used to put on their cheaters and shakily make their mark opposite their typewritten names in the ship's articles. I refer to quondam crew members like myself who sounded around until they had found a ship that stood three watches and served filet mignon with mushroom sauce except on those days when the menu called for toasted quail and champagne. They're out of the market too. Rather than ruin their digestions with flapjacks and scrambled eggs they stay ashore. And a good place for them. But their defection does nothing to relieve the crew situation.

I used to think that with four children of my own I had the key to the solution. As I slaved on my hands and knees putting my cutter *Hotspur* in commission I looked forward to the halcyon days when they would be so mature that I could sit back and order them about. But what do I do and what do I find? During the lovely weeks of spring, while college and school are in session, I go down to the boat and sand and varnish, scrub and paint, whip and splice. And I find the young ones spending their week-ends with their noses in their books. Now that summer has come and the boat is in the water, do I gather the clan together and take a little cruise as skipper emeritus? I do not. I gather myself on the landing float and wave the young goodbye as they sandwich a short cruise in between two summer semesters. No wonder I hate education.

But now I'll tell you about the personal characteristics, traits, habits, and mannerisms of people that I would avoid if I were able to acquire a crew for a cruise or a race. In their way they're every bit as bad as the bull-voiced brass knuckle skippers that Mr. Taylor contemns. And they're more numerous. First and foremost is the person who asks if I can't stow him away as a cabin boy. The question itself reveals the depths of his—or very likely her—ignorance. What would I be doing with a hand who had so little experience with small boats that he thought there was room for a cabin boy? What I want from the crew—besides ceevility—is knowledge. What I don't want is to have to say: "This is the tiller—sometimes called the helm—and it is connected to the rudder, and the rudder is what steers the boat, just the way the front wheels steer a motor car." And go on from there. What I do want is a man with the know-how and the intuition to say: "Skipper, you've done all the work so far, so if you'll let me take over and you go below and sack off I'll call you when we get to port." Where, oh where, is there such a paragon?

I don't want anybody who whistles—especially through his teeth. Or sings. Or hums. Or talks. I once knew a man—I strangled him years ago—who plumped his fanny down on my chart as I was entering a tricky channel and began to tell me about the tenets of the Mormon faith. I am strictly one who can leave religion alone until the anchor is down and the sails have been given a harbor furl, and so he perished without the sanction of the church.

If you incline to the belief that this incident has been caressed by the fond fingers of exaggeration, perhaps I can restore your faith by telling about the artist who talked. Sitting at the tiller of my boat he told me that it was the artists of the nation—the painters, the musicians, the poets—who had performed the really fine deeds of heroism and inspiration in the late war. From that he branched into a discussion of modern art which happened to be raging in the cockpit at the moment. A dull fellow I—inartistic, inarticulate and pragmatic—I watched the course the artist steered while talking. Now he had the wind abeam and now he had the headsails ashake, and never did he do as he had been previously instructed and sail her by the wind. Finally I took over. But not before informing him that not even the most gifted artist in the world could prattle on about art and at the same time steer my boat.

So he won't sail with me any more. And neither will the bird who thirsts for knowledge by day, by night, and at other undesignated times. The one who says, "Skipper, when you're reeving off the deadeyes of a vessel's shrouds, do you start your lanyards from inboard or outboard?" Or, "What is a cesser clause?" What, I ask you, in return, has either of these topics to do with sailing the boat?

Then I'll never extend a second invitation to the man who comes aboard for a cruise carrying his gear in a large square suitcase that has to be moved from my bunk every time I want to turn in. Or the one who brings no gear at all and borrows my leather coat half an hour or so before I want to wear it myself. Or the sloppy Joe who leaves his wet clothes in a heap at the foot of the companionway ladder. Or the one who lays all his socks, shirts, and sweaters out on deck to dry just as we're sharpening up for a thrash to windward.

I want to avoid the man who spends all his waking hours in

reminiscence—but I guess we can skip that as it comes under the aforementioned head of talking. And I have little room for the man who lies on his back looking aloft for an entire watch, saying nothing, and remarks as he is about to be relieved, "Some time when you think of it, Alf, it would be a good idea to renew the chafing gear on the lee spreader. I notice quite a bad hole being worn in the mainsail." Contrarily, I disapprove of the seagoing doctrinaire who spends all his time rearranging things according to lessons he learned in books. For example, he has read that you must never half hitch a halliard, and he goes about substituting myriads of round turns for single half hitches, with the result that when you want to get a sail down in a hurry it's just too bad. (If I'm aboard another man's boat and find that he doesn't half hitch his main sheet I mutter sadly to myself: "Different ships, different long splices," and respect the owner's principles. And when a sea comes aboard and floats all the round turns off the cleat so that the sheet pays out to the knot in the bitter end I say nothing—at the time.)

I take issue with the learned Mr. Taylor when he advises you to pick a skipper who has accumulated a spare tire around his middle. That skipper didn't get that fat going to sea in a small boat. On the contrary he goes cruising in order to reduce, and he ships a cook of his own turn of mind and curve of belly. Come chow time and the fat cook, enjoying the sunshine while waving greeting to passing boats and airplanes, rubs his fat pot affectionately and declares: "It's too good a day to slave in the galley, so what say, Boss, if I toss up a couple of cans of peaches and let the crew help themselves?" The fat skipper, who could exist for days on his accumulated stores, says: "That's a swell idea, Doctor. Time enough for a hearty meal when we get ashore. In the meantime, Alf, if you're going below you might break out my special cheese and a box of crackers and a bottle of beer."

No, for a cook give me the Cassius who requires 5000 calories a day merely to keep soul and body together. He's up with the larks to brew a pot of coffee. By the time he has followed that with a pitcherful of orange juice he turns to eagerly on the bacon and eggs, and the rest of the boys barely get the table cleared of the breakfast things before the starving cook has popped twelve pounds of beef into the oven for the noonday meal. This amazing creature—he exists only in my imagination and is a professional cook at that—adds strawberry shortcake and whipped cream to a dinner of soup, meat, and three vegetables, and by supper time practically has the boys in tears begging him to serve nothing more hearty than cold consommé, salmon timbale, and alligator pear salad, with fresh baked Boston cream pie as a gastronomic epilogue. . . . These, I may say, are the ravings of a lean and hungry skipper who can dream without being able to afford to set a Lucullan table.

If I were looking for a navigator for my crew I would want one who is the reverse of me in many particulars. For example, I would want a man who is young, neat and methodical. I would want him to keep his big mouth shut in matters that did not concern him—such as the trim of the main, and whether or no to let go the jibtopsail sheet as the helmsman calls "Hard alee." But in his own field—and here I shall not continue to offer myself as a horrible example—I wouldn't care whether he took three sights a day or thirty as long as he made his landfall precisely when and where he expected it.

On the other hand, I wouldn't want a navigator who was more interested in helping out in the galley than he was in the practice of his art. Or one who says: "Navigation? Nothing to it. Snap a couple of stars and there you are." I've known that kind of free and easy navigator to make a slight arithmetical error that cost him his landfall and a wasted day at the termination of a Bermuda Race. What's more, I don't want a navigator who learned compass courses and bearings in degrees while in the Navy and doesn't know offhand the difference between windward and leeward.

I can get along also without a navigator who talks all the time—or have I previously mentioned the besetting sin of garrulity in long distance racing and cruising? I particularly don't want a navigator who believes it to be his duty to set a course and try to make the boys steer it, irrespective of whether the boat is being pinched to death. Let such a man do his pinching in night clubs, say I, where everybody can enjoy it.

If that sums up my feelings about navigators let me sink a dart in the shipmate who has an excess of enthusiasm. You know the type. We're standing forward looking things over and I say quietly, "Give me a hand sweating up this halliard." Instantly this energetic egotist rouses out of the cockpit, charges forward and knocks us out of the way, doing the job himself. Or he is forward watching the headsails and I'm aft and require a slight trim of the main sheet. He senses the situation, leaves his post and takes such a mighty strain on the sheet that he shakes the wind out of the sail and the sail out of its boltropes. Or when we're running in a soft air I say I'd like one to trim the spinnaker pole a trifle aft—and this vicious volunteer and his twin brother and a coupla other guys just like them man the fore guy, the after guy and the spinnaker sheet and halliard and ruin the set of the sail before I can lay hand to the sounding lead or any other lethal weapon.

Of course, I'll take him as a crew member in preference to the one who has never been seasick in his life but spends his time crawling from one lee bunk to another and on bright sunny days lies on deck blocking the companionway. Or the congenitally lazy loafer who has to be shown where the ice, ice pick, tumbler, whiskey bottle, and galley pump are before he can hand me up a highball. Or the improvident one who comes aboard without cigarettes or matches.

As you see, the list of non-indispensable crew members is as long as a piece of sail twine, and if I were interested in spinning out my objections until they reached approximately the dimensions of a new jib for *Hotspur* I could, like William Hardcase Taylor, write on forever. But let me be honest and present the reverse of the picture in a few short, cogent sentences.

I'll take a crew of experienced sailors. Each of them will know intuitively where all the gear is stowed. He knows the perils of drinking or eating too much. Or too little. He can steer, pilot, handle sail, and navigate. He never drops shaving brushes into the toilet bowl. He has single-handed it on occasion. He is neat and seaman-like. Silent without being morose. Doesn't whistle. Knows how tired I am and stands my watches without complaint. Naturally, my ideal crew would consist entirely of skippers.

(ED. NOTE: *The opinions expressed in the above article are those of the author and not necessarily those of the editors of this magazine. It seems to the latter that this is a type of cantankerous skipper that might well have been mentioned in Mr. Taylor's masterpiece on employer-employee relationship, entitled "Skippers We Can Live Without."*—THE OLD MAN)

"100 Tons of Bronze, Son"

Cleveland Amory

A Walter Mitty-like fantasy of the author's recollection of his America's Cup "career"

Cup Defenders! Schmup Defenders! Don't talk to me about these modern Defenders. Tenders, that's what they are, landlubbering tenders! Why, boy, before you were born, I shipped on a Defender in the days when they *were* Defenders. A J-boat, that's what she was, son, the *Vanitie*. And as a matter of fact, if I do say so myself, she was the largest J-boat ever built.

And would you like to know how old I was, boy, when I took the helm of *Vanitie*? Twelve, son, that's what I was, *twelve*. And don't think I was just out for the air, either. I was out for the Auld Mug, that's what I was out for. And not just against one other boat either—like these modern trials. "Boat-to-boat," they say. Children, I say. Those aren't races, boy, those are yacht club dances. No, boy, I was up against five other boats—you count 'em, *five—Resolute, Yankee, Enterprise,* never mind the others. And do you know who won, son? Do you know who won?

But I am getting ahead of my story. It all started one morning off ol' Marblehead. We were lying at anchor, there—on the good ship *Leonore*. A Q-boat she was, built in ol' Norway. I had shipped on that summer to give my father and brother the benefit of my experience. I had taught my father as much as I could and I was bringing my brother along nicely. Regular doses at regular intervals regularly repeated, that's the way I saw it. Not too much at any one time.

And, if I do say so myself, I ran a taut ship. They were coming along fine. Ship-shape. Then, lo and behold, that morning, if young

Gerry Lambert doesn't heave by on his big launch *Utilitie*, tender of the *Vanitie*. "On board *Leonore*," he hollers over his megaphone. "Ahoy there."

"Ahoy there yourself, Gerry my lad," I hollers back. And then, out of the clear blue, he asks the question. "Any body on board can sail a J?" he wants to know. "I'm shy a skipper."

Well, it called for some quick thinking. I took a look at my father. Much as I loved him as a man and had high hopes for him as a sailor, I just didn't think he was ready. A Q, yes—50 feet overall. But *Vanitie*, 84 on the line and 126 overall, no. Then I looked at my brother. Why the little shaver had just turned 15. I couldn't take the chance. No, this was one for the old man. It had to be me.

All this thinking, of course, took far less time than it takes to tell it. A good sailor man, I've always said, thinks in seconds. But with a good racing man, it's split seconds. I picked up the megaphone. "I'll go, Ger," I volunteered.

In a moment the big *Utilitie* was hard by. They were going to lower a boat, but I stopped them. "It's blowin' pretty pert," I said matter-of-factly, "fer to lower"—and, with a quick vault, I was on *Utilitie*'s deck. I landed lightly. In a moment Lambert was at my side. "Have you had much experience," he asked, "in J's?"

"Enough," I said quietly. "What's your trouble?"

On the way over to *Vanitie*, Gerry gave me a brief rundown of our situation. It was not good. But I'll always be grateful to Ger that he gave me the bad along with the good. The skipper never lived, I've always said, who was any better than the mate on the watch ahead of him.

In a word, the story was this. We were to be up against the Big Five that day—and for all the marbles. This was the big one—the one we had to win for the Big Skipper Upstairs—I mean, of course, On Deck.

Four of the boats were obviously newer than *Vanitie*—and just built for this—and one of them, *Yankee*, had the best skipper in the business at the wheel. "Charles Francis Adams?" I asked grimly. Lambert nodded. I didn't say anything, but to myself I was thinking, "Well, good ol' Charlie Ad is going to have a fight to the finish this day." As for the rest of them—we went rapidly down the list—they were all trouble. *Enterprise*, backed by New York money and sailed by Mike Vanderbilt—there was no soft touch there. *Whirlwind* was comparatively untested, it is true, but *Weetamoe*! Well, the sardine in the scuppers there was that Gerry himself had been part of the Syndicate that built her.

Again I didn't say anything, but I did plenty of thinking—to myself.

"Ger, my lad," I thought, "it looks like today you're going to beat yourself."

Finally there was *Resolute*—as tough as her name implied. And here, as if things weren't tough enough, we had to give her a time allowance. "We've got to give her," Lambert told me nervously, "2:11."

I calculated quickly. "All right," I told myself, "we'll beat her by 2:12."

By now we had reached *Vanitie*. The crew was all lined up, but I permitted no piping the skipper on board. Instead I shook my head and once more leaped lightly to the deck. But, as I did so, I caught the eye of every man jack of that crew—man by man, mate by mate, even the boatswain's mate. "Aha," I thought, "Norwegians all."

"Captain," I joshed, "you're pretty pronounced toward the Norwegians, aren't you—for a Yay-boat?"

The crew got it, as well as the captain, of course. There's nothing to ease the tension of a Norwegian sailor, I always say, like a skipper that knows when to yoke.

But now there would be no more jokes. "Let's go, boys," I said quietly. "Pass the *Utilitie* forward. Mind the tow line."

That did it. That crew might have thought when they first saw me that I didn't know a jib from a jibe or a beat from a batten. But once they got their first order, they knew. A crew just knows those things, that's all. It's the habit of command, I've always said.

I went aft and took the helm. I don't mind saying a lot of green water had gone over the side since I'd had a wheel like that in my hand. But the years seemed to roll away the minute I put thumb and forefinger on her.

"Head 'er up," I said. "Ready on the main halyard." And while I barked out the commands, 23 of those 26 men pulled up that main as if she were a baby. "Clear away," I shouted. "Let go *Utilitie*." And then, as I spun the wheel, I shouted, "Let go the boom crotch."

I put her over on the port tack. But before we came up on the wind again, and I gave orders to hoist the headsails, I took a moment to size up my opposition. First, Mike Vanderbilt. I could see him, out of the corner of my eye, watching me even as I watched him. And then I saw him look at his watch. "Aha," I thought, "the best starter in the business. Well, today he's going to be the second best." And then I spied Charlie Adams. Lambert had warned me—I knew how he loved to bluff—even when he didn't have right of way. "Well," I thought, "if there's any bluffing in this race he'd better have right of way—or Mrs. Charles Ad's a widow tonight."

By now we had the headsails up. And just as the jib started to draw—bang, went the warning gun. I jockeyed up wind, paying no attention. All the time before the second gun I just rode easy, testing and getting the feel of her. And all this time the others couldn't for the life of them figure what I was doing—which was, of course, exactly what I wanted. What I was doing was testing that starting line. "Aha," I thought, "a better fetch on the port tack. They'll all try that. Well, now."

Bang, went the second gun. Now they were all four of them pulling off—I could see all four skippers with their watches. They were crowding each other—jockeying for the same position.

"Let go the mainsheet," I hollered. The Captain looked up. The crew hesitated. Everyone thought I had lost my senses. "I believe, Captain," I said quietly, "I said something about letting go the main-sheet."

The captain repeated the command and the crew hopped to. I sawed off and ran down on the port tack and away from the line. By now they thought I was really crazy. There was one minute left. Out of the corner of my eye I could see all five boats now and on the port tack.

"Ready about," I hollered. We came around. And then, with just 20 seconds left, we were bearing down on five boats—all by our-selves—on the starboard tack. "My God," muttered the boatswain's mate, "ol' Cleve is sweeping the line on the starboard tack."

But I had more important things to think about. "Right of way," I shouted, "right of W-A-Y." You could hear the groans as one by one *Whirlwind, Weetamoe, Enterprise* and *Resolute* had to tack away from the line. Finally there was just old Charlie Adams left. "Right of way," I holler again. Charlie seemed to be pretending he didn't hear me. By now there wasn't 50 feet between us. At last he looked. "You wouldn't," he shouted.

"Charlie," I said quietly, "I've got 100 tons of bronze that says I would."

At the last possible second, Charlie came about—the starting gun went off—and the race was on. But by then, of course, we had such a lead that, almost from that moment, we had nothing but clear sailing.

I should say clear sailing except for one incident. It happened on the second leg, when we were close reaching for the second mark—and we were caught by a wicked puff.

I should explain here that in a light breeze, *Vanitie* handled, as Gerry himself had said, like a violin. But in a breeze of wind, off wind, she could be a wild beast—it took plenty of strength to handle her.

In any case, when that puff caught her, even my strength wasn't enough. It was some puff—one of those green ones that blows the tops right off the waves. And, when it hit us, we had green water right up to the companionway and we started to have bad lee helm. I kept slammin' it to her and I never changed expression. I was trying, obviously, not to let the crew know that even the old man himself had doubts about this one.

But I did have doubts and I knew we were in trouble. We had to let that jib sheet off to make her head up. But how to do it? Worst of all, those other boats astern had seen what had happened to us. They were heading up to avoid the squall, and if we couldn't get *Vanitie* headed up, too, we'd never get near that second mark. Every darn one of those tugs would go by us as if we were tied to a mooring. It was good bye Auld Mug.

The crew was willing, I'll say that for them. They knew how important it was to let that jib sheet go, and one after another they tried. But those cleats were four feet under green water—the best crew who ever sailed couldn't get near them. I remember the last kid who was going to try. I just couldn't let him. "Watch out for that damn kid," I heard myself say.

I was cracking. But I couldn't. It was now or never. With a sigh I reached in my pocket and took out my knife. "Captain," I said, "take the wheel." "My God, Cleve," he says, "you're not going to cut that sheet. We'll lose that way too." "No, Captain," I smiled, "I'm not." And in a twinkling I dove down there into that hell, green water and all, and cut—not the sheet, of course, but the jib *whip*.

That was all there was to it. The crew cheered, but it wasn't anything really—nothing any one of them couldn't have done if they'd had the guts and the know how and the experience and set their mind to it and kept moving. In any case, immediately the jib eased, and we headed up and—but, well, there's no need to tell the rest. It's all there, in the books. For the record, though, we beat *Resolute*, as I remember, by 2:23 and not, as some have it, 2:13.

And on the run home, for a brief moment, I allowed Gerry to take the wheel. For one thing, by that time we had the race won 40 ways to Sunday—and, for another . . . well, I just knew it was something he'd remember all the rest of his life.

PART VI
Cruising

Cruises, both daring and adventurous and routinely relaxing in tame waters, have been a major subject in every issue, practically the backbone of the magazine, and a subject of enduring interest to a majority of readers, according to surveys taken over the years. It was a practice in the early years to carry book-length serials of interesting cruises, most of which defy excerpting in an anthology like this. In one issue, we would leave Slade Dale in his 23-foot sloop Postscript at sea on his way to circumnavigate Cuba on a precedent-setting voyage, and pick him up in the next issue for another stage of the passage. Fortunately, one of the epic small boat adventures of all time, Fritz Fenger's voyage through the Caribbean in a sailing canoe, appeared in condensed form and can be included here. It later ran as a book-length serial and book and became a classic sea yarn. From the great wealth of cruising material that has appeared in 80 years, the selections here give an idea of the great variety of the cruising experiences that have been such a colorful part of Yachting's *editorial tradition.*

1917

The Cruise of the *Yakaboo*

F. W. Fenger

One of the classic small boat voyages of all time, by sailing canoe through the Windwards and Leewards

One learns little of the geography of the earth from a school book. I found no mention of the vast Atlantic shelf, that extended for hundreds of miles seaward of Hatteras, where the sperm whale comes to feed in the spring. Nor was there scarcely any mention of the Lesser Antilles, a chain of volcanic peaks strung out from the corner of South America. Yet it was on these peaks that my thoughts clung like dead grass on the teeth of a rake and would not become disengaged.

My first plan was to ship on a whaler bound on a long voyage. From Barbados I would sail the 90 miles to Grenada. A wise Providence saw to it that there was no whaler bound on a long voyage for months. I did find a British trading steamer bound out of New York for Grenada. She had no passenger license, but it was my only chance and I signed on as A. B. On the top of the cargo in the hold was the crated hull of the *Yakaboo*, the pretty "mahogany coffin" as they named her, that was going to carry me 500 miles of the most delightful deep sea sailing imaginable. The *Yakaboo*—a sailing canoe 17 feet long had a beam of 39 inches. From a plan she grew in a little shop in Boothbay, and the finished hull weighed less than her skipper—147 pounds.

On the eighth day out we spoke the lonely island of Sombrero and we steamed between Saba and Statia to lose sight of land for another day—my first in the Caribbean. The warm trade winds, the skittering flying-fish chased by tuna and the rigging of awnings proclaimed we were now in the tropics. The land under a rusty old fort melted away before our eyes and we slipped into the harbor of St. George's. The houses, some of them white but more often washed with a yellow, were of the French type, their weathered red tile roofs in pleasing contrast to the green of the surrounding hills. A last breakfast with the Captain and Mate and I was ashore with my trunk and gear. The *Yakaboo* was lifted from the hold and as the nature of my visit became known I was given all possible aid in preparing for my voyage.

When all articles of my outfit, tent, clothing, provisions and numerous other supplies were compactly stowed away in the compartments, *Yakaboo* sat on the water as jaunty as ever. I have come into the habit of saying, "we," for next to a dog or a horse there is no companionship like that of a small boat.

After a delightful morning spent in coasting past the green hills of Grenada, I hauled the *Yakaboo* up on the jetty of the picturesque coast town of Goyave and here loafed through the heat of the day and spent the night in the cool barracks of the native constabulary.

On the second day my log reads: "After beating for two hours in a stiff wind I found the canoe was sinking by the head and leaking in the forward compartment. I was about a mile from shore and when the water began to pour in through the centerboard well I found the bailing-plugs in the cockpit floor were useless and that every drop of water coming in was retained. Making for shore with all speed I made Duquesne Point where the canoe sank in the small surf."

After the *Yakaboo* had been bullied into some semblance of tightness we reached Tangalanga Point—the extreme northern end of Grenada and I now set sail for the first time in the open sea. When I ran past the wicked reef and reached Sauteurs, the surf was piling up on the beach five feet high and the cockpit was full of water. A figure on the jetty directed me to a sloop, and my outfit was quickly transferred to the larger craft and the canoe trailed off on a long scope of line, and I jumped into the whaleboat sent out, and was soon on shore. One of the men who assisted me was Jack Wildman, a Scotch cocoa buyer who owned a whaling station on Ile-de-Caille, and he arranged for his whalers to convoy me to the island where I could stay as long as I liked and overhaul my outfit for the fight through the rest of the islands. After ten days spent in whaling on Ile-de-Caille, I resumed my cruise and late in the afternoon stepped out of my canoe on the uninhabited island of Mabouya, lying off Cariacou, where I camped for the night. The next day I ran alongside the jetty of Hillsboro on the shores of Carriacou where I enjoyed the hospitality of Whitefield Smith the Commissioner.

On the fifth day I sailed for new islands and landed on Frigate, which lies off Union. Here I found plenty of wood and soon had my campfire going. It was good to be a Robinson Crusoe again if only for a few hours. While I was cooking my chocolate, a little open boat came down the wind from the eastward. As she beached two black men jumped out and a third—a white man—unfolded his length and I recognized Walker, famous as the tallest man throughout these islands. The British government had but lately taken over Union Island and it had been Walker's duty to survey and divide up the land so that it could be sold in small tracts to the natives. During our conversation I admitted some knowledge of drafting upon which Walker said, "Come over and help me finish a map of the island" and so I became an inhabitant of Union for a few days.

From Union I reached Mayero, one of those romance islands where in its stagnation one can trace a past once beautiful, now pathetic. At the time of the unrest in France, a cadet branch of the Saint-Hilaire family came to this island, thrived, and finally died with the ebbing fortunes of sugar cane. The last descendant of this famous old family still governs the island under a sort of feudal system.

The next day I left the island, Walker insisting upon accompanying me in his sloop. After three hours of sailing we ran shore on Cannouan to cook our luncheon. Here it was that Walker taught me a new trick. The natives of the island had come down to have a close look at the strange man who was sailing about the islands in "de canoe." They handled everything, examined my dishes and one of them even started to open my food bags. I swore at them but they did not seem to understand.

"Oh, I'll fix 'em," said Walker, at which he swept one arm toward them and then pointing at me yelled: "Get out! or 'de mon' will put a curse on you."

The words were magic. With one bound they cleared the place and for the rest of our stay I could see the tops of their woolly heads and the gleam of their white eyeballs, curiosity and fear holding them at the nearest point of safety.

The moon swung over its zenith, I could make out little huts and trees on the island and I finally saw a small fire on the beach, and it was after eleven when I rowed up to the jetty. The curiosity of the natives was unappeased, for I tied my painter to a sloop at anchor and I was ready to turn in when a native policeman drove the crowd inshore. I had hardly fallen asleep when Walker sailed alongside and awoke me. He had lost track of me in the darkness and had been looking for me by moonlight. He left me at five in the morning, and after spending a few hours ashore with Old Bill Wallace the Nestor of whalemen in the Grenadines, I resumed my voyage and set sail for Saint Vincent and the Carib Country.

My entry into the port of Kingstown was spectacular, but hardly to my liking. The mail sloop from Bequia had spread the news of my coming and as I neared the shore, I saw that the jetty and the beach were black with black people. A rain squall came down from the hills, but it did not seem to dampen the interest of the people nor dim the eye of my camera. I had scarcely stepped out of the canoe when the crowd rushed into the water, lifted her on their shoulders and she continued on her way through a sea of bobbing heads.

Among the officials in the patio was one who pushed himself forward and gave me a package of mail. He was His Majesty's Postmaster, *Mr.* Monplaisir.

"Is there anything I can do for you?" asked H. M. P. M., addressing me by my first name. "Yes, Monty,"—he was pleased at this—"you can lead me to a fresh-water shower."

On the 22nd of March, I sailed out of the roadstead of Kingstown before a stiff breeze which the trade sent around the southern hills like a helping hand. It was only natural that the wind should become contrary off Old Woman Point where it hauled around to the North. Then it changed its mind, crawled up and down the mast a couple of times, and died out in a hot gasp.

So far, I had done but little rowing in smooth waters and the sense of stealing quietly along the lee coast to enjoy its intimacy was a new pleasure. All these islands, especially the lower ones, have more or less the same formation—Grenada, Saint Vincent, Saint Lucia, and Dominica. This information consists of a backbone which rises to a height of from two to three thousand feet and is the main axis of the island with spurs which run down to the Atlantic and the Caribbean, east and west, like the veins of a leaf.

As I rowed out into the bay, I nearly ran down a diminutive craft sailing across my bows. There was something about that double rig—the *Yakaboo* turned around to look at it as we slid by—and sure enough it was *Yakaboo*'s miniature! Not far off a small grinning boy sat on a small bobbing catamaran. He had seen the *Yakaboo* in Kingstown and had made a small model of her—and so she was known to a place before she herself got there. I left a shilling on the deck of the *Little Yakaboo*, but she was not long burdened with her precious cargo.

Rounding DeVolet Point, which corresponds to Tangalanga on Grenada, and I once more felt the roll of the trades. A sea slopped over the gunwale and wet my leg which I drew into the canoe. We were now all island savages together holding up our ticklish craft by the play of our bodies. I looked across the channel to Saint Lucia with her twin Pitons rising distinct, thirty miles away.

March 30th found me once more in the *Yakaboo* rowing out of the bay of Chateau Belaire half an hour after sunrise. I had a lurking suspicion that I had made a grievous error when I had designed the *Yakaboo*; I had perhaps erred on the side of safety and had given her a too powerful midship section in proportion to her ends. That was the feeling I had while sailing in the channels of the Grenadines. I was still travelling eastward as well as northward, and I knew that it would only be by the most careful windward work that I should be able to fetch the Pitons, thirty-one miles away. The wind on this day was the same trade that I had met with lower down, but the seas were longer than those of the Grenadines, and, if not so choppy, were more vicious when they broke; there would be less current to carry me to leeward.

I had scarcely got her under way and was still under the lee of the land when the first sea came, like the hoary hand of Neptune himself and we turned to meet it. Aft I slid, she lifted her bow—just

Caribbean landfall

enough—and the sea broke under us—and we dropped down its steep back, with lighter hearts.

My mainstay was the jelly coconut or water-nut as they called it. This is the coconut that has not yet reached the stage where the meat is the hard, white substance which we meet in the kitchen pantry in the shredded form, but is still in the baby stage when the meat is soft and jelly-like. In this stage the milk is not so rich as later on, but is a sort of sweet coco-tasting water. I never wanted for a supply of coconuts.

When my supply of pilot bread ran out I carried soda crackers and sometimes the unleavened bread of the natives. Raw peameal sausage helped out at times and there was, of course, the chocolate of which I have spoken before. I also carried other tropical fruits besides coconuts, mangoes, bananas, pineapples, but I never ate more than one sort on a run. The coconut was my mainstay, however, and that with a little bread and a piece of chocolate would make an excellent stop-gap till I could reach shore and cook a substantial evening meal.

Sailing as I did—seated only a few inches above the water—I had an excellent opportunity to observe the flying fish which rose almost continually from under the bow of the canoe. Although they were smaller than those I have seen in the channels off the California coast—they were seldom more than about nine inches long—their flight did not seem to be appreciably shorter. Their speed in the water immediately before they emerge must be terrific for they come out as though shot from a submarine catapult; their gossamer wings, vibrating from the translated motion of the powerful tail, make the deception of flight most real.

It was dark and it was raining when I reached Martinique and Fort de France. My clothes were already wet and I sloshed along the narrow sidewalks like a dripping Newfoundland dog. Fort de France was as new and strange to me as St. George's had been and far more interesting. An impending week of rainy weather decided for me and I made up my mind to spend that week here. Until I was ready to put to sea again and sail for Dominica I could not take my outfit away from the customs office. Camping along shore, then, was out of the question. There was no alternative for me than to become for the time a part of the life of the town.

My walks about town were for the most part sallies from the hotel during intermissions between showers—for it rained almost continually for the entire week. These sallies I alternated with periods of writing in the quiet little cabaret where an occasional acquaintance would sit down for a chat, my French taking courage from day to day like an incipient moustache. I usually occupied a marble-topped table under an open window by which bobbed the heads of passers-by.

In the evening, after dinner, I would walk out across the savanna to the still waters of the carenage—I was living in such a civilised state that canoe cruise, whalers, and Caribs seemed to have slipped back into the remote haze of memory—where an aged steamer, clipper-stemmed and with a ship's counter, lay rusting at her moorings, her square ports and rail with ginger-bread white-painted life-net, a delight to one who revels in a past that is just near enough to be intimate. From the carenage my walk would continue along the quay, past the barracks of the naval station across the street from which a tribe of cosy little cabarets blinked cheerfully into the night through open doors and windows. But this life in Fort de France was becoming too demoralising and I should soon be too lazy to cook another meal. The rainy week was over and I bade adieu to the statue of Josephine, extracted my outfit from the jealous care of the duanes, and sailed for the ruined city of St. Pierre, and the thread of my cruise was once more taken up and I was back into the canoe, enjoying the lee coast panorama with my folded chart in my lap for a guide book. It was early in the afternoon when I made out the little beacon on Sainte Marthe Point beyond which lay the roadstead of St. Pierre.

Reviewing these things in my mind, I ran alongside the new jetty built since the eruption and hauled up the *Yakaboo* under the roofing that covers the shore end. There were about ten people there, nearly the entire population of what was once a city of forty thousand.

Looking up at Pelee from the streets of St. Pierre, one felt that surely no destruction from a crater so far off could reach the city before safety might be sought; but as I sat upon the very slope of the crater I could easily imagine a burst of flaming gas that could roll down that mountain side and engulf the city below it in a minute or two of time. That night I read myself to sleep in the cockpit of the *Yakaboo* with my candle lamp hung over my head from the stumpy mizzen mast. I awoke in the morning to find that I had carelessly slipped into the second day of a windy quarter. There was no doubt about it; the trade was blowing strong at six o'clock. I was impatient to be off shore before the surf would be running too high even for the thirty-foot dugout.

The lee coast of Dominica stretching away to the north was in brilliant light. You have probably gathered by this time that the Lesser Antilles are decidedly unsuited for camping and cruising as we like to do it in the North Woods. In a few isolated places on the windward coasts one might live in a tent and be healthy and happy, such as my camp with the Caribs; but to cruise and camp, that is travel and then rest for a day on the beach—this is impossible. In this respect my cruise was a distinct failure.

I tried to sail in those shifting puffs but it was a waste of time. The lee coast of Guadeloupe is noted for its calms and on this May day when the trade to windward must have been very light, there was at times not a breath of air. I settled down for a long row. The heat did not become intense till eleven when what breeze there had been ceased and on all the visible Caribbean I could detect no darkened ruffle of its surface. My long pull at last came to an end when at six o'clock I rowed into a beautiful little bay and beached the canoe at the very doorsteps of the village of Deshaies. The bay was a deep pocket walled by green hills on three sides and open to seaward where the sun with a guilty red face was hurrying to get below the horizon so that he could sneak around again as fast as possible in order to have some more fun scorching inoffensive canoe people.

The bay, a snug enough harbor for small coasters, struck into the land like a tongue of the ocean mottled with shoals and coral reefs while the green of the hills was barred from the blue water by a narrow strip of white sand. The charm of the place was strong and I forgot the hot toil of the day while I stood on the beach by the *Yakaboo* and looked about me. Scarcely two canoe lengths from the water's edge stood the outposts of the village, those meaner houses of the fishermen, the beach combers, and the keepers of small rum shops.

There were iron grills and balconies and bits of paved roadway and courtyard and there were faces among those easy-going people that took my mind back to Mayero and the descendants of the Saint-Hilaire family. But the banded Anopheles were coming from the Deshaies River bed in millions and I returned to the beach where I found the acting mayor waiting for me. He had borrowed a sheet of my note paper which he now returned, a neatly written document to the effect that I had landed that evening in Deshaies—on my way to Montserrat. Then he showed me a great iron key and led me across the street to that "hotel" which is less sought after than needed. It was the town lock-up!

We left the beach in a dead calm. The sun was nearly an hour above an horizon of trade clouds and even as I rowed I could see the wind that was coming begin to darken the water in patches to the eastward. In half an hour the wind caught up to us and soon after I set sail. We were scarcely free of Guadeloupe when the canoe began to move with the first light breaths, over a long easy swell. Montserrat was a hazy blur on the horizon, and I should have to look sharp lest I miss it. As far as I could see to windward, north and south, squalls were now chasing down as though there were two conditions of wind; one a stiff breeze and the other a series of squalls moving independent of and through the first. The canoe was travelling so fast—we were making a good six knots—that I could easily dodge most of the squalls by tacking down the wind like a square rigger. Once I was actually running off on the port tack WSW while the course from Deshaies was NW ¼ W. There was no harm in being thrown off my course to the south and west for it ultimately served to place Montserrat all the more to windward.

There was not much in Montserrat for me. Thirty miles to the northwest lay Nevis and St. Kitts—stepping stones to St. Eustatius and Saba. A nearer invitation than these was Redonda, a rounded rock like Diamond off Martinique which rose almost sheer to a height of a thousand feet out of deep water with no contiguous shoals, a detached peak like those of the Grenadines—a lone blot with Montserrat the nearest land, eight miles away. On the 10th of November in 1493 Columbus coasted along Guadeloupe and discovered Monserratte, which he named after the mountain in Spain where Ignatius Loyola conceived the project of founding the Society of Jesus. "Next," says Barbot, "he found a very round island, every way perpendicular so that there seemed to be no getting up into it without ladders, and therefore he called it Santa Maria la Redonda." The Indiana name was Ocamaniro.

There was just enough breeze to allow me to lean with my elbow on the weather deck. Sharks were as far removed from my thoughts as the discussion of the Immaculate Conception—I believe I was actually deciding that my first venture upon escaping the clutches of the chosen few who guard our national customs would be a large dish of ice cream which I would eat so rapidly that it would chill the top of my head and drive from it forever the memory of the calms of Dominica and Guadeloupe. My mind was fondling this chilly thought when suddenly the flash of a yard of rainbow under my bows announced the arrival of a Dauphin or, as they called them in the days of Labat, a Cock Dorade. By shape of its square-nosed head I could see that it was the male of the species. I have often wondered whether this was not the dolphin of the dying colors—it surpasses even the bonito in the marvellous changes in its hues when expiring.

These fish are common near the northern coast of Martinique. Pere Labat says that in order to catch the dorade without bait one must troll with a fly made of two pigeon feathers on each side of a hook and smeared with dog grease. I watched him leasurely cruise for a while back and forth under the bow when suddenly there was a mighty swirl under the nose of the canoe and I saw the greyish white torpedo form of a huge shark heave after him. The dauphin was not to be caught unawares—the Lord knows how long Mr. Shark had been watching him from under the shadow of the *Yakaboo*—and the pair tore away through the sea, the shark a lagging second. After a hopeless dash the shark gave up the chase.

I left Nevis on a hot calm Sunday morning for Basse Terre, the port of St. Kitts. The row was twelve miles and the calm hotter than that of Guadeloupe. There was no perceptible breeze, just a slow movement of air from the northeast—not enough to be felt—a sluggish current that stranded a ponderous cloud on the peak of Monkey Hill, its head leaning far out over the Caribbean where I rowed into its shadow. When I was still half a mile from the town I stood up in the cockpit and took off my clothes. After I was thoroughly cooled I enjoyed a shower bath by the simple expedient of holding one of my water cans over my head and letting the water pour down over my body. Then I put on my "extra" clothes.

"Don't waste your time here," he said in the swinging dialect of the northern islands, "you will be among your own at Statia and Saba." I had met this Saba man on the jetty, Captain "Ben" Hassel of a tidy little schooner, ex-Gloucester, and he told me of the Dutch islands and their people. He was my first breath of Saba and my nostrils smelt something new. From her earliest days Statia belonged to the Dutch, who, before the British, were masters of the sea and for long years were supreme in maritime commerce. They have always been sailors as you shall see. The policy of the Dutch has always been for free trade and by this they became rich in the West Indies. Oranje-town, on the lee side of the island, half on the cliff, half on the beach, Upper and Lower Town as it was called, with its open roadstead where at times two hundred trading vessels have lain at anchor, possessed no advantages except those of free trade. Statia became a port of call. When our thirteen colonies broke away from the mother country the old Dutch Republic sympathized with the young one and the Dutch made money in the commerce that followed. When the struggle for independence broke out Statia was one channel through which the colonies procured munitions of war. Every nation has its blackguards and it seems that English traders at Statia actually supplied to the American Colonists powder and cannon balls which were made in England and sent to them in Statia.

As in Fort de France, I became a part of the life of Statia; here was a place where I could live for a time. In six hours I had boon companions. There was the Doctor—he would always come first and there was that inimitable Dutchman, Van Musschenbroek of Hendrick Swaardecroonstrasse, the Hague, who had an income and was living in a large house in the town which rented at $8.00 the month and was doing—God knows what. His English was infinitely worse than my German and it was through this common medium that we conversed—Dutch was utterly beyond my ken.

The Bay was only habitable during the early morning hours, before the sun got well over the cliff above. The rest of the day I spent on the plateau where the sun's heat was tempered by the trade which blew half a gale through the valley between the humps, a fresh sea wind. The active men of Statia go to sea; there is little agriculture besides the few acres of cotton and sisal that cry for the labor of picking and cutting for here the negro is unutterably lazy.

I became attached to Statia as I had become attached to Point Espagnol and Fort de France, but I found that little by little my eyes sought the sea more and more. The channel was calling again and peaked Saba became an aggravating invitation. With all the fascination of the old fort and the batteries, the stories of the privateers and the brisk companionship of the Doctor, the call was stronger than the present love, and so one morning I took to the shimmering channel and left the island of England's wrath for her sister where the Dutch rule the English.

To land at Saba in a small boat you must choose the right kind of weather. If there is no wind you cannot sail, if there is too much wind you cannot land, for the seas swinging around the island will raise a surf on the rocky beaches that will make a quick end of your boat. Saba one might call the Pico of the West Indies; not as high by half, but the comparison may stand for all that. From a diameter of two miles she rises to a height of nearly three thousand feet, her summit lost the loftiness of this old ocean volcano.

Here was a town walled in by Nature. The cleft into which the path was built ended in a small ravine that broke into the level plain of the Bottom and it was across this ravine that Freddie Simmons pointed out the ultimate anchorage of the *Yakaboo* and the asylum of her skipper. Our procession started again—we stopped once or twice to meet a Simmons or a Hassel—to make a starboard tack along the western side of the ravine, a short tack to port, and we put the canoe down on the after deck—I should say the back porch—of a cool airy house where we were to keep in the shade for a matter of ten days. Here then was the end of my cruise in the Lesser Antilles. I had swung through the arc from Grenada to Saba and in the doing of it had sailed some six hundred miles. My destination was the Virgins and their nearest island lay a hundred and ten miles away, and I was finally persuaded to take the trip in Capt. Ben's schooner.

We awoke with the Virgins dead ahead. We were approaching them as Columbus had—from the eastward. His course must have been more westerly than ours, but had he seen them first in the morning light as I did the effect must have been very nearly the same—a line of innumerable islets that seemed to bar our way. Herrera says, "Holding on their course, they saw many islands close together, that they seemed not to be numbered, the largest of which he called St. Ursula (Tortola) and the rest the Eleven Thousand Virgins, and then came up with another great one called Borriquen (the name the Indians gave it), but he gave it the name of St. John the Baptist, it is now called St. Juan de Puerto Rico." The largest island to windward he named Virgin Gorda—the Great Virgin.

It was Thursday, June 22nd, the Coronation Day of George Fifth and Queen Mary when we dropped anchor in the pretty harbor of Road Town in Tortola. How ancient will it all sound should someone read this line a hundred years from now! I put on respectable dress, for I had with me my trunk which had followed by intermittent voyages in sloops, schooners and coasting steamers, and from its hold I pulled out my shore clothes like a robin pulling worms of a dewy morning. Shaved and arrayed, I was taken to meet the Commissioner, Leslie Jarvis, who, like Whitfield Smith deserves better than he has received.

It was from Gorda Sound that I began my little jaunt about the Virgins. I had been looking forward to sailing about in the Drake Channel, for in many ways it is ideal canoe water. Here is an inland sea with a protected beach at every hand, blow high or low. Columbus may have been far off when he named them the "Eleven Thousand," but as I sit here and glance at the chart I can count fifty islands with no difficulty, all in range of forty miles. The Virgins are mountainous but much lower than the lesser Antilles and while they are volcanic in origin they do not show it in outline and must be of a much older formation than the lower islands. They are the tail end of the range which forms Cuba, San Domingo, and Porto Rico.

In the morning I was again on the summer sea of the channel. We had cleared Virgin Gorda and were lazing along toward Ginger when I saw the mottled fin of a huge devil fish directly on our course. I was in no mind to dispute his way—not being familiar with the disposition of these creatures, I hauled up a bit and let him pass a hundred feet or so to leeward. I stood up and watched him as he went by and swore that some day I would harpoon just such a fellow as that from a whale boat and take photographs of the doing. Just now I was leaving him alone. His fin, mottled brown and black like the rest of his upper surface, stood nearly three feet high and I judged his size to be about eighteen feet across from tip to tip.

On the afternoon of July Fourth I was bundled aboard the *Lady Constance*, together with the *Yakaboo*, and in the evening we sailed into the Danish port of Charlotte Amalia. So here ends the cruise of the *Yakaboo* after nearly six months of wanderings in the out-of-the-way places of that arc which swings from Grenada to St. Thomas. Six months may seem a long time to you of the office who at the most can get a month of it in the woods or along shore, but to me these months had been so full of varied interest that they were a kaleidoscope of mental pictures and impressions, some of them surprisingly unreal, that I had gone through in weeks. Had it not been for the heat I should have kept on and cruised along Porto Rico, San Domingo, and Cuba, crossing the large channels by steamer if necessary.

1935

Discovering Islands

Irving Johnson

When this famous skipper first started his fabled circumnavigations in vessels named Yankee, *there were parts of the world that were still not properly charted, and he found them*

"No, we won't see any new islands. They have all been charted long ago," I explained to my wife as she sat beside me on the squaresail yard, fifty feet above the deck. "There certainly are plenty of uncharted reefs around here, but islands are a different matter, although some of them already on the charts are as much as fifteen miles out of position. But you can see islands for miles and they would all have been charted and named for some years now."

We were on a round-the-world cruise in the schooner *Yankee*, doing masthead piloting among the islands of the Admiralty Group which lie about two hundred miles north of New Guinea. On the chart these islands looked sufficiently out of the way to be especially inviting, as they proved, in fact, to be. We found most of the natives living in villages built on shallow reefs just offshore from the main island of Manus. This isolation gave them greater protection from the wild Manus raiding parties. These houses of the natives were almost invariably built on piles over the water, and quite often the only ground close by was that which they had built up artificially by throwing all the loose coral rocks they could gather into one pile. This custom provides deeper waterways for canoes, but the islands themselves were seldom used for any purpose whatever. In going from one house to another, the natives always use their canoes, although the water is nowhere deeper than two feet. Even four-year-old children have their own tiny dugouts, without outriggers, in which they stand up and paddle along the watery streets of their village as confidently as do their fathers.

Leaving our first anchorage in the group, we headed west along the coast of Manus, the large island, through a maze of reefs seventy miles long and twenty-five miles wide. This would mean two whole days aloft for me, as it is safe to move only when the light is suitable. Piloting in a region such as this is a strange procedure; the chart is absolutely useless except to keep track of approximate position in relation to the various islands of the group, and no soundings are shown on it. This was an unusual experience for me, after doing most of my navigating along the American and European coasts and the Atlantic Ocean, where soundings and aids to navigation are dependable. Here there is nothing to trust but one's eyes. The difference between the reefs and clear water is plain enough when the sun is behind and a light breeze is ruffling the water, provided there is not some large light-colored cloud above which reflects its light on the water just ahead. When this happens, or when the sun is ahead, it is most difficult to distinguish a reef until you are almost upon it.

Many times I have found the appearance of the water misleading as to depth, and I found this change was probably due to differences in the transparency of the water even more than to the character of the bottom. Whenever approaching a shoal in a new group, I have a man on deck take several soundings to give an idea of what depths to expect with different shades of green. When a light brownish color is seen, you may be sure that the reef is practically awash because it is the growing coral and seaweed that make that color. The next deeper water shows a very light blue; this color is the reflection from the white sand through four to eight feet of water. Then, as the reflection from the white sand gets darker, you have to be especially careful in gauging depth as it is necessary to take into account the character of the water in which you are sailing. There are usually many dark, almost black, coral patches spotted here and there on the white sand, but one always gauges the depth by the appearance of the sand itself. Even in the South Seas it is difficult at times to see the bottom in four fathoms. Off Pitcairn Island we could easily see the bottom at a hundred feet; in the Marshall Bennett Islands we let go the anchor in ninety feet and watched it hook into the coral as we backed the ship towards a reef to see if there was room to swing.

Another thing to watch for in doing such work is the approach of a squall which brings such a downpour of rain that to move at all would be folly. When a squall is seen approaching, the procedure is to bring the bow of the ship up to the lee side of some reef and drop the hook in from two to five fathoms of water. Here the bowsprit is hanging over the reef, which may be just awash, but under the stern there is no bottom at twenty fathoms. Sometimes the anchor will have to be placed two or three times before it will hook on some projection to keep it from sliding off into the deep water.

It was just after getting under way from one of these forced stops that I saw a tiny speck ahead on the horizon. Because of its bearings it could not be an island as the chart showed none. Standing up with the binoculars, I thought I made out the bridge of an approaching ship. What a ship would be doing in those waters I could not imagine, but there are many stories of Japanese shell poachers who go around to isolated islands and often steal large quantities of the shell that natives, or white men, have collected to await shipment. They have large crews and are so heavily armed that they are able to steal from these smaller islands without fear of resistance.

Soon two more specks appeared on the horizon and the first one, growing larger, now looked more like a clump of trees than a ship. We took more bearings and I had the chart brought aloft to me, but there certainly were no islands charted where these specks appeared. However, with such a mess of reefs as showed up ahead, even brand new islands would have to wait to be investigated. It was now afternoon and the sun drawing ahead caused a glare on the water which made the reefs hard to see. But perhaps the most disconcerting thing was the strong current that caused tide rips which made even deep water look like a breaking reef. I had planned to leave the Admiralty Group on this day, so, with the moderate breeze, we were now making our utmost speed under power and sail, trying to get clear of all the outlying reefs before the light failed. Even the squaresail was set and we were bowling along at a great rate. Suddenly a long reef appeared ahead.

"Stop her!" I yelled, and the Diesel was shifted into neutral, but the sails still kept us piling along. Then, over to starboard, a heavier tide rip showed where the water was probably deeper.

"Starboard, six points. Brace the yard!" And we skirted along the reef. Deeper water showed up.

"Port four. Let her go ahead!" Now, just off our starboard bow there appeared a queer looking, oval shaped atoll which showed above the surface only in two long sandbars at one end. The remainder of the symmetrical oval was a narrow, light brown strip of live coral with even narrower strips of light green bordering it inside and out. There was no pass in the reef but in the center, as well as all around, was deep water.

"Port four more. Square the yard and jibe the mains'l over!" We

Brigantine *Yankee*, successor to the Johnsons' schooner

had found a pass only two hundred feet wide between the long reef
to port and the partially submerged atoll to starboard.

Now it looked as though we were at last clear and we turned our
attention to the new islands. By this time another pair of them had
appeared, making a total of five, all stretched out along the outside
of the main group where the chart showed open ocean. I was just

thinking how glad I was that we were clear of the reefs as, with the sun so far ahead, we could see nothing under water more than one hundred feet in front of the ship. Suddenly I looked down and saw several flashes of dark green. And we were racing along with the bottom appearing right under our bow as plain as day.

"Let her go astern! Hard astarboard! Heave the lead!"

The mate, Fred Jackson, had the lead ready and called out in quick succession, "Eight fathoms; seven fathoms; five fathoms." Now it looked even shallower to starboard.

"Stop her and hard aport!" Slowly she swung back before the wind. "Steady at that!" The depth was still five fathoms. We might get across, but there was no telling how wide the reef might be. Now it looked shallower ahead. "Hard aport!"

And the soundings came, "Four and a half; three and a half; three fathoms."

"Clew up squaresail and douse jib!" I bawled. "Get the anchor ready. Full speed astern. Haul mainsail amidships as she rounds up!" Still getting three fathoms, and we draw about two.

"Let go the anchor!" The chain hardly rattled, it was on the bottom so soon, but we paid out sixteen or eighteen fathoms because of a strong current which held us broadside to the wind.

"Clew up topsail. Down foresail and mainsail. We'll stay here for the night and find out in the morning how much more of this reef we've got to cross." It was still only 2:30 P.M., but looking ahead into the sun we could see no more than if it were midnight.

The rest of the afternoon was spent taking bearings of the new islands and observations of the sun. More observations in the morning put us in Latitude 2° 08′ S and Longitude 146° 23′ E. The lines of position from these observations came out exactly on the D. R., which was computed from bearings of two of the charted islands nearest us, while two more islands, which were also in sight, were definitely charted a couple of miles out. This gave me a good position from which to chart the five new islands.

We felt greatly relieved to be anchored even if it did look as if we were in the middle of the ocean except for the small islands in the distance.

From the masthead in the morning the shoal at which we were anchored proved to be extensive, with a depth of three fathoms over a large area, but I doubt if there was less than three fathoms anywhere. We got under way about 9:30 with the sun behind us showing up every reef within miles.

On the way out past the new islands, dozens of bearings and cross bearings were taken by the mate, while from aloft I was able to get a fairly accurate idea of the size, shape, and depth of the various reefs. As we approached the first islands, several natives climbed into an outrigger canoe and paddled out to us. We slowed down, thinking they might have something to trade, and also to learn the native name for the island. But in answer to our question, in Pidgin English, "What name belong this fella island?" they yelled back something which we could not make out. Apparently they didn't live there.

Most of the islands seemed to be of fairly recent origin; two of them had only bushes on them, two more showed trees thirty-five or forty feet high, and another bore larger trees and many coconut palms. They were composed of sand and probably at no point were they more than eight or ten feet above sea level. A chart I have drawn shows better than any description their situation on the long shallow reef.

After these were all charted, arguments and suggestions fell thick and fast as to what we should name the new islands. The atoll is so different from the usual coral formations in this vicinity that we felt it also should be named. We therefore called it Rufus Reef for the ship's doctor, Rufus Southworth, who was at the wheel when we ran between it and the long reef. Besides, we all liked the sound of it. One island of course had to be Yankee Island for the ship. The other four were named for several people who made the cruise possible: Arthur Island, Exy Island, Roger Island, and Search Island. The family names may sound a little strange, but they are in good company with others to be found on the charts of these waters: Annie Florence Island, Violet Patch, Katharine Bay, Lizzie Weber Islands, Marie Louise Reef, Clarence Strait, and Bassett Smith Shoal. Besides, we felt that no name we could choose could possibly be objected to when the chart has already admitted two such as Boo Island and Blupblup Island.

1960

Icebound in the Far North

Donald MacMillan

Few vessels have had more passages in the Arctic than the schooner
Bowdoin, and this was one of her most dangerously challenging

"If you would bring back the wealth of the Indies, you must take
with you the wealth of the Indies," goes the saying.

The arctic explorer is unable to do this. He must penetrate a new
country, where people have lived for hundreds of years, whose
language is strange, whose attitude towards life is wholly different
from his own. He must prepare his ship to stand crushing icefields
and winds of unknown velocity. He must anchor where no ship has
anchored before. He must select his men with greatest care for they
will be pitted against depressing darkness for one, two or three
years—perhaps even four, as we were from 1913 to 1917.

The real explorer is on his own. His life, and that of his associates,
depends upon his ability as a leader and, most important, *careful
preparation*. Careless selection of a single item has caused the death
of every member of an expedition!

As I recall my 30 trips into the Far North, and the tense moments
when all seemed lost, one touch-and-go affair in 1924 stands clearly
in my memory. It wasn't the lives of my men at stake. It was the life
of a ship with over 300,000 miles of arctic work to her credit, my
schooner *Bowdoin*.

My objective on this expedition was a safe little nook in the Far
North from which, after establishing winter quarters, I could drive
my dogs over the heights of Ellesmere Island to Eureka Sound, to
Axel Heiberg Land, to unexplored Ellef and Armund Ringnes Islands, and even out on the unknown Polar Sea.

There were anxious moments long before we reached the Far
North. The *Bowdoin*, built by the Hodgdon Brothers of East Boothbay, Maine, was considered one of the strongest wooden ships afloat,

double-timbered and planked with native white oak, reinforced by two watertight bulkheads, with 21 tons of cement moulded into her frame and a spoon bow armored with ponderous steel plate.

To reach the Far North we had to thread our way through the rocks and ledges sprinkled along the Labrador—thousands of these from the Straits of Belle Isle to the entrance of Hudson Bay. And our last 400 miles was sailed without a chart of any kind. Only vigilance and skill in estimating depth of water by color brought us safely through the intricate inside waterways to the various Eskimo villages tucked away in remote corners of the coast. Greenland itself presented fully as many difficulties. This forbidding coast had for a century been closed to traffic by international agreement, and charts were not available.

We were more at home when we reached the land of the Polar Eskimos in North Greenland, for I had lived there for five years and knew every rock and island, every bay and inlet along the coast. Furthermore, I had sledged over each foot of it with my dog team, and detected rocks, boulders and shoals by the bulge they made in the sea ice at dead low water. Not an ideal method of charting dangerous spots!

Eventually we rounded Cape Alexander, exactly half way between the Arctic Circle and the North Pole. From my "ice barrel" lookout, at the foremast head I surveyed the ice-covered waters of Smith Sound and Kane Basin beyond. There were no lanes or leads. No ship, however strongly constructed and powerfully engined, could conquer such a mass of ice.

We were navigating in a dangerous part of the Arctic, first seen by that tough old seaman William Baffin more than 300 years before. South of this point it was child's play compared with what lay to the north. Almost from this point Baffin had turned his little *Discovery* south to announce to the world what he had seen—and he was not believed. The consensus of the most learned geographers of England was that he could not have sailed that far north in his little ship of 55 tons—incidentally, the size of my *Bowdoin*. Baffin was called a plain liar. His sketches and surveys were deleted from all circum-polar charts, and remained removed for more than 200 years!

In August, 1852, England's Captain Inglefield in the screw-schooner *Isabelle*, 149 tons, steamed gaily in, the first steamer to enter these waters. But, as he wrote, "A strong northerly gale with low temperature" compelled him to return southward.

One year later our own explorer, Dr. Elisha Kent Kane, rounded Cape Alexander in his ill-equipped schooner *Advance*. With more courage than judgment, he drove his vessel into the ice pack. He zigzagged from shore to shore; even moored his ship to rocks to prevent her from being carried southward. She was aground a dozen times. Still undaunted, he continued into unknown waters and discovered a harbor where he spent two winters. His ship is there now under the ice—a sacrifice to ignorance of conditions.

Seven years later another vessel was seen by the Eskimos approaching the Cape. It was the *United States* from Boston under command of Dr. Isaac Israel Hayes, who had the idea that he could do better than his former commander, Dr. Kane. After struggling for several days against violent winds and that invincible polar pack, he crept into a sheltered nook where he stayed for the winter. After that he was glad to return south to Port Foulke. His ship was practically a wreck—her topmasts and bowsprit gone, her planks bruised and broken, her rudder torn from its pintles!

My *Bowdoin*, heading north, finally reached the spot where another famous ship, the *Polaris*, was nipped and 19 men, women and children began their 1500 mile drift to the shores of Labrador—on an ice cake! From October 15 to May 30 they drifted through the Arctic night! They were found by Captain John Bartlett.

Off Victoria Head, which I could barely discern in the distance, the gallant *Proteus* had been crushed into a shapeless mass. With solid ice pushing through her greenheart sheathing and planking into her engineroom, she disappeared, leaving her crew bewildered on an icefloe.

In 1906 the SS *Roosevelt*, one of the strongest ships ever built, limped south badly wounded in her first fight with the polar pack. Only Peary's experience and Captain Bob Bartlett's masterly handling could have brought her back.

So we of the *Bowdoin* were now on the battleground of those explorers and our job, like theirs, was to find a home for the winter. Near us was Pandora Harbor, where the British exploration ship *Pandora* was threatened with destruction 47 years before. And just ahead, to starboard, were Etah and Port Foulke, the former headquarters of Robert Peary, 1899–1900, and the latter of Dr. Hayes in 1860–61. I had lived at Etah for four years, fighting everything the Evil Spirits of the North could conjure up against us—drift ice, blizzards, drifting snows, low temperatures, shortage of food, and those terrific cold winds which sweep down from the ice cap.

A harbor at Cape Sabine, where 18 of the Greely party died of starvation years before, was beyond our reach at present. North of Etah on the Greenland side there was only one possible nook where we might find shelter. Only one ship had ever entered it, and for only a few hours. With its back to the hills and its face to the south, Refuge Harbor certainly justifies its name, especially during July and August. From my sledge expeditions north and west in late fall and early spring, I had known it as a beautifully sheltered round hole among the hills, with its covering of ice and snow as smooth and level as a floor. I had never visited it during the summer. Two important questions were: when does Refuge Harbor freeze over in the fall? When does it break out in spring?

At half speed I entered the "door" of the harbor, a narrow passage with the water black and deep, and with no change in color ahead that denoted shoal ground. We coasted on to within a few yards of the northern shore and anchored in five fathoms on a mud bottom. Excellent holding ground!

Lines of soundings, criss-crossing in every direction, failed to detect a single ledge or boulder throughout the bowl, making it a perfect shelter from violent north and northwest winds. It also offered ideal protection from heavy polar sea drift ice, resting so innocently in Kane Basin yet ever ready to tear a ship to pieces. I decided to risk it, and thereby add a bit more to our knowledge. In future years some other ship might need just such a harbor.

Swinging the bow of the *Bowdoin* into the north, from which direction I knew the prevailing winds to blow, I let out some 20 fathoms of chain. A 500-pound kedge with an equal amount of chain in the opposite direction assured me that the *Bowdoin* would be right there in the spring when the sun returned. We soon discovered fresh water among the hills, a deep, beautiful little lake within 300 yards of the harbor, that could be kept open throughout the winter. Thirty gallons of water were to be brought each day from the lake to the ship.

Within a week our non-magnetic station was constructed and occupied by our two men from the Carnegie Institution of Washington. Eskimo hunters were in the field supplying us with meat from land and sea. Our work got under way.

The winter passed almost too quickly. We were always comfortable under our blanket of snow, and could go below protected by the snow houses erected over our three cabin entrances. Eskimos from the south were frequent visitors; music from home a constant delight. Our radio, first to be used by any arctic expedition, kept us in daily communication with home. Hundreds of American boys sat up nights sending—sending, and hoping their calls might be received and answered by W N P (Wireless North Pole), our radio call.

Darkness slowly gave way to dawn, then to the warm, sunlit days of spring when little ringed seals lay basking in the sun. White glaucous gulls circled against the sky. Musical notes of millions of dovekies filled the fjords. A happy time of year, for food was plentiful. We harnessed our dogs and set out on a thousand—even a two-thousand—mile journey across Smith Sound and over the hills of Ellesmere Island into the unknown. We trusted that the country would furnish food both for the dogs and ourselves.

June is the melting month in the North. Snowbanks disappear; water trickles down the face of cliffs; brooks run merrily through valleys. In June pools and puddles appear on the surface of the sea ice, followed by a rapid breakup of the harbor ice, and a drifting away of various sized pans. Blue water is here again, and summer has come.

But no such change occurred in our surroundings that year. As the days passed I grew alarmed. Was it possible that Refuge Harbor did not break out each summer? It wasn't wise to let time answer that question, when it might be too late. Since we were not provisioned for two years, if caught it would be necessary to abandon ship and retreat south to the underground igdlus of the Smith Sound Eskimos.

Ice is easily but slowly cut by placing a dark object on its surface. Acted upon by the warm rays of the sun, the object sinks itself deeper and deeper as the days go by, gradually weakening the whole structure. To aid in the melting, parallel lines of ashes from our galley stove were strewn upon the harbor ice from the bow of the *Bowdoin* to the nearest point of land dead ahead. This black path led to a margin of open water bordering the shore—a narrow lane leading to the harbor entrance, now our only exit. Just such a bordering lane of water, caused by the radiation of heat from the land, is found around the banks of lakes every spring here in our country.

I had sounded out every foot of the way, and had found sufficient depth through the entire passage to float the *Bowdoin* on dead high water. I was confident that such a plan could be carried out successfully. Rather than having to remain a second year, there was but one thing to do—chance it!

The *Bowdoin*, too, seemed to realize that it was now or never. She smashed that ash-strewn lane into smithereens, gaining the open water along the shore. Now came the real test. Thirty yards ahead there was a ledge which was exactly ten feet under water at high tide.

Ordinarily the *Bowdoin* drew ten feet; now, relieved of weight during the winter, possibly only nine. It was high water. By giving the ship full speed ahead, I might, if caught, bounce her over the obstruction.

I jingled the engineroom for full speed ahead. A puff of black smoke shot from the exhaust and we were away! A moment more and—BANG! She hit that ledge and stopped dead. I rang for reverse at full speed. She never budged. I rang for full ahead. No result. We were caught on "dead high" water, a serious condition at the top of the world with no possible help in sight.

On the low tide my ship would be completely out of water, probably perched on top of a rock, possibly with a broken back. The rock, as far as I could judge, was exactly amidships. I was aware that few ships could take such punishment without serious injury. To save the *Bowdoin* the only possible line of action was to balance her on the rock to prevent her falling over on her side into deep water when the tide went down. If that happened, there she would lie submerged—a total loss!

We ran the peak halyards to a huge rock on the side of the cliff, the throat halyards to a hole in the harbor ice. Then we tightened up, starboard and port. With a level on the chart table in my cabin, I watched the bubble move slowly from right to left, meanwhile yelling instructions to my men to tighten up, now starboard, now port.

Badly worried, I ordered the cook, the oldest man on board, to leave for a safer place on the harbor ice. Fastening a rope around his waist, the Mate and Engineer lowered him to an ice cake alongside, on which he paddled away, followed by one of the other men who had injured his arm a few days before.

When the *Bowdoin* was half out of water, we were whispering and tip-toeing about the decks and cabins as if afraid of awakening her from sleep. I had planned to have the boulder on the cliff take the major part of the strain, rather than the harbor ice, which might be "pulled home."

I slid down to a small pan and paddled aft to the main body of ice. As I stood there lining up the two masts, and noting the small angle of heel, I heard the rattle and thud of rocks tumbling from the cliff—she had broken loose.

On board all was instant confusion. Everything not tied down went flying from the decks over the port side with a tremendous splash. A man in the air plunged into the water. I saw my Mate pop out of the after cabin and frantically grab at the binnacle for support. He missed it, and landed flat on his belly in the water. I ran along the edge of the harbor ice and grabbed him by the collar as he came within arm's reach, puffing and blowing. Tom, my second mate, had rescued the engineer, who swore that the ship "went out from under him."

The *Bowdoin* had all the appearance of a complete wreck. She lay on her side with water nearly up to her cabin doors, and her keel still up on the rock. "She's gone!" my men declared. "When the tide comes back, she'll fill and that's the end of her. We can never get her up."

They might be right. And yet, why not give her a chance? When designing the *Bowdoin* with William H. Hand of New Bedford, Massachusetts, I had repeatedly warned him to guard against this very thing. I knew that in uncharted northern waters I would have her on the bottom, high and dry a dozen times.

I ordered my men to drop both of our heavy anchors over the bow with our 125 fathoms of chain, to empty all water tanks, remove all heavy weights, to caulk all hatches and portholes. She must be turned into a corked bottle. Now let the tide return and do its worst! All we could do would be to wait and see.

With far more than passing interest, each of us watched the incoming tide creep up the slanting deck toward the midship hatch. Was it caulked sufficiently tight? Now the water was playing along the sides of the cabins, beginning to lap the portholes. Now it had reached the cabin doors! Tense moments!

When all seemed lost, the *Bowdoin* awoke as if from sleep and began to struggle to her feet. Inch by inch she floated on her side to an upright position as the tide made.

We breathed once more.

"Everybody aboard!" I yelled. "John, start your engine."

John did. She refused to budge.

"All right, boys," I said, with a forced smile, "that was a rehearsal. We'll do the thing all over again, and maybe better."

So we did it over again, except that we compelled the *Bowdoin* to fall over on her *other* side, toward the land. It was not so far to fall and there was no danger of her toppling into the deep water of the harbor. It was a bit hard on the ship, however, for she fell into a bed of rocks which crushed three planks in her bottom. But since I had moulded into her frames when she was built twenty-one tons of cement as inside ballast, I wasn't concerned over her safety.

Familiar with the phases of the moon, and consequent action of the tide, I was encouraged by the fact that the next tide would be at least a foot higher. With my Eskimo helpers, their wives and children, their dogs and all their possessions littering our decks, we awaited the crucial moment of dead high water. When the rising tide reached the waterline, I pulled the engineroom bell and breathlessly awaited results.

The *Bowdoin* evidently had had enough grief to make her wish to go home. She had been frozen in the ice for nearly a year; she had flopped over almost flat in the water; she had been cruelly stabbed by rocks; her shoe had been torn from the keel. With vibrations of her diesel engine, she seemed to tremble in her eagerness to start home. We were off!

Cautiously she picked her way along the edge of the harbor ice toward the entrance. Then something else happened! A small iceberg, driven in by a southwesterly wind, popped around the corner of the bluff. Like a stopper in a bottle, it completely closed our exit!

From the ice barrel I studied the situation. On the starboard side the berg pressed against the shore. Not even a kayak could squeeze between. But on the port hand it might be done, where part of the old winter ice impinged against the berg—if I could crack that ice and shove it to one side before the berg was aware of our intention.

"John," I yelled to the engineer, "I'm going to back the *Bowdoin* to the very end of the channel, give her full speed and bust that ice ahead. We may be able to split it, push the broken part aside, and sneak out before the berg closes it up again."

Grabbing a halyard, I slid down to the deck.

First at half, then at full speed, we charged down upon the locked gate of the channel that was trying to keep us in the North another year. Every man was on deck, braced and prepared for the shock. She hit—and stopped dead! The ice was harder and much thicker than I had thought. When 100 tons are stopped instantly, something is bound to suffer. Everything on deck and below shifted. I ran for'ard to inspect damage. The *Bowdoin* stood there looking innocently down on what she had done—a fine crack directly through the center of the pan. Her heavy oak stern, shod with steel plate, was not even dented.

I ran back to the open hatch leading to the engine room and yelled, "Give it to her."

If ever a ship knew what she was called on to do, or tried to do it, that ship was the *Bowdoin*. As I watched, the inch crack widened to a foot, then to a yard. The large, flat ice pan began to move, without the berg apparently being aware of the fact that we were escaping. It may have been aground. We didn't stop to investigate. Instead, we shot out into open water, into a strong southwest wind and heavy sea. We exulted at finding ourselves actually on the open road home. Our Guardian Spirit had finally thwarted Old Tornasuk, God of the North, who has guarded its ramparts down through the ages.

1973

Into the Solomons

Harold LaBorde

One of the highlights of a well-executed circumnavigation by a young Trinidadian family in a 40-foot ketch home-built from plans that first appeared in Yachting

I had always been enthralled by William Albert Robinson's 1930 book "Deep Water and Shoal," so it is not surprising that when our self-steering gear broke down on the passage from Vila, in the New Hebrides, to Port Moresby, in Papua, that we opted not to keep on with a hand at the helm. I put up the twin jibs and *Humming Bird II* ran for Guadalcanal before a fresh southeasterly. On board were my wife, Kwailan, our two sons, Pierre, 7, and Andre, 14 months, and myself. Even though we were running late for the Indian Ocean and all the places we wanted to see there, we looked forward to a few days in the Solomon Islands.

In four days we were off Rennel Island, near where we hove to for a while as I fixed the socket of the trim tab of the self-steerer. Finding no secure anchorage, we again headed toward Guadalcanal.

Robinson talks about the Solomons' "evil reputation," and I could well believe in the malevolence of the area as we screamed along under shortened sail, through black squalls and tide rips. About nine in the morning the rain ceased and, signaled by a great roll of thunder, a curtain of mist lifted to reveal not six miles away the veiled Cordilleras of Guadalcanal, surmounted by towering 8,000-foot Mt. Popomanasiu. The land stretched interminably across the horizon.

A sight to check on this, my most dramatic Pacific landfall, put us some 30 miles west of our dead reckoning, although I had made a generous allowance for the west-going current. The wind dropped right off and the sea calmed, so we cranked up the engine and headed on. It soon packed up, however—the first time this had ever happened since it was installed in Trinidad almost seven years earlier. I checked the oil level to find the sump almost dry, topped off the tank with an extra gallon of oil and started the engine again. It ran for about half an hour before sputtering to a complete halt.

I was all for giving up on the Solomons (harbors there are too difficult to enter under sail alone) but Kwailan told me that if we headed for Port Moresby we would be admitting defeat. I tried the engine again and it worked, and we kept on toward Guadalcanal.

The moon that night dispelled any black thoughts of failure as we beat against a light breeze. The dawn was not spectacular and the sun came up not like thunder but slowly, first sending out rosy hues that pushed the darkness farther and farther west until at last it danced like a golden pagan god on the steel-sharp horizon. Visibility was perfect: we could clearly make out the islands of San Cristobal, 30 miles to the southeast, and Malaita, 45 miles to the northeast. Guadalcanal itself was turning from hazy blue to dark green. We tacked to lay Graham Point, the island's eastern extremity that lies opposite the many small islands in the reef-strewn Marau Sound.

In perfect, almost storybook conditions, we sailed past the main reefs which we could see clearly with the sun at our backs, shot through the narrow passage between Graham Point and Maraumibina Island and dropped anchor in Danae Bay in six fathoms and a mud bottom, close off a jungle shore. At dusk natives paddled out in sleek canoes, some to fish and others to "look-look at ship bilong brown pela." I am a Trinidadian, and these were only the first of many confused natives used to seeing only whites in foreign yachts.

Our three days in Danae Bay were most enjoyable. We bought snappers from the native fisherman. Pierre spent much of his time with the local kids, paddling around in their dugout canoes. And we came to know the Irish priest, Father White, and his native Brothers and Sisters in the Catholic mission. At nights it was deadly still as the fisherman came paddling out. One evening there was beautiful singing, which, we learned from a Father, was that of children celebrating the opening of a new toilet. It was a neat toilet, thatched and hanging over the water's edge, and only added to the scenery.

The Mission was a school for about 100 children, 60 of whom live there. They spend half the day at classes and the other half tending the gardens that provide their food. In most of the smaller villages we found that the Catholic Church was doing fine work in education. The government helps with grants, but there are still not enough schools and education is not compulsory. There are over 400 primary schools, the vast majority of which are Church-run, but only five secondary schools.

Running before a fresh southeasterly *Humming Bird II* headed for the main port of Guadalcanal, Honiara, 50 miles on, drifting in at dawn with limp, dew-soaked sails and anchoring near the main wharf. Customs cleared us quickly and efficiently and we shifted our anchorage to the Point Cruz YC, which is sheltered to the east but open to the west. During the monsoon season boats must be prepared to move around to the commercial harbor in the event of a hard northwester.

Members of the yacht club made us welcome. Although the Solomons is still a British Protectorate, there was no hint of a colonial atmosphere and planters, government officers and ship captains descended on the club every night to slake their thirst. There were a few yachts and many stumpy-masted cutter boats in the bay. It is a hubbub of activity, with these little vessels, all now pushed by power, and long dugout canoes equipped with outboard engines moving in and out at all hours. The Solomon Islanders are very much a maritime people constantly on the move from island to island. They think nothing of making a 100-mile canoe passage to visit friends or the hospital or to catch a plane for Honiara. One can hear on the radio frequent reports of some voyager's misadventure—a capsizing, a shark attack, a mission of mercy or a heroic rescue. Like the cowboy and his horse, it is unheard of for a coastal native to be without his canoe.

Humming Bird, visited by Solomon Islanders

The natives were curious about *Humming Bird II* and her origins. "Which place bilong you?" they would ask.

"This pela bilong place him name West Indies," I would answer.

"Ah! Indonesia!"

"Look this pela bilong place close America."

"Ah! America!" they would cry. "Why you no say first time?"

A competent engineer fixed the engine and we motored 25 miles north to Florida Island to try to get some painting done away from the congenial club atmosphere. On the way we came across a native towing a large dead shark behind his outboard-powered dugout. I asked him why he did not haul it into his canoe, and he answered, with a lot of incomprehensible pigeon talk, that it was tabu in his village. Later, after the monster had been hauled on board *Humming Bird* with the mizzen halyard, the young, heavily-tattooed native told us that although he was a Christian his father was a shark priest who could communicate with the fish. Only a few weeks earlier, he said, a "devil priest" had died on Malaita and immediately many giant rays and crocodiles that had once responded to the man's call had come and stayed by his house for several days. I did not scoff; many level-headed Europeans who have lived all their lives in the Solomons tell the same kind of story.

After five days of painting masts, cockpit and cabin trunk we powered back to Honiara. It was August Bank Holiday and the yacht club organized a race, which work on the steering vane forced us to miss. The race winner, George Ermtage, later took us for a drive along Guadalcanal's shoreline, on which we saw dozens of engineless World War II American landing barges.

We enjoyed the comforts of Honiara for another few days before leaving for Gizo, capital of the Western Solomons, intending to visit en route some islands and lagoons. Savo lies 20 miles northwest of Honiara and seismologists believe that the small circular island will one day blow its top. Here William Albert Robinson found that a shotgun shell would buy both a cock and a woman. But nightfall caught us before we could make port there and we continued on toward the Russell Islands. The islands on the way are ringed by white sand and turquoise lagoons and on many stand coconut plantations owned by Lever Bros.

We anchored at a couple of islands for a night and a swim and then headed for the Marovo Lagoon on Vanguna Island in the New Georgia group. What attracted us to the lagoon were the warnings of many sailors at Honiara. Said to be the largest lagoon in the world, Marovo is a mass of reefs and islands. There are no Admiralty charts of the area, but the Solomons Marine Department in Honiara has compiled an excellent set of charts and, armed with these, we poked into narrow Tongoro Passage in search of the lagoon and some of the best wood carvers in the Pacific.

An unforgettable sight met us: dozens of tiny islands, some supporting solitary houses, lay scattered in every direction; the different colors of the water ranged from the brown of exposed coral to the yellow, light green and dark blue of increasing depth. Though our charts proved to be correct as we ticked off the islands, I could appreciate how a bad chop or cloud cover would hide the reefs and turn the lagoon into a navigator's nightmare. At noon we brought up in the small bay of Batuna on the main island of Vaguna and dropped the small Danforth on rope and chain in 2½ fathoms in sand. I felt that the fisherman and heavy Danforth were too much of a bother for an overnight stay.

But a terrific rain squall from the exposed north bore down on the boat after Pierre and I went ashore to inspect a sawmill. The lagoon was turned into a mass of whitecaps and, despite the sawmill manager's assurances, *Humming Bird*, with Kwai and little Andre aboard, dragged. I got aboard as soon as possible, but increased scope did not help and the engine was of little use against the 40-knot wind. With Kwai at the tiller holding the screaming Andre, I let go the 60-lb. Danforth. It finally held 20 yards short of the rocks. A big native and his wife brought Pierre out in a canoe and the native conned us into a small, deep, well-protected cove where we anchored in ten fathoms. He was a Seventh Day Adventist and would not accept a drink, but I had a double rum. He eventually accepted some canned goods as a token of our gratitude.

We moved on to other islands in the lagoon, which is quite well buoyed. Much of the navigation can be done by sight, as long as there is enough sun to see the changes in water color that indicate shoaling, but to be safe I always laid off courses and distances. At Telina we were met by natives trying to sell us wonderful carved fish, inlaid with mother-of-pearl. We traded cash, watches, clothes, canned goods and other items for a few good items, including an ebony bust of a woman. The local pastor sold us this carving. The natives of Telina and several nearby islands are all Seventh Day Adventists who may not eat crayfish, scaly fish, turtle and pig. Of course, tobacco, liquor and coffee and tea are also prohibited. Adventist missionaries enforce these embargoes by preaching, as Robinson put it, "a very material hell, preying upon the converts' fear of a horrible after-life." But they say nothing about visitors, and we glutted ourselves on crayfish and turtle during our three-day stay.

Two natives joined us for our passage to Sege, on New Georgia.

They were quite amazed when, using preset courses, we picked our way from marker to marker in rain and poor visibility. The natives spent the night with us and motored back to Telina in their canoe, which we had towed over. A day later we powered up the Blanche Channel through a fleet of 50 canoes, all manned by singing children commuting to the mission school at Sege, to Hele Bar. It was quite frightening to pass from the deep blue of 30 fathoms to the light green of two fathoms over the bar. A depth sounder would be handy when navigating among coral except when the shelf rises sheer to the surface. Here, as Eric Hiscock says, "Eternal vigilance is the only watchword." Time and time again I have gone up the ratlines and made out shoals invisible from the deck. The hours between 0900 and 1500 are the best for reef navigation; should the sun get low and in the navigator's eyes, extreme care should be taken. Polaroid sun glasses are a help.

We had New Georgia and Vaguna to starboard and the great number of small reef islands astern. To port were Rendova and Tetipari, some 20 miles away, and ahead was the towering 5,450' cone of Kolombangara. Off the entrance of Viru harbor we bought a huge tuna for the equivalent of $1 from a passing fisherman. The only access to the harbor is through a winding channel under high cliffs, and a borrowed wartime Japanese chart was useful.

The harbor was a hive of activity as the Kalena Timber Co. had a loading facility there. A native in a dugout showed us a good anchorage on the eastern side of the bay. We gave him one-half of the tuna for his trouble and he reappeared at 1700 with an old man who had carvings to sell. Our guide, Chillon, explained that since it was Friday the old man, a Seventh Day Adventist, had only until 1800 to sell his carvings. Business would start again Sunday. We bought some carvings, offered our guests some tea, which, of course, they refused, and they left us. We left Viru at 0700 the next morning to the crowing of village cocks, the barking of dogs and the squawks of parrots trying their wings in the early morning sunlight. To leave a peaceful harbor at dawn before anyone ashore stirs is to me a most wonderful experience, even though it may be selfish to enjoy something sublime while others sleep, oblivious.

Anyone cruising in this area from July to April must do a fair amount of powering, as the winds are light to non-existent. Although I enjoy a good sail, with short hops I prefer to mosey along under power, taking in the sights, lazing and reading. So we powered to Rendova, 25 miles away, and entered Renard harbor there with the aid of my rapidly disintegrating Japanese chart. We anchored in seven fathoms, a little deeper than I would have preferred. I always hope to find an anchorage of about three or four fathoms in sand or mud, but this is impossible near reefs. We carry four anchors on *Humming Bird II*, three Danforths and a fisherman, and though we have had them caught on coral heads many times, we've always been able to get them up, albeit sometimes a bit bent. In most cases the chain gets caught, especially if there is no wind, and I look through my face mask to see which way to motor to free the chain.

From Rendova we motored the ten miles to Munda Bar, the main entrance to the Roviana Lagoon on New Georgia, and almost went aground when I became more interested in photographing a school of porpoises than in finding the channel. "Daddy," Pierre said, "I can see bottom." I continued to snap pictures until he finally convinced me to take a look. I put her hard astern, the whole boat reverberated, billows of black smoke emitted from the exhaust—but there was no crash. Complacency has no place aboard a cruising boat.

Inside the lagoon the stacatto beat of a big wooden drum called people not to a feast but to Sunday worship. The next day, with Andre in his pram, we walked the short distance to the township of Lambetti (site of a small airport and the Munda administrative seat). Part of the road was in the open and quite hot, but much of it passed through cool coconut groves where natives sat in front of their thatched huts either weaving baskets or doing wood-carving. Like Tahiti there was an abundance of flowers, but no corrugated iron marred the scene. We were so impressed by this section of the Roviana Lagoon and by its part-native part-European residents that, after returning to the boat, we shifted to the lovely, completely protected anchorage off Government Rest House.

One day Frank Wickham, a Solomon Islander of mixed races, came over in his 30′ dugout from his plantation on Rendova Island, bringing with him two enormous coconut crabs, looking like a cross between a lobster and a crab and with claws the size of a man's fist. The Rest House housekeeper stewed them in coconut milk and, while we ate them by the light of a Tilley pressure lamp, Frank told us something of his family. His uncle and father, he said (and proved with clippings), had revolutionized swimming in Australia by winning every race they entered there with a stroke some called the Australian Crawl. "In fact," he said, "it was the Raviana Crawl before my uncle and father took it down south. All the kids here used to swim that way. The stroke got its name when an Australian reporter saw my uncle win his first race and said, 'Cripes, look at that kid crawling over the water!'"

On our way to Gizo, we chose to go through the Diamond

Narrows to the north of Arundel Island. This area is steeped in World War II history, and here John F. Kennedy's PT boat was cut in half by a Japanese destroyer. The well-marked channel leading to Diamond Narrows has a quiet, almost sinister beauty. Thick mangroves come down to the water's edge. All is still among the many islands, almost like in a large swamp. Now and then a large fish leaps and falls back, leaving rings on the water surface. The engine noise sends flights of parrots and parakeets soaring. There are no houses, no shouting, friendly people on these shores.

We plunged into Diamond Narrows, feeling as though we were in a canal lock with walls of green jungle instead of concrete on either side. From the mile-long Narrows we entered Hawthorn Sound, and not far to starboard lay the village called Paradise by the followers of an alleged messiah called Holy Mama. But Paradise would have to wait, and we swept through maelstromic tide rips in Blackett Strait. A mile from Ringi Cove a rain squall caught us with main and jib up and threw *Humming Bird* over on her beam ends as she narrowly missed a native cutter, and the dinghy was swamped.

Standing into Ringi Cove, we hit hard enough to knock Kwai and Andre down into the cockpit, but backed off easily enough, and at the Lever Bros. wharf natives told us that we had found the only projecting reef in the cove. Blackett Strait was calm the next day, but full of logs, and we kept a sharp lookout as we headed out. Halfway to Gizo a fresh following breeze sprang up and we were able to sail toward our last Solomon harbor.

Gizo is far different from any of the other Solomon towns. Here more than anywhere else in the chain was a real South Sea port, with supermarket, hotel, Chinese stores and the coming and going of all types of craft, not just canoes. But there were the same curious, gentle, honest people, the same quiet stirring of the palm trees in the evening breeze. At least for *Humming Bird II*, the evil reputation of the Solomons had been all bluff.

1976

Deep Sea Passage

Frank W. Hamilton, Jr.

An account of a pleasant, rather routine passage from the Caribbean to Bermuda that recreates the very essence of the joys of being afloat

It seemed to me that the cocks had crowed most of the night. They were quiet now, and the sun rising in a cloudless May sky was well above the eastern arm of Road Bay. The area of the harbor where we had anchored was empty except for our boat and a native schooner moored alongside the quay. Her crew were unloading bananas, lemons, and brightly colored vegetables. On the quay several women were arranging a display of the fresh cargo as it landed. A taxi moved slowly along the waterfront and pulled up by the schooner. The driver, the women, and the schooner's crew exchanged cheerful greetings. The lilt of their voices and laughter flowed over the water to the boat. Somewhere up in town a church bell began to toll softly and then ceased suddenly as if it had forgotten what it had wished to say.

Some of our crew were stirring now, and I stopped to pull on some pants before anyone appeared on deck.

We ate breakfast in the cockpit. Communication at breakfast was limited to requests for the salt and tea bags, and an observation by Amy that I was sitting in her egg. We dispatched the meal quickly. Amy gathered the remains of it and took it below with instructions to make a final inventory of our provisions. One passage had ended—a leisurely trip up the chain of islands from Grenada; another passage was about to begin—the voyage back to the States. Although we had no schedule to keep, we were all caught up in the preparations for departure as though we had some urgent deadline to meet.

While we worked, fluffy white clouds were forming over the channel to the east of the bay. The first of them moved in over the saddle in the hills. When it reached the harbor, some invisible hand reached out and wrung a shower from it. By the time the little cloud had arrived over the western arm of the bay, its fleece was dry again, but the following cloud was in position to begin the cycle again. And beyond it, over the channel to the eastward, there were other clouds forming up to advance in equally spaced intervals through the saddle in the hills—pieces in some automated watering process shaped by celestial hands. All the while the sun bathed the town and the waters of the bay in intense light. The natives on the quay took little notice of the showers or the rainbow that arched continuously over the green ridges back of the town.

No more did we. We checked our life jacket stowage, our safety harnesses, our flares. We tested our running lights and binnacle light, and made sure our horseshoe life preservers slipped easily out of their brackets. We removed our vents and screwed in the plates to cap the throughdeck openings. We dogged the forward hatch. Then Amy came on deck to announce she would like to go ashore to purchase some fresh native bread. It would keep for perhaps six days and would be most welcome for snacks on the night watches. We decided on ten loaves, and Jim accompanied her to look for some ice for the deck box. In between showers they hurried for the beach. The rest of us continued with our check-off.

Amy and Jim returned soon. We could smell the fresh loaves as the boat came alongside. The delightful smell of the bread somewhat compensated for the ice, which was wrapped in a burlap bag that appeared to have once been employed to carry goat manure. We swung the dinghy aboard on the mizzen halyard and secured her right side up on the after deck. We filled her up with sail bags and the outboard motor and lashed each item individually to the boat and the deck.

There came a point when we could think of nothing more to inspect or secure. We paused then, all of us, soaking up the light, the warmth, the smells and sounds of the port. Perhaps the others were struck as I was at that instant by the thought that we were about to let go of those islands and that southern sea. We would be gone, most of us, for at least a year and, although we looked forward to sailing in New England waters again, these were sights and sensations we did not want to forget.

We had a farewell beer and I pressed the button. The windlass groaned. The cable clanked. Soon the anchor, dripping mud, was clearing the water. We hosed, scraped, and secured it carefully and motored slowly out into the bay setting our main, mizzen and #2 jenny as we went. A fresh breeze swelled our sails. We cut the engine and soon were clear of Road Bay. We jibed then and came full before the wind for a run down Sir Francis Drake Channel. It was warm running before the wind. Nick got out the wash-deck hose and washed the dust and grime of the land from our decks. Some of us bathed our feet in the cool hose water as it flowed down the warm teak. The feel of the water was so refreshing that we held the hose over our heads and let the cool stream part our hair, slosh down our ears, and slide down our chests and backs. When we had had enough, Nick coiled up the hose and shouted to Cuthbert to take down the Red Duster which still flew from our starboard spreader.

"I didn't know you permitted anyone but yourself to handle those colors," I said to Nick.

"Frank," he replied, "you know very well that for years now we've been permitting the Colonials to haul down that flag all over the world." It was no use my trying to kid that Englishman. He topped me every time.

We were passing Little Thatch now. Once by, we sheeted in, cut in between Great Thatch and West End, and reached out towards the north end of Jost Van Dyke. The breeze came down strong off the Tortola hills. Cat's-paws raced across the water. The big island provided us with a lee from the Atlantic rollers to the northeast. We sped along. Our bow made a tearing sound as it parted the rippled water. The sun shone on a light shroud of rain hanging beneath a cloud coming over the ridge of a hill, prismatic lights dancing within the rain.

Almost before we knew it, we had crossed the Windward Passage and were off Little Jost Van Dyke. A small yacht lay at anchor in the lee of Sandy Cay. A man on her deck, who had been rubbing himself down with a towel, paused to watch us through binoculars as we broke free of the island chain and surged into the Atlantic. We took Little Jost Van Dyke as our point of departure and I stepped down into the chart house to make a proper entry in the log.

I turned the log to a fresh page. I listed the crew. I noted the weather. I recorded our time of departure and entered our course and speed. I left our destination open. A good friend and a fine sailor once told me that he made it a practice to enter his destination only when he had arrived in port and his anchor had a secure hold on the bottom. It seemed prudent, he remarked, to be humble in the face of the elements. I headed the page "Passage from B.V.I."

When I stepped on deck again, the wind appeared to have hauled far enough aft to allow us to fly our mizzen staysail. We had aboard no other sail with as large an area. With its great belly full of air it was a proper sail for riding the Trade winds home from the Spanish Main. I suggested we prepare to raise it. Groans followed from every quarter. It was not a popular sail with the crew, but we had it up and drawing quickly. It added three-quarters of a knot to our speed.

We had an assembly then in the cockpit and discussed the watch list. Amy, my 16-year-old daughter, would stand watch with me and also cook. Jim would be Royce's watch partner and Cuthbert, the fisherman from Carriacou, would stand with Nick. We agreed the night watches beginning at 1800 would be three hours long until 0600, when we would stand four hours until 1800. The three-hour night watches were not tiring, and the schedule resulted in staggered watches. At 1800 each evening the crew would assemble in the cockpit for one drink unless the weather was inclement, in which case the watch would have their drink on deck and the rest of us would gather below. We reviewed our man-overboard procedure once more, and it was time for our drink.

We did not linger over it. The cook called up through the galley port that dinner was ready. The meal was a good one, but Nick, Jim and I fled to the deck after the first course. We had been sailing for three weeks, much of the time closehauled, but the great Atlantic rollers as they swept around the islands this evening acquired some form or motion that got to our stomachs. It was a delightful evening to have dessert and coffee on deck. Royce and Cuthbert below may have had more to eat than we, but we had the better view. The sun was close to the horizon. The cumulus clouds that rode the Trades were a pearly white now and under each cloud the water was a lighter grey. Far out to the east, shafts of light from the setting sun caught the clouds near the horizon and colored them with the soft rose shades of conch shells. Reflections fell from the clouds and spread like spilled wine on the surface of the water beneath. Purple mounds—all that remained of the Tortola hills—lingered on the southern horizon.

It was difficult to stir ourselves, but we did. We dropped the mizzen staysail. Wind conditions had not changed, but they might during the night. We wished to keep sail handling to minimum after dark.

As it turned out, during the 0300 to 0600 watch our course brought us across the path of a bank of black clouds. Large drops of rain began to spatter down before the clouds reached us and shut out the stars. Then the wind flowed out from the dark hole beneath the clouds. With increasing weight it poured over us and held us over. I wrestled the wheel and we bore off. The effect was that of a train switched from a siding to the main line. We began to pick up speed. Soon we were hurtling down the track. One rudder angle kept her steady with no change of helm.

We settled deeper on our lines. The rain and wind flattened the sea. Our bow wave roared and gurgled and flung out blobs of phosphorescence that rushed down our sides and lay glowing in our track astern. The wind whistled through the rigging. We vibrated with energy. It surged up from the deck through the soles of my feet. I danced a jig at the wheel and whooped and hollered into the wind in a manner unbecoming a man of my age. In about ten minutes we had gained the edge of the black canopy above us and we slid out from beneath the overhang into the light where the stars, not the clouds, formed the roof of the sky. The boat slowed, and we moved again to the more deliberate rhythm of the Trade winds.

As the morning twilight grew, I got some sights of Jupiter and a couple of stars. When the next watch relieved us, we set the mizzen staysail again. Amy went below to prepare breakfast and I worked out my sights. The star sights did not plot well. The shots of Jupiter fell in where I thought they should. By chance, one of them was on the local meridian. There was no reason to believe it was more accurate than the others, but this was the one I saved on the plotting sheet.

When Nick got up, he could advance it and cross it with a morning sun line. As on other passages, Nick and I seemed to specialize in our sights. I liked the planets, the moon and Polaris. Nick took great comfort in the local apparent noon observation. When the opportunity offered, we both took sun sights several times during the morning and afternoon. Of these, we would work out the ones which could be most conveniently advanced or retired to provide us with a running fix. Our star sights were only occasionally a success. No doubt we would have been more successful with the stars if we had given proper preparation to obtaining approximate altitudes and azimuths.

Bright sky, small cumulus clouds, evenly spaced seas, and a steady wind on our quarter were with us the entire day. We occupied ourselves as we have done so often in fair weather on other passages. We read, we slept, we took salt water showers on deck (the temperature was 109° below), we accomplished small chores.

In the afternoon, Nick was checking out some circuits on our radio and heard a boat talking to some other vessels back at Peter Island. The boat gave a position which placed her about 68 miles ahead of our own. Nick called her and we learned that she was a schooner bound for Gibraltar by way of Bermuda. We arranged a daily schedule with her to exchange weather and position. She was considerably larger than we were, and would be out of range before many days. The information on the weather, however, would be helpful to us as long as we could pick up her transmissions.

Amy and I had the mid-watch that night—our second night out. Amy was in a mood to talk and I was in a mood to listen. We made congenial watch mates.

The next day we approached the northern limit of the Trades. The winds were still easterly but light. They were enough to keep the sails drawing, but our speed dropped occasionally below four knots. The sea smoothed out and the heat, during the middle of the day, was oppressive. Our friend up ahead of us reported she had been encountering heavy thunderstorms, but the weather was clearing with light, variable winds and mares' tails at high altitudes. We were unable to transmit a reply until we discovered our mainsail was bearing on the shroud which included our antenna. We regained operation when we sheeted in.

Our daily observation of LAN had taken on the aspects of a pagan rite. Nick and I were the high priests and Jim was our acolyte. Each day just before the local apparent noon, Jim bore a radio and a watch to the cockpit with considerable ceremony (we had no chronometer but kept a wristwatch of mine which had a constant error rate in a card box in the chart room). When Jim snapped on the set and the disembodied voice and the ethereal ticks and tones sounded the time, the crew assumed a serious mien and began checking their own watches as though they were participating in some profound and mysterious act. Then Jim would arrange himself cross-legged on the after deck with stop watch and notebook and prepare to record the sextant readings as Nick and I called them out.

On this particular day, I was puzzled because I was able to bring down the sun to the horizon on any bearing. I looked up and saw Nick sweeping his sextant around the horizon. Then it occurred to me that the declination of the sun was the same as the latitude: The sun was directly overhead and our altitudes were all close to 90°. Since our course was close to true north, the distance between our LAN lines was the day's run. The announcement of the day's run was made in solemn tones, and thus the ceremony was concluded, following which the crew became their normal raucous and disrespectful selves.

Late in the afternoon of this the third day, the sky became overcast, and grey thunderheads towered up ahead of us. They loomed motionless on the horizon, and so dark was the sky beneath that it was difficult to distinguish where the clouds left off and the sea began. Yet from time to time we thought we sighted even darker columns of waterspouts spiraling down from the cloud mass to the water below. The sea quieted and grew a leaden color. No wrinkle of wind showed on its surface yet somewhere above it there was moving air that kept our sails filled and the boat sliding ahead. Great beds of sargassum weed lay on each hand and suppressed the labored undulations of the sea. The heat remained oppressive.

Shortly before dinner, Cuthbert, the fisherman, sighted the spouts of two whales about a mile off our port bow. The whales were swimming on a southerly course, parallel and opposite to our own. When they were almost abeam they sounded and reappeared on a westerly course. We fell off and sailed after them. They sounded again and we maintained our course. Cuthbert stood lookout on the bowsprit, his feet on the top rail of the pulpit, holding with one hand to the head stay. With his body arched forward and one arm stretched ahead pointing the course, he looked like a figure out of an old whaling print.

As we waited it was strangely silent. Our bow wave whispered. Our spars and rigging creaked and groaned softly. When someone spoke to ask Cuthbert if he still saw something, his voice sounded strangely loud and lonely on this empty expanse of ocean. Suddenly there was a disturbance in the water ahead. An immense back rose majestically to the surface. A long hump broke the glossy water and sent waves rolling out from each side. The humpback appeared motionless yet drifted forward slowly. We moved abreast of him until we could see beneath the surface the full extent of his vast bulk and the crustacea and marine growth that mottled his great back. As our boat drew ahead, the flukes moved with deliberate grace and the enormous hulk slid beneath the water from our sight. We resumed our normal course. Some minutes later we saw again two spouts side by side. The whales had resumed their passage south.

Before dinner the wind died. We took down all our sails and bagged the jib. We lay with no way upon us during dinner and for an hour after. The light faded imperceptibly. No thing moved on the ocean, in the air, or in the sky. We were alone on a great desert of water, but snug and secure on our small boat. There was a feeling of timelessness. Ties to the life and concerns of the shore had never seemed so remote.

Without warning it began to rain. The drops came so quickly and in such volume that we felt smothered by them, and yet each drop made its own distinct hole in the surface of the sea as it hit. Each drop bounded up again from the water, carrying with it a drop of sea water to form an hour-glass-shaped droplet. All these hour-glasses bounced to the same level, and a trim counterpane of white droplets was snugged around our boat and across the water for as far as we could see. We switched on the engine and began motoring. As we progressed it grew darker, and soon we seemed to be entering a cave of impenetrable blackness. Thunder crashed above us and rolled around us, yet no lightning flashed. Occasionally small patches of phosphorescence winked in our wake, but only the dim glow from the binnacle and running lights survived the darkness.

The rain lasted several hours, and then we were in clear, cooler air. Stars peeked through mare's tails high in the sky, and a freshening northeast breeze sprang up. When the mid-watch came on deck to relieve the watch, we put up our sails again and ceased motoring. At 0600 the wind had made up to the point that we changed the #2 jenny for a working jib. As the day progressed, the wind increased. The schooner ahead of us reported she was hove to in a full gale. She had made only 46 miles since the day before and had been set 20 miles west of the rhumb line. By 1400 we felt we were overpowered with the sails then set. We took down our mizzen, which on our boat is a good-sized sail. The boat eased and there was no perceptible difference in speed.

It was oilskin weather. The spray whipped across the cockpit and hit the other side like a handful of gravel on a drumhead. During the course of a watch, water got down and through to the skin one way or another, and it got below decks. It came below on dripping boots and oilskins. It oozed through hatch gaskets and vents. It worked its way into bunks and lockers and packaged food. It created an atmosphere below with the relative humidity of a rain forest. Those on watch developed Machiavellian strategies to ensure themselves the least soggy leeward bunk.

Two hands were better than one for holding on. The boat was short-rigged and stiff. The motion was abrupt and immoderate. Getting from one place to another was strenuous and bruising. Shooting the sun was an athletic event. Sleeping was fatiguing. But the crew's spirits and appetite remained hearty. The cook provided us with hot soup often and served us mulligan stew topped with sliced tomatoes and lettuce for dinner. We balanced, dodged and clung as we ate. We cleaned the gravy and juices out of the bowls with good Tortola bread. We swilled beer or tea or coffee in accordance with our personal preference, and no one passed up his drink at happy hour.

That night after our watch, as I lay half clinging, half bracing in my sleep, a sudden motion tossed me clear of my bunk into the bunk straps. I awoke, hung on with both hands and feet, and listened to the many voices of the wind working—the moans as it labored to pile the sea up, the roars as it buffeted and shook the boat, the shrieks and wails as it attacked the sails and rigging, and the smaller voices, the murmurs, the groans, the sighs, the whispers, the chuckles. I listened to them all, and it seemed the moans had grown deeper, the roars more savage, the shrieks and wails wilder than when I had come below.

I felt for my flashlight under my pillow and slipped through the bunk straps to the cabin sole. I groped forward to my foul weather gear, holding on all the while with both hands to whatever solid surface provided a hand hold. I sat down on the sole, braced myself in a corner, and began my struggle with my foul weather gear and boots. Yes surely, I thought, the motion is more violent now. I became engaged in a personal struggle with the demonic forces that were throwing the boat about. I braced my elbows in the corner to keep from being rolled over, but the instant I had to lean forward to pull on my boots, something was watching and flung me on my side.

Finally I was ready, and crawled up the ladder. I slid back the hatch and looked out. Jim was on the wheel. Royce was packed into the forward lee corner of the cockpit under the dodger, his feet on the steering pedestal, his head lowered, sou'wester down over his eyes. He raised his head as the hatch squealed on the slides.

"There's François," he shouted above the wind.

"How is it?" I shouted back.

"No change," said Royce.

"Has the wind increased?"

"The wind's the same," said Jim, "but the watches get longer every night."

I glanced out on the sea. Through a mackerel sky a wan moon shown on riotous and foam-streaked water. We had a thousand fathoms under our keel but from the look of the sea, we could have been running inside a line of breakers in shoal water. A wave swelled up on our beam. Its dark shoulder loomed above us. The wind swept the top off the wave. The tumbling water frothed and foamed toward us. The boat began to rise. The froth and foam slapped the hull, and we ducked as the spray shot into the cockpit. The boat shook herself, and the wave passed under us. It was an awesome and beautiful sight in the moonlight. The boat was riding well. Royce and Jim were correct. There had been no change.

"I drank too much tea on our watch," I explained.

"A beer would go good while you're up, François."

"Tea and some of the Roadtown bread for me," said Jim.

I pulled the hatch over my head and wrestled my way down into the galley.

The norther lasted about thirty hours. Then the wind began to moderate and hauled around to the southeast. We put up our mizzen, our #2 jenny and finally our mizzen staysail. It was as fine sailing as we had ever had on *Free Spirit*. Under a brilliant sky we surged along the white-capped waves, our sails swelling with the wind. Our bow roared as it drove through a sea and hissed as we settled into the trough that followed. As the boat yawed and bucked, the jib dumped air on the wave at the lee bow. The air raced out to rejoin the wind, and as it sped away made wrinkles like grained leather on the top of the waves. Royce festooned our lifelines with bed sheets and foul weather gear to dry. We abandoned all pretense of chores and surrendered ourselves to the pleasures of the day.

From time to time schools of porpoise frolicked across the boisterous waves to join us. They played in our bow waves for perhaps 30 minutes at a time. They appeared to be the happiest creatures on the planet and certainly among the most graceful. They streaked through the azure water seemingly without effort. Sometimes in sudden bursts of speed they sped far ahead of the boat. Sometimes, as they leaped from the water, they rolled completely over in the air. Some were brown, others, possibly older, were speckled with grey like the muzzle of an old dog. Each had a gloss-white tip on the end of its bottle nose. We noted that the air hole in the porpoise's head was closed while it swam beneath the water, but the instant it cleared the water, the hole opened to admit air. As the bowsprit dipped to touch the top of the waves, we had the sensation of being among them. Nick could not resist temptation. He reached out with a broom and swept it along the back of a porpoise as it plunged by. The porpoise brought his tail down with a slap as he reentered the water, and the resulting splash soaked Nick thoroughly.

We must be a brave sight, I thought, bounding home over the foam-topped seas, our sails swollen with wind, our wake boiling, the porpoise sporting in our bow wave. Had we been Argonauts, I could have believed that this condition of sea and wind and sky and this gift of porpoises were signs that we were voyagers on the deep with whom the gods were well pleased.

We expected to make our landfall that evening about midnight. The cook had been holding back the best of her larder for this occasion. We had for dinner roast beef, Yorkshire pudding and pumpkin pie. We demonstrated our admiration of the cook's effort by sending back for helpings until no scrap remained. Leaving Jim and Royce to help with the dishes, I went on deck to try for a good running fix before we started in. We had had some good afternoon sun lines, and although the boat's motion made star sights difficult, I thought I should try for a shot of Polaris.

Since we were on a course that swung the bow through an arc centered on true north, the sails were in the way of a sight except from a point forward of the headstay. I put on a harness and, shielding my sextant under my foul weather jacket, ran forward to the main mast. The spray line was forward of the mast. I clung to a halyard until the bow was on the rise and the water running off the deck before struggling forward to the bowsprit. Once there I clipped my harness to the pulpit. Here I was beyond the spray. Kneeling on the bowsprit, knees hugging a stanchion and back braced against the headstay, I clung. With the liquid thunder of the bow wave in my ears and the throbbing power of the boat pulsating through my back from the tensed headstay, I prepared to stalk the North Star. The bowsprit reared and dove, but I trapped that tiny crystal of light in my glass. I held it captive like a firefly in a bottle and watched it streak from side to side until I had rocked it down to tangential contact with the dimming horizon.

The cook and I were scheduled for the 2100 to 2400 watch that evening. Amy, however, had turned in for a nap after dinner and Cuthbert, when the time came to call her, said he would like to stand her watch in appreciation of the special meal she had cooked for us. He took the wheel while I worked out my Polaris sight and crossed it with our sun lines. The fix indicated we were close to our DR position and no change of course was necessary for our run in. The wind had moderated as the light waned. There were occasional sibilant whispers as whitecaps frothed near us, but no longer were we crashing along at full speed as we had been during the day. The atmosphere was so clear you seemed to be able to look deep into space beyond the near stars to the far ones, and to sense the planet's roll toward the morning constellations and the distant dawn. Scorpius appeared with stinger raised, and Antares, his great red eye, fixed us with a baleful stare. After a while the moon came up. It placed a burnished sword of light upon the black water and diminished the stars. I steered by the North Star. Cuthbert sat in the cockpit looking out on the water. Finally he broke our silence.

"A man muss have a trade."

He spoke not to me and I did not respond. The wind was drawing farther aft. We slacked the sheets until they luffed, then sheeted in.

"I don't know why it is," Cuthbert said, "but I like the water more than land."

There was still a luff near the head of the jib and he cranked the winch a couple of turns.

"A fishermon has a trade, but fishermon muss have a boat. I know a mon with a boat. He has two sons but they don't want to stay in Carriacou. They want to go to Trinidad to learn to make automobiles. I think this mon likes me."

The mizzen staysail was becoming a nuisance. We dropped it. It fell with a rustle and we gathered its soft damp fabric into a bag.

"The fishermon has a daughter. She goes to church on Sundays and is full of serene tranquility. She has no mon. I believe she likes me."

The wind was so light now it was difficult to keep the jib full.

"Someday a mon muss take a woman and responsibilities. The woman muss cook and keep the children clean. A mon can fish. I believe the hotels in Grenada need fish now."

Cuthbert sighed and began to beat the palms of his hands on the seat of the cockpit as though it were a bongo drum.

Amy appeared in the after hatchway. She was disheveled and groggy.

"Cuthbert, why didn't you call me?"

"Because you are a star, a super-star."

"Cuthbert, you stand your watches and I'll stand mine."

"You are a star, a sunshine cool super-star."

"Let's take down the jib," I said. "It's doing us no good now."

They went forward, Amy still scolding and Cuthbert chuckling. When Cuthbert chuckled, he lowered his head, wagged it back and forth and pumped his elbows up and down as if he were playing a concertina. They were a great foredeck crew, but they got the jib down soon enough. Nick and Jim heard them and came on deck to join us. About 2300 we sighted the loom of the lighthouse light where it should be. The wind had faded so that we just had steerage way, but there was no advantage in hurrying our arrival. We used the air as long as it lasted. When we had no way upon us, we strapped in the main and mizzen and prepared to motor. Jim asked us to wait before pushing the button until he could check below. He went down into the engine room and we knew he was dip-sticking and switch-flapping until he was happy all was well. It was a good feeling to have somebody aboard who felt about engines the way Jim did.

Royce joined us when we switched the engine on. We motored in watching the shore lights come over the horizon. We found the sea buoy. The color of the light and the flash were right but its paint and number were gone. We followed on in the channel and missed the turn to the entrance of the harbor. We found ourselves half way to Fort St. Catherine before we turned and motored back.

This time we found the line of buoys leading in and motored in toward the cut. A large ship was anchored up ahead inside the harbor. She was lighted from stem to stern, but no one moved on deck. A light breeze sprang up as we passed through the cut. It felt soft on our cheeks and it carried land smells with it. We searched for a channel buoy with a flashlight. Wherever the spot of light showed on the water, the surface boiled and silver-sided fish leapt through air.

We went a short way beyond the harbor buoy and turned out of the channel. I rounded her up into the wind and backed her down. Nick dropped the anchor. The cable rumbled. Royce released the brake on the halyard winch. The main rattled down. I backed her hard for several turns. Nick called back that we had a good bite. I shut off the engine and the boat swung quietly at the end of her tether. We furled the main and took down the mizzen. Amy and Jim went below. Royce got three beers, and he and Nick and I drank them as we looked out on the few lights in the hushed town.

We said nothing, but we were pleased with ourselves. We had accomplished nothing of value that you could put a name to. We had completed a milk run, an uneventful passage such as hundreds of yachtsmen make each year. But there it was—we had a feeling of accomplishment anyway. We were sailors who had come in the night across the water in our own staunch boat, and for a moment we had the harbor to ourselves. In the morning the yachts and commercial craft would furrow the water. The streets would fill with rasping motor bikes and taxis bulging with tourists. We would be a few among many, but for a short time, at least, we would savor the sensation that from all those who rode in overstuffed chairs far above the weather to this patch of land in the ocean, we were a breed apart.

We finished the beers and went below. It was 0400. We were five days and ten hours out of B.V.I. I recorded the final entries for the passage in the log, and completed the heading: "Passage from B.V.I. to St. George, Bermuda."

1981

A Dream Comes True, the Hard Way

Jack A. Somer

A fine day for cruising, but the unexpected occurred. Knowledgeable crew saved the situation ... and the dream.

I have a friend—call him Alex—who had a dream: to take his beautiful Swan 44 sloop to the Virgin Islands for the winter, to escape New York's snows, and perhaps evade the onslaught of a deep emotional crisis.

Alex has years of sailing behind him, in one-designs and big boats. He's an accomplished ocean racer; he won his class in the 1976 Bermuda Race. He's an experienced navigator. He's sailed thousands of miles on the east coast, the Caribbean and Mediterranean. He's a man with strength of purpose and singleness of mind.

But the mind is a curious device: it can take curious paths. Under routine circumstances it can produce poetry or turn a neat business profit. Under stress it can abandon critical judgment, lose reason and turn from reality. On land that's a problem; at sea it's dangerous.

On the occasion of this delivery to the Virgins, Alex was distracted. Some months before, he'd lost his wife in a hideous accident. His home, possessions and much of his past went up in flames. He was justifiably distracted. And he looked to his boat for possible salvation.

On the morning of January 17, 1979, we were on the final leg of the journey, one day out of Nassau, Bahamas, heading for St. Thomas. We were crossing Exuma Sound, in 1,000 fathoms, beating easily on port tack in about 10 knots of breeze. A few remnant clouds from a passing storm scudded overhead, but the trend was toward clearing. My two tickets for the opera that night were safely in the hands of music-loving friends up north. I was content.

At 0600 Alex replaced me at the helm, and we consulted by dawn's early light on our strategy. Ahead, at about 18 miles, lay Conception Island and its well-charted Southampton Reef. If the wind held direction, we would have the reefs on our bow. Prudence dictated that we tack at 0800, take a one-hour hitch to the north, then return to port tack to leave the reefs well to the south. To play it safe we agreed to tack when the island came into view. That would give us plenty of room, and with the island in view we'd always know where we were. No need to take chances in these unfamiliar waters. I told Alex to wake me when he saw the island, and I'd help him tack.

I went below, logged, and stretched out on my bunk for a nap. I slept easily, as did Larry, our other crew. In these gentle conditions rest comes sweetly. But, as I've said, Alex was distracted. Alone on deck at the helm, in the undemanding lull of an easy sail in good weather, he had time to think, and to look at his badly scarred hands. Perhaps he relived his entire life. So, as the sun rose higher, and Conception Island appeared on the horizon, he forgot our plan, forgot the reef and didn't wake me. He sailed on into the gentle morning. The breeze held; our track was straight; the boat sailed steadily.

A few minutes past nine we struck the reef.

The impact was horrific. The noise thundered through the hull like a great bass drum being demolished by an over-enthusiastic percussionist. The grinding sound from below sent deep chills through me: it grated inside my head like a dentist's low-speed rasp. We struck, bounced a few times, then stopped.

For only a moment there was silence.

I rolled out of the bunk and instinctively lifted the floorboards over the deep bilge to check for water, still not certain that this was reality or nightmare. The bilge held only a bit of water, so I flipped the pump on to empty it for later reference. I instructed Larry, who was now vertical, if not awake, to check the forward bilges for damage and water. He found neither. Assured, for the moment, that we weren't sinking, I scrambled on deck to learn the truth.

It was a glorious morning. The sun was high, the water glistened merrily. The skies were a rich wintry blue with patchy clouds. The moderate northeaster filled the sails nicely, but with no purpose now. A swell was running, and small breakers lapped foamy crests all around us. The boat, standing erect, was lifted in each wave then dropped with sickening new shocks. And there was coral everywhere: rust-brown and ochre heads peeked above the surface in every direction.

We were a full boat length inside the reef, and the hull was surrounded by a crowd of coral like a celebrity in a sea of autograph hounds. I couldn't see any way to sail off. After my fast survey I addressed Alex, who was still at the wheel, frozen. I comforted him with the news of the dry bilges. But there wasn't much comfort. The swell was pounding us, the sails driving us harder on. Each impact rattled the rigging to worsen the impression. We first had to stop the drive, so we luffed the main and furled the genoa quickly.

With the forces eased a bit, we could calmly make plans. Could we back off under power? We had obviously entered through an opening in the coral, so why not back out the same way? It seemed logical. On the other hand, the boat is a thoroughbred racing machine with a folding propeller, notoriously powerless in reverse. Still, we tried.

We couldn't use the mainsail to heel the boat because its drive would counter the engine, so Larry and I rocked the boat while Alex revved the engine. But we were apparently wedged so tightly the boat wouldn't heel, and didn't even budge with 3,500 r.p.m. of reverse power. Even when we timed the rocking and power with the swell, to use its lifting, the reef maintained its grip. Despite the nearness of deep water astern—considering the risks to the rudder—we abandoned the idea of backing out directly.

But there were several channels behind us, so we trimmed the main flat to drive the bow up and turn the boat to a more favorable direction for powering out. There was no response, so we furled the main. I then suggested that we could drive the stern down by setting a sail on the backstay, and (improbably) sail off. My companions scoffed, so I set the storm jib despite them. The stern did move, but the swell repeatedly shoved the bow around negating the effect. (I now wish that I'd set a big genoa instead of the storm jib; we might have sailed to glory backwards and made the *Guinness Book of Records* at the same time. But glory was elusive, and we were still stuck hard.)

Clearly, we had coral *behind* the keel, keeping us from backing out. This might have been the right time for me to dive under the boat to determine the best way out; but with sharp coral everywhere, my vulnerable flesh suggested that I wait. We elected, then, to drive forward, clear of the obstruction, and back off around it. With full power forward we moved, and for an instant we floated. But the prop struck hard on the coral, which must have occupied the entire space between the keel and rudder. The engine stalled. When we started up again, the prop wash was almost nil. The prop was certainly damaged.

At that moment, and for the first time, I thought that the end was near: that there was no way we could extricate this beautiful craft; and that as the wind and sea increased she would sustain increasingly greater damage, and eventually break up. The impacts were, in fact, becoming more severe, and with no propeller our prospects looked dimmer. But, of course, we never gave up.

Despite the limited value of the engine, we again tried to drive forward, using the swell to break us loose. We were even able to swing the bow a bit toward a small clearing in the coral, so we were encouraged. But the same swell that helped us now did its final dirty work. One particularly long sea lifted and swung us; as we dropped, the entire impact was taken by the rudder. The wheel spun as a sure indicator that the rudder was in the grip of an unseen adversary.

Now the situation looked bleak again. We couldn't move, but the rudder kept striking, and the propeller wouldn't propel. Kedging was our only remaining solution. We had thus far rejected kedging because we believed we could work ourselves out without an anchor. But there was no choice now. We'd been on the reef for three hours, the tide was falling, and the wind and swell increasing. The prospect of spending the night on the reef was not inviting.

Larry pumped up the inflatable dinghy while I readied the 35-lb. Danforth by adding chain scavenged from the other anchors. The nearest deep water into which I could drop the hook was well off our starboard quarter. We might have tried to kedge off stern-first, but the density of coral behind us was too great to risk further rudder damage. (I still don't know how we came *in* that way.) We decided to kedge the bow toward the nearby clearing, and work out from there, going forward. We launched the dinghy.

The wind was piping now. As long as I could remain in the boat's lee, I could progress toward deep water. But out of the lee I was driven away from my objective. Inflatables are tough enough to row in light conditions. But in heavy going, loaded with ground tackle, and trailing a heavy, water-logged rode, steering is nearly impossible, and it's usually three lengths forward and four aft.

My first attempt failed. The anchor rode prevented my steering, and I fell off in the wrong direction. And the rode snagged coral in several places, so as Larry hauled me back I had to progressively unsnag it. (Polypropylene, where were you?)

My second try was no easier, but I'd developed some expertise. I reached the end of my tether and tried to drop the anchor smartly. Dropping an anchor from an inflatable with no floorboards is difficult. There's no lifting leverage, so it's not hard to put a fluke through the boat. And no matter how carefully you've stowed it, the rode, chain and anchor want to tangle. The few moments of delay in getting the rig over the side can cost precious distance. I confess that this dropping was no exemplary operation; and it wasn't improved by Alex and Larry shouting at me to get the anchor down. But it went. And that's when I lost my watch.

Back on the boat Larry tailed and I ground the winch, while Alex applied judicious bursts of power despite the prop. Slowly we swung. In half an hour we managed a 45-degree turn and were headed for the clearing. At no time did the impact against coral diminish, so periodically we checked the bilge and found nothing, despite the music of destruction that filled the air.

In an hour we were across the clearing and within twenty feet of the reef's edge, having made an agonizing semicircular turn through the heads. The anchor now lay abeam, and was no longer much help to forward progress. Further winching would have pulled us too far around and back to denser coral. But, by alternately pulling and slacking to rock the boat, we inched forward. The propeller struck a few more times, as did the rudder; but we pressed on. The terrible impacts continued; the strain on the rode (and crew) was enormous. But, finally, after five hours on the reef, the boat lurched forward and slipped into deep water. I paid out the entire rode and snubbed it, as the boat fell off and lay to the anchor out of danger.

For a moment no one spoke. The horror was behind us, but that was no cause for celebration. I just took one very deep breath which made me realize how exhausted I was from rowing and winching. But there was no time to relax.

My final bilge inspection proved that Nautor builds the finest boats in the world—I truly believe that many other craft would not have survived the pounding. Through five hours and hundreds of impacts, we didn't take a drop of water. Nonetheless, I donned mask and fins and went over to inspect the underbody.

As I went under and cleared the mask a cloud of reef fish scattered in the sunlight, their silvery sides glinting at me in mockery of my clumsy entry into their world. What I then saw was awesome; the usually graceful hull was a mess. The entire leading edge of the keel was gouged and pocked, completely stripped of gelcoat. Long gouges crisscrossed the keel's sides. The keel bottom, reinforced by a stainless steel shoe, was dented but intact. The knife-edge after end was totally blunted. Odd white patches spotted the hull where coral was embedded in the fiberglass. Small cracks appeared where the hull and keel faired.

The propeller was so badly twisted, it looked like a large bronze cotter pin that had been used too many times. The blades were jammed closed, which explained our loss of powering, but I was able to spread them which later enabled us to power at two knots.

The rudder looked bad as well. Repeated impact had stripped away large areas of fiberglass matting, and a new rudder extension was partly torn away. The skeg also had cracks along its fairing. Worse, though, the rudder was jammed hard at the top and no amount of wheel turning could move it. Fortunately, I was able to cut and file away enough of the rudder top to free it. We would be able to sail on.

Over hot coffee I urged Alex to turn around, and sail to Florida. The wind would be fair, the mileage short and the shipyards known quantities. I was the only one who knew the extent of the damage below, and I didn't feel easy about the rudder. But, as I've said, Alex had a dream. And who am I to deny a man his dreams? So, after consulting Virgin Islands guidebooks and reading between the advertising lines, we set a course around the reef and on to St. Thomas's east end where we would haul for repairs.

One week later, after some heavy sailing, we made our landfall and had a curious postscript to this exhausting madness. We were a few miles from the channel between Tobago and Thatch keys: the entry to St. Thomas' east end. The sun had set with the promise of a moonless night. Still, with good night vision, I could make out the channel so we headed for it. A sudden tropical squall blew in with howling wind and traditionally torrential rain. But the roller furling gear jammed, as it always does in a crisis, and we couldn't roll in the genoa. I went forward, in the dark maelstrom, to turn the headstay while Larry winched the furling line. After much struggle we brought it in only halfway, so we decided to leave it there and heave-to to wait out the storm.

When the blow passed we were all so tired, wet and grumpy we elected to have dinner and remain hove-to overnight, and enter fresh in the morning. The wind obliged by completely disappearing. For the first time in my long sailing life I hove to in a dead calm.

In the morning I had the final shocker. Our furling effort, heroic to say the least, had put a full turn-and-a-half twist in the metal twin headstay. I do not, as one might guess, believe much in roller furling any longer.

At any rate, we made a smooth docking at Johnny Harms' and hit the showers. And Alex was able to realize his dream. That, after all, was what he paid me for.

Index

A

Admiralty Islands, 242–47
Advance, 249–50
Ailsa, 8, 9, 13
Airplane trip to Bermuda, 45–49
Alderman, James Horace, 81–82
Alexander, W. H. "Bill", 45–49
Allcard, Edward, 136
Aluminum alloy masts, 122, 124
Amberjack II, 50–58
America's Cup Race, 23–29,
   95–104, 221–25; 1920, 3–5;
   boat design, 107–11, 118–24
Amory, Cleveland, 221–25
Anderson, Charlie, 60–61
Annie Oakley, 133
Apache, 9, 11, 12–14
Arctic cruise, 248–56
Ariadne, 22, *21*
Aries, 15
Atlantic, 9–13

Aura, 93
Australia, 95
Australia II, 23–29
Aztec, 34–36, *35*

B

Baffin, William, 249
Barr, Charles, 9, 11, 12
Bartlett, Bob, 250
Bartlett, John, 250
Bavier, Bob, 95, 97
Beckers, Roy, 194
Bedloe, 200–6
Bennett, James Gordon, 34, 36
Bermudian lug, 132
Bertrand, John, 24, 26–29
Billings, C. K. G., 34
Bimini, 77–78, 80
Bluejacket, 188–89
Blue light, 134

Bohlin, Tom, 10
Bond, Alan, 23–24, 27
Bootlegging, 68–73, 77–85
Bouck, Zeh, 45–49
Bouzaid, Chris, 16, 17, 19, 22
Bowdoin, 248–56
Bowen, Catherine Drinker,
 112–17
Bowker, Peter, 17, 86, 89, 92–94
Brassey, Lord, 8, 9–10
Briggs, Arthur, 62, 63
Briggs, Benjamin, S., 62–67
Briggs, Sophia Matilda, 63
Bruce, Peter, 20
Burgess, Charles P., 122
Burgess, Edward, 101, 119–21
Burgess, Starling, 101, 118–24
Burrage, A. C., 34

C
C.D.B., 113–17
Cambria, 152
Canoe cruise, 229–41
Cape Alexander, 249
Cap Horn, 151
Captains Courageous, 184
Cardinal Vertue, 151
Caribbean cruise, by sailing
 canoe, 229–41, *233*
Carolina, 132
Challenge, 12, 24
Chaperone, 99
Chichester, Francis, 151–57, *152*
Chute, 133
Cicely, 6
Clark, Robert, 151, 154
Coast Guard, and Prohibition,
 78–85
Cobb, Oliver W., 62–67
Cobb, Sarah Everson, 62–63

Columbia, 95, 101, 121, 126
Columnists, 207
Communications, single-handed
 ocean crossings, 139–40
Condor, 17, 18–19
Conner, Dennis, 23, 25, 26–29
Connolly, J. B., 10
Constellation, 101
Corsair, 36, *38*
Costs of yacht ownership, 1907,
 39–40
Courageous, 96–97, 101, 103
Cox, Woody, 94
Crane, Clinton, 122, 123
Crews, views of, 215–20
Crosson, Marvin, 195
Cruises, 227, 265–77; Arctic,
 248–56; by canoe, 229–41;
 Caribbean, 278–83; Solomon
 Islands, 257–64; South Seas,
 242–47
Cudmore, Harry, 19, 24
Cunningham, Briggs, 95, 100,
 102
Cuyahoga, 52–53, 55

D
Dauntless, 152
Davidson, Kenneth S. M., 123,
 125–29
Davis, Norman, 58
Davison, Ann, 135–41
Dawson, Joe, 112–13
Defender, 101, 121
Dei Gratia, 63
Devil, 133
Diamond Narrows, 264
Drawbridges, 116–17
Dry Armada, 78

du Moulin, Edward, 25, 102–3
du Moulin, Richard, 101

E
Eclipse, 15, 20
Edgecomb, L. J., 97
Edward, Prince of Wales, 6
Edwards, Antone, 41–43
Edwards, Joseph, 41, 43
Eira, 151
Elan, 95, 96–97
Ellis, 52–53
Endeavour I, 122, 123
Endeavour II, 123
Endymion, 9, 10, 13
Enterprise, 96, 98, 99, 101, 104,
    122, 133
Enterprise syndicate, 102–4
Erin, 37

F
Fastnet disaster, 15–22, *16, 21*
Felicity Ann, 136–41
Fenger, F. W., 229–41
Fleet racing starts, 142–49
Fleur-de-lis, 9, 10, 12, 13
Florida, smuggling, 77–85
Flying Fox, 170–71
Food, single-handed ocean
    crossings, 138–39
France II, 95–96
Frers, German, 89

G
Gardner, William, 34
Genesta, 120
Genoa jib, 133
Gilling, Andrew, 63, 66

Gilpin, George, 194, 195
Gimcrack, 128
Gipsy Moth III, 151–57
Gizo, Solomon Islands, 264
Glaser, R., 10
Goddard, Brenton, 197
Golden Apple of the Sun, 19
Golwobbler, 132–33
Gould, Howard, 36
Gould, Jay, 102
Grant (*Wakiva* Captain), 161,
    166, 173, 175–82
Gray, David, 73
Great Lakes, boat racing, 110–11
Green, Alan, 15, 21
Greene, James Brent, 197
Greenland, 249
Gretel II, 95
Griswold, F. G., 68, 69
Guadalcanal, 196, 257–60

H
Haggerty, Clarence T., 182–83
Hainge, R. F., 200–206
Hamburg, 7, 9, 10, 13
Hamilton, Frank W., Jr., 265–77
Hand, William H., 254
Hauoli, 36
Hawthorne Sound, 264
Hayden, Sterling, 184–92
Hayes, Issac Israel, 250
Head (toilet), 133
Hebbinghaus, H. G., 11
Helfrich, Bunky, 91, 94
Hereshoff, Halsey, 101
Hereshoff, Nathanael, 98, 101,
    119, 121
Higgins, Eugene, 34
Hijacking, 82–83
Hildegarde, 9, 13

Hinman, George, 101, 95–97
Hiscock, Eric, 262
Hohenzollern, 7, 7, *8*, 14
Holland, Ron, 19
Hood, Ted, 97–98, 102, 103, 104
Hummer, Lloyd, 196
Humming Bird II, 257–64, *259*
Hurricane, 200–6

I
Illingworth, John, 154
Imp, 15
Impetuous, 15
Independence, 97, 98, 103
Indianapolis, 58
Isabelle, 249
Islands, discovery of, 242–47
Istria, 131, 132

J
Jackson, 200–6
Jan Pott, 18
J class yachts, 131
Jester, 151
Johnson, Irving, 242–47
Jones, Warren, 24
Jubile, 15

K
Kanawha, 36
Kane, Elish Kent, 249–50
Kennedy, John F., 264
Kialoa, 17, 18, 92
Kid Boots, 84
Kidnapping, 74–76
Kilroy, Jim, 18
Kona, 68–73
Kuharski, Teddy, 193

L
LaBorde, Harold, 257–64
La Plata, 188
Lawson, Peter, 97, 100
Legg, John, 195, 199
Lexcen, Ben, 24, 25
Liberty, 23–29
Lipton, Sir Thomas, 37, *109*;
    and America's Cup, 3–5,
    107–11
Long, Shorty, 196
Longley, John, 24
Loomis, Alfred F., 207, 215–20
Loomis, Lee, 103, 104
Luxury yachts, 1907, 33–40
Lysistrata, 34, 36

M
McDonald, J. H., 9, 12–13
McLaughlin, Terry, 24
MacMillan, Donald, 248–56
Mae West, 133
Manus Island, 242–43
Marconi rigs, 131–32
Margaret, 41–42, 43
Marovo Lagoon, 260–61
Marshall, John, 103
Marshall, Wilson, 9, 14
Mary Celeste, 62–67
Match racing starts, 142
Mattingly, Jim, 94
Maxwell, J. Roger, 108
May, Charlie, 196
Mayflower, 101, 119, 120
Meldner, Heiner, 100
Meteor IV, 6
Meyer, Randy, 102
Moley, Raymond, 56
Montgomery, Alan R., 193
Morehouse, Captain, 63, 64

Morgan, J. Pierpont, 36
Mosbacher, Bus, 142, *143*
Munroe, R. M., 68

N
Nale, Leon, 195
Navigation, Admiralty Islands,
    243
Navigators, views of, 219
New Bedford whalers, 41–42
New Georgia Island, 263
New York Yacht Club, 25–26,
    102–3
Niagara, 36, *37*
Nicholson, Charles, 4–5, 131
Nikoloric, Leonard A., 197
North, Lowell, 96–100, 102–4
Norwood, Alfred, 198

O
O'Daniel, Elvie, 194, 195
O'Malley, Frank, 195
O'Meara, Marty, 90, 93, 94
O'Neill, Bernie, 199
Ocean crossings: single-handed,
    135–41, 151–57; World War I,
    161–83
Ocean cruises, 184–92, 265–77
Off-the-wind starts, 148–49
Oretha F. Spinney, 184–92

P
Panama Canal passage, 184–92
Pandora, 250
Park Avenue booms, 122
Parrish, Ben, 198
Patisson, Rodney, 19
Pearle, Owen, 197

Peary, Robert, 250
Peterson, Charles, 184–92
Peterson, Doug, 20
Peterson, Halward, 195
Pilot Radio, 45–49
Plant, Morton F., 37
Polaris, 250
Police Car, 15, 16–17
Porpoise, 274
Potter, John, 92, 94
Prestige, 98
Presto boats, 68
Prince, Bill, 74–76
Priscilla, 120
Proteus, 250
PT boats, 193–99
Puritan, 101, 119, 120

Q
Quad, 133
Queen, 108

R
Racing starts, 142–49, *147*
Ragamuffin, 15
Rainbow, 98, 101, 102, 122–23
Randolph, Edmund, 9, 11
Ranger, 98, 101, 123–24, 125
Reliance, 98, 101, 121
Resolute, 3–5, *4*, 98, 121
Rich, Tom, 28
Richardson, Albert G., 63–65
Robinson, Hugh M., 197
Robinson, William Albert, 260
Rogers, H. H., 36
Rogers, Jeremy, 15
Roosevelt, 250
Roosevelt, Franklin D., 50–58,
    51

Roosevelt, James, 52, 53, 58
Rounding bouys, 142, 149–50
Roviana Lagoon, 263
Royal Perth Yacht Club, 23
Rum-running. *See* Bootlegging
Russian, 170
Rust, Paul D., Jr., 50, 52, 53

S
Safety regulations, British, 22
Sails, for 12-meters, 99
Sanderlin, Sydney, 80–81
Savo, Solomon Islands, 260
Schnackenberg, Tom, 24
Schneider, Franz, 94
Seasickness, 139
Self-steering wind vane, 153, 155
Seventh Day Adventists, 261
Shamrock, 3–5, *4*
Shamrock II, 125–26
Shamrock V, 98, 121, 122, 133
Shipyards, 112–15
Single-handed ocean crossings,
    135–41, 151–57
Skippers, views of, 209–14
Sleeping arrangements,
    single-handed ocean crossings,
    135–38
Smith, F. M., 36
Smuggling, 77–85
Solomon Islands, 257–64
Somer, Jack A., 278–83
Soul of ship, 59–61
Southerly, 93
South Seas cruise, 242–47
Spanish Marie, 79, 84
Steam yachts, 33–40, 161–83
Stephen, Olin J., 25, 101, 123,
    125–30, *126*

Stephens, W. P., *Traditions and
    Memories of American
    Yachting*, 131
Stevens Institute of Technology,
    123, 125–29
Stone, Herb, 31
Stuffert, Arthur, 196
Sunbeam, 8, 9, 10, 13
Sverige, 95
Syndicates, America's Cup, 103

T
Tank tests, in yacht design, 123,
    125–30
Tar, Sherman, 114, 117
Taylor, William H., 209–14
Tenacious, 15, 17, 86–94, 103
Terminology of yachting, 131–34
Thistle, 9, 13, 121
Thomas, Stanley C., 196
Tietjens, Adolph, 7, 10
Tina, 20
Transatlantic race, 6–14
Treharne, Hugh, 24
Triangular mainsail, 132
Trouble, Bruno, 24
Tufts, Charlie, 196
Tulagi, PT boat squadron,
    193–99
Turner, R. E. "Ted", 15, 17,
    86–94, *87*, 96–97, 98, 101–3
12-meters, computerized, 98–101

U
United States, 250
Universal Rule, 121–22
Utowana, 9, 13

V

Valentijn, Johan, 25
Valhalla, 8, 9, 10, 13
Valiant, 34
Vanderbilt, Harold S., 98, 121–23
Vanderbilt, W. K., 34
Varuna, 132
Venetia, 37–39, *38*
Victory '83, 24
Vigilant, 101, 121
Vim, 99, 146
Viru, Solomon Islands, 262
Vocabulary of yachting, 131–34
Vogel, Scott, 28
Volunteer, 101, 119, 120–21

W

Wakiva, 161–83
Wanderer, 41–44
Watson, George L., 121, 125–26
Webb, J. Beavor, 120
Webster, Robert K., 80, 82
Weech, Robert K., 81–82

Weetamoe, 122, 123
Whales, 271
Whaling fleet, New Bedford, 41–42
Wicks, John, 199
Wilhelm, II, Kaiser, 6–7, 14
Williwaw, 15
Wing, Herbert, 196
Wisdom, Hobart Denzil, 193–94
World War I, ocean crossing, 161–83
World War II: hurricane, 200–6; Panama Canal passage, 184–92; PT boats, 193–99

Y

Yacht design, 118–24; tank tests, 123, 125–130
Yakaboo, 229–41
Yancey, Lewis A., 45–49
Yankee (sail), 133
Yankee (schooner), 242–47, *245*
Yankee (12-meter), 102, 123